D1605832

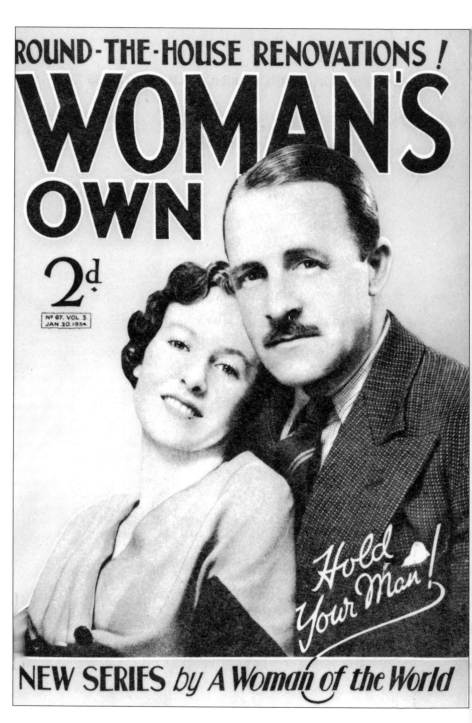

The cover of *Woman's Own*, January 1934 (no. 67, vol. 3) featuring Barbara
Hedworth's series 'Hold Your Man!' (By permission of *Woman's Own*. Photograph
of cover reproduced by permission of the British Library, shelfmark 691.)

Sisters and Rivals in British Women's Fiction, 1914–39

Diana Wallace

First published in Great Britain 2000 by
MACMILLAN PRESS LTD
Houndmills, Basingstoke, Hampshire RG21 6XS and London
Companies and representatives throughout the world

A catalogue record for this book is available from the British Library.

ISBN 0–333–77400–0

First published in the United States of America 2000 by
ST. MARTIN'S PRESS, LLC,
Scholarly and Reference Division,
175 Fifth Avenue, New York, N.Y. 10010

ISBN 0–312–23433–3

Library of Congress Cataloging-in-Publication Data
Wallace, Diana, 1964–
Sisters and rivals in British women's fiction, 1914–39 / Diana Wallace.
p.   cm.
Based on the author's thesis (Ph.D.).
Includes bibliographical references and index.
ISBN 0–312–23433–3
1. Triangles (Interpersonal relations) in literature. 2. English fiction—Women authors—History and criticism. 3. English fiction—20th century—History and criticism. 4. Women and literature—England—History—20th century. 5. Women in literature. 6. Love stories, English—History and criticism. I. Title.

PR888.T76 W35   2000
823'.91209352042—dc21
00–023347

This book is printed on paper suitable for recycling and made from fully managed and sustained forest sources.

10   9   8   7   6   5   4   3   2   1
09   08   07   06   05   04   03   02   01   00

Printed and bound in Great Britain by
Antony Rowe Ltd, Chippenham, Wiltshire

For my sisters,
Linda and Dawn

Contents

Acknowledgements

Marion Shaw was a generous and constructive supervisor of the thesis on which this book was based and I am enormously indebted to her for her support throughout. I would also particularly like to thank Gill Spraggs and Jeni Williams for reading and commenting helpfully on sections of the book, and the members of the Feminist Research Group at Lough-brough University for their responses to the work in progress. I am grateful to my colleagues at Glamorgan University for enabling me to have an invaluable period of study leave in which to finish the book. Finally, for their support and encouragement I would like to thank my parents, Anne and Nigel Wallace; and, most especially, Jarlath Costello.

DIANA WALLACE

The author and publishers wish to thank *Woman's Own* for permission to reproduce the cover of *Woman's Own* (no. 67, vol. 3, January 1934) which appears as a frontispiece. The photograph of this cover is reproduced with the permission of the British Library (shelfmark: 691).

Abbreviations

Vera Brittain

DT: *The Dark Tide*, London: Grant Richards, 1923
TY: *Testament of Youth*, London: Victor Gollancz, 1933
HE: *Honourable Estate*, London: Victor Gollancz, 1936
TF: *Testament of Friendship*, London: Virago, 1980 [1940]

Winifred Holtby

CS: *The Crowded Street*, London: Virago, 1981 [1924]
SR: *South Riding*, Glasgow: Fontana, 1974 [1936]

Rosamond Lehmann

DS: *Dusty Answer*, Harmondsworth: Penguin, 1936 [1927]
IW: *Invitation to the Waltz*, London: Virago, 1981 [1932]
WS: *The Weather in the Streets*, London: Virago, 1981 [1936]
EG: *The Echoing Grove*, London: Collins, 1953

May Sinclair

TS: *The Three Sisters*, London: Virago, 1982 [1914]
MO: *Mary Olivier*, London: Virago, 1980 [1919]
HF: *Life and Death of Harriett Frean*, London: Virago, 1980 [1922]

Rebecca West

RS: *The Return of the Soldier*, London: Virago, 1980 [1918]
J: *The Judge*, London: Virago, 1980 [1922]

Note: Unless enclosed in square brackets all ellipses in quotations are as in the original text.

Introduction

> Cleopatra did not like Octavia. And how completely *Antony and Cleopatra* would have been altered had she done so! As it is [...] the whole thing is simplified, conventionalised, if one dared to say it, absurdly. Cleopatra's only feeling about Octavia is one of jealousy. Is she taller than I am? How does she do her hair? [...] how interesting it would have been if the relationship between the two women had been more complicated.
>
> (Woolf, 1977c, 78–9)

Cleopatra and Octavia, of course, never met, at least not in Shakespeare's version of the story. Their conception of each other is always that of the 'Other Woman' in the triangle – wife or mistress – and is mediated through their relation to the man for whom they are rivals. This is, as Virginia Woolf implies here in *A Room of One's Own* (1929), the male plot of female rivalry – 'simplified, conventionalised'. It is the stereotype that Bertrand Russell accepted when he wrote that 'women regard all other women as their competitors, whereas men as a rule only have this feeling towards other men in the same profession' (1930, 85). It is based on the assumption that getting a man is every woman's *raison d'être* and that this will over-ride any other loyalties or interests.

What would have happened if the relationship between the two women had been, as Woolf suggests, more 'interesting'? If they had met, perhaps liked each other, become friends, even fallen in love with each other? Or if they were already friends before either met Antony? Or if they had worked together, like Chloe and Olivia, the two friends in the imaginary novel Woolf famously goes on to discuss? Or if Octavia had been Cleopatra's sister rather than Caesar's? Such questions involve a shift in perspective which centralises the two women and their relationship. Over a decade earlier Woolf had addressed the question of this 'difference in view' in 'Women Novelists':

> no one will admit that he can possibly mistake a novel written by a man for a novel written by a woman. There is the obvious and enormous difference of experience in the first place [...] And finally [....] there rises for consideration the very difficult question of the difference between the man's and the woman's view of what constitutes the importance of any subject. From this spring not only marked differences of plot and incident, but infinite differences in selection, method and style.
>
> (Woolf, 1979, 71)

This book will be concerned with the female plot of rivalry between women which is the result of that difference in view and experience. And it will focus on the time when Woolf herself was writing, between 1914 and 1939, when, for complex historical reasons, the subject of female rivalry was very much in the public eye.

Woolf's contention in *A Room of One's Own* that 'Chloe liked Olivia' (1977c, 78) has led to a substantial body of work which has explored female friendship as an important theme in women's writing.[1] 'Sisterhood' as an ideal of equal, supportive, female friendship, both political and personal, has been a productive metaphor for the feminist movement. The political need to valorise relationships between women, however, has led to an unease around the equally central theme of female rivalry in fiction and meant that its complexities remain underexplored. Ironically, women's fiction is not only more complex in its treatment of the subject than male-authored texts, but often franker than feminist theory or criticism.

One assumption that underlies much early work on female friendship is that while female rivalry supports patriarchal structures by dividing women, female friendship *per se* threatens them by uniting women. This is, I think, too simple. Female friendships, far from automatically threatening the status quo, can work to sustain it. They may provide solace and guidance which help to assimilate woman into heterosexual relationships. They may also help to police 'unfeminine' behaviour and rebellion against the accepted social mores by excluding 'transgressive' women, or women who are 'different' in age, sexuality, race or class. In the nineteenth century, Gill Frith argues, the concept of 'sisterhood' was used to support dominant ideologies. Hence, she suggests,

We need to disentangle the concept of sisterhood, to see that it is not
a unitary or transhistorical idea, and to recognise that the bonds
between women cannot always be celebrated as potentially subversive, as mysteriously 'outside' ideology.

(1988, 17)

Black and Asian feminists have, of course, from the 1970s onwards, been
pointing to the fact that white feminist notions of sisterhood, far from
being 'unitary or transhistorical', have been deeply problematic.[2] The
notion of 'female friendship' is also a contested area in terms of sexuality. The focus on *non-sexual* friendship has involved some theorists in
definitions of 'sisterhood' and 'friendship' which, in attempting to
reclaim them from the 'taint' of lesbianism, border on the homophobic.
This is particularly clear in the debates surounding the friendship of
Winifred Holtby and Vera Brittain.

A second assumption is that if rivalry and competition are 'masculine'
characteristics, a definition of women that excludes these implies that
we are, therefore, 'nicer' than men. Sara Lucia Hoagland has suggested
that the so-called 'feminine virtues' of altruism and self-sacrifice are
actually part of 'femininity' as a 'concept which makes female submission to male domination seem natural and normal' (1988, 69). If we
need to question the gendering of altruism and self-sacrifice as 'feminine' and 'good', I would suggest that we should also question that of
rivalry as 'masculine' and 'bad', and even consider the possibility that
some kinds of rivalry might be productive or beneficial for women. Most
crucially, women have traditionally been discouraged from rivalry in the
workplace, both with each other and with men, but have been encouraged to see other women as rivals in romance. Not only are friendship
and rivalry not mutually exclusive – they can co-exist in the same
relationship – but friendly rivalry can be, as in the case of Vera Brittain
and Winifred Holtby, a spur to greater professional achievement.

One of the possibilities I want to explore is that female rivalry can be,
as Elizabeth Abel describes friendship being, a 'vehicle of self-definition'
(1981, 416), a process of self-identification. It can reflect, not the dominance of patriarchal structures, but the primacy and power of female
bonds. It can be the result, not of competition over a man, but of a need
to separate from another women, to assert difference, and to resist the
'merging' of ego boundaries (which Abel and other theorists idealise). As
such it can even, paradoxically, threaten male power structures.

This book will focus on the years between 1914 and 1939 in the belief
that it is through the specificity of historical contextualisation that we

can best understand the complexity of representations of female rivalry. These years were, for historical reasons which I shall outline in Chapter One, a period when rivalry between women was encouraged and even manufactured by the dominant ideologies. The result is that rivalry between women, especially in versions of what is popularly known as the 'eternal triangle' (here where two women who are rivals for the same man), appears repeatedly in inter-war women's fiction. These versions – the rival friends or sisters triangle, the lesbian triangle, the wife and mistress triangle, the second wife triangle, and even the mother-and daughter-in-law triangle – can all be closely linked to their historical specificity. In looking at how these texts relate to the reality of relationships between women during these years, I shall be bearing in mind the fact that, as Rachel Blau DuPlessis phrases it, narrative is 'a version of, or a special expression of, ideology' (1985, x). Or, to put it another way, that fictional conventions reflect societal power structures and attitudes.

The 'eternal' or 'erotic triangle' plot was first schematised by René Girard in *Deceit, Desire and the Novel* (1961). He asserts that it is often the relationship between the rivals which is the determining factor in such a triangle, rather than the bonds between either rival and the beloved. Hence, 'the loathed rival is actually a mediator' (1976, 14), and the object of desire is often chosen precisely because it is already the choice of the rival: 'The mediator's prestige is imparted to the object of desire' (1976, 17).

Eve Kosofsky Sedgwick's critique of Girard's paradigm in *Between Men: English Literature and Male Homosocial Desire* (1985) uses the work of Gayle Rubin (1975), Lévi-Strauss (1949) and Luce Irigaray to expose its gender-blind nature. She points out that in the majority of the triangles Girard discusses the two rivals are male and the love object female and analyses this pattern as an instance of what Rubin, following Lévi-Strauss, calls the 'traffic in women' (1975). Patriarchal society, Rubin argues, is structured around bonds between men (legal, economic and social) which are cemented by the exchange of women who function as symbolic property (for instance, in marriage the woman is 'given' by her father to her husband). Drawing attention to the radical disruption of the continuum between male 'homosocial' and male 'homosexual' behaviour in our society (1985, 1–2), Sedgwick uncovers what she calls the 'male homosocial desire' (a phrase which reinserts the concept of desire into 'homosocial') in these exchanges. This triangular structure is reflected in literature and Sedgwick reads a range of canonical texts to argue that their subject is not, in fact, heterosexual desire but the (hidden) bonds between men. The woman in the triangle functions as a mediator between men in order to evade the tabooed area of male homosexuality and the threat it offers to patriarchal stability. She is used as 'exchangeable, perhaps symbolic, property for the primary purpose of cementing the bonds of men with men' (1985, 16) and thus is never an equal subject in these exchanges, but 'a "conduit of a relationship" in which the true *partner* is a man' (26).

The 'erotic triangle' as Sedgwick explores it is not the ahistorical, ungendered structure delineated by Girard, but

> a sensitive register precisely for delineating relationships of power and meaning and for making graphically intelligible the play of desire and identification by which individuals negotiate with their societies for empowerment.
>
> (1985, 27)

It is this concept of the 'erotic triangle' as a locus for the play of desire and gender identity through historically specific relationships of power which informs my own project. (I use the term 'erotic triangle' rather than the popular 'eternal triangle' because the latter term implies a transhistorical paradigm.)

However, the female-authored novels I will examine use a triangle of two women and a man, reversing the paradigm examined by Girard and Sedgwick, and allowing those 'complicated' relations between women which so interested Woolf to be centralised. They set up a test of gender-loyalty: is the woman's loyalty to the man who offers her the possibility of sexual fulfilment, or to the other woman, sometimes a blood-sister? The triangle of two men and a woman (the 'two suitors convention' analysed by Jean Kennard (1978)) offers the woman a choice between two men but this is ultimately a choice between alternative forms of heterosexuality. Ironically, it is the female rivals plot where relations between women can become influential and even determining.

The blind spot in Sedgwick's work is precisely, as she remarks, 'the isolation, not to mention the absolute subordination, of women' within the triangle, which is 'a distortion that necessarily fails to do justice to women's own powers, bonds and struggles' (1985, 18). As Terry Castle asks in a critique of Sedgwick's work in her illuminating essay on Sylvia Townsend Warner's *Summer Will Show* (1936): 'Within such a totalising scheme, with its insistent focus on relations "between men", what place might there be for relations between women?' (1992, 131). In *Summer Will Show*, set against the 1848 Paris Revolution, wealthy, aristocratic Sophia Willoughby pursues her unfaithful husband Frederick to Paris, meets his mistress, Minna Lemuel, a Jewish actress and story-teller – and falls in love with her. Castle brilliantly reads Warner's novel as a self-conscious revision of Flaubert's canonical *L'Education sentimentale* in order to show how Warner destabilises and collapses the male homo-social triangle and replaces it with a triangle of female desire. As wife and mistress become lovers, Frederick, the now isolated male, occupies the subjugated position of mediator 'between women'.

The issue of canonicity is crucial here. While both Girard and Sedg-wick choose their almost exclusively male-authored texts from the tradi-tional canon of European literature, *Summer Will Show*, as Castle acknowledges, is not only not canonical, it was until recently very little known at all. Girard argues that 'triangular desire is the basis of the theory of the novelistic novel' (1976, 52). Sedgwick, gendering his argu-ment, provocatively contends that the entire European canon itself is 'a male-homosocial literary canon' which is 'most so when it is most heterosexual' (1985, 17). The equation works both ways. As Castle glosses it: 'Literature canonises the subject of male homosociality; in return, it would seem, the subject of male homosociality canonises the work of literature' (1992, 131). In contrast, Castle's concern is with the question: 'What is a lesbian fiction?' (1992, 128). She calls Warner's novel 'an exemplary "lesbian fiction"' not simply because it depicts a sexual relationship between two women but precisely because it figures this as a breakup of the canonical male–female–male triangle and, Castle suggests, 'it is exactly this kind of subverted triangulation, or erotic "counterplotting" that is in fact *characteristic of lesbian novels in general*' (1992, 134, my emphasis).

I want to take issue with Castle's conclusion that this revision of the erotic triangle is 'characteristic of *lesbian* novels in general'. My own argument is that the female–male–female triangle plot is one which has a particular resonance for *women* writers in general and is widely used in women's fiction, especially in the inter-war period. Indeed, it crosses categories of genre and style as well as sexuality in women's writing, being used by 'modernists' such as Virginia Woolf and May Sinclair, as well as by so-called 'traditional' writers such as Winifred Holtby, 'popular' writers like Daphne du Maurier, and 'lesbian' writers as different as Sylvia Townsend Warner and Radclyffe Hall. Their focus on the bonds and powers of women is one reason why so many of these novels have not become part of the canon but are variously seen as 'middle-brow', 'women's novels' or 'romance'. Not only has literature failed to canonise the subject of female homosociality, but the subject of female homosociality seems actively to mark a text as *not* canonical. This applies not just to 'lesbian fiction' but also to texts which explore the power of female homosocial relations without confining them to the comforting cover of the heterosexual romance plot.

Romance novels often (although not always) use a version of the erotic triangle. The 'other woman' as rival then becomes a key structuring element and the heroine's identity is ratified by the man's choice of her as *different* from her rival. Where the 'other woman' is often older and overtly sexual, the heroine is chosen because she is younger and more innocent. The romance plot thus presents rivalry as 'a vehicle of self-definition', but it is ultimately one which inscribes the woman into the status quo by separating her from other women and imposing a 'virgin'/'whore' dichotomy. The romance plot, as Rachel Blau DuPlessis (1985) and Carolyn Heilbrun (1988) have argued, has exerted a stranglehold over women's narratives: 'women have been deprived of the narratives, or the texts, plots, or examples, by which they might assume power over – take control of – their own lives' (Heilbrun, 1989, 17). With its marriage ending, the romance plot works not only to obscure the importance of female relationships but to reinforce the stereotype that rivalry between women is both inevitable and always over men.

One of my concerns will be to examine how the dominance of the romance plot affects representations of women's rivalry. The five writers I concentrate on – May Sinclair, Rebecca West, Vera Brittain, Winifred Holtby and Rosamond Lehmann – all use versions of the triangle plot to explore relations between women. With the possible exception of May Sinclair, each of these writers was also involved in a triangle in her own life. My strategy here is to read the fiction against autobiographical and biographical writings in order to examine the disjunctions between the texts. My interest is in how the narrative structures or conventions of fiction, especially the romance plot, shape and distort the accounts these writers give of their own lives and of their sisters and rivals, not only in fiction but also in their non-fiction writings.

While the concept of sisterhood has been central to feminism, the kinship bond which underlies this metaphor has been under-examined.[3] My own feeling is that it is precisely the fact that the friction and tensions of blood sister relationships so often conflict with the ideal of sisterhood which makes this concept so suggestive, and allows for a more complex consideration of rivalry. Studies of sister relationships show that they are distinguished by a complex tension between similarity and difference, closeness and separation, friendship and rivalry. The sister relationship, as these studies show, is a primary and formative element in a woman's sense of identity. Moreover, like the bonds of female sexual desire Castle examines, sister bonds are both primary and powerful and as such can disrupt and collapse the supposedly canonical male–female–male triangle and offer another form of counterplotting. The rival sisters novel is a special version of the triangle novel where the complex play of similarity and difference between women is doubly intensified.

This tension between similarity and difference is also evident in the use of the sister metaphor to figure the relations of writers themselves. The writers of the inter-war period were concerned especially to locate themselves in relation to nineteenth-century women writers, particularly the Brontës, and often did this, as Woolf does in the following passage, through familial metaphors:

> it is by no means certain that every woman is inspired by pure envy when she reads what another has written. More probably Emily Brontë was the passion of her youth; Charlotte even she loved with nervous affection; and cherished a quiet sisterly regard for Anne. Mrs Gaskell wields a maternal sway over readers of her own sex; wise, witty and very large-minded, her readers are devoted to her as to the most admirable of mothers; whereas George Eliot is an Aunt, and, as an Aunt, inimitable.
>
> (1979, 75)

Noting the number of women who produced critical or biographical commentaries on the Brontës during this period (among them Woolf, May Sinclair, Rebecca West, Phyllis Bentley, Elizabeth von Arnim and E. M. Delafield), Patsy Stoneman has suggested, following Woolf, that the 'combined prominence and ambiguity of the Brontë inheritance meant that coming to terms with the Brontës, like killing the Angel in the House, was "part of the occupation of a woman writer"' (1996, 78). Writing about their predecessors, either critically or by using their novels as intertexts, was a way of both locating themselves in a tradition *and* marking difference from earlier writers. While Jane Austen, Elizabeth Gaskell and George Eliot were also important, it was specifically the Brontës who offered models of three women writers as 'sisters', with all the connotations of sisterly support and rivalry that implies. Equally important in this period, the Brontës offered models of the woman writer as unmarried, yet conversant with sexual passion.

Thus the rewriting of the *Jane Eyre* plot, a 'paradigmatic romance' (Stoneman, 1996, 92), is a widespread and important phenomenon in this period. The economic and class differentials in this plot – the lower-class woman in love with a wealthy, upper-class man with a big house and a mad, invalid or dead first wife – demonstrate the potential of the triangle as, in Sedgwick's words, a 'sensitive register' of relationships of power and meaning, and of the 'play of desire and identification' by which women 'negotiate with their societies for empowerment' (1985, 27).

In the next chapter I will look at the historical context of these years in order to explore how female rivalry was both manufactured and encouraged by the dominant discourses. One of those discourses was, of course, the newly emergent Freudian psychoanalysis. In Chapter Two I will consider various possible ways of theorising rivalry, starting with an examination of the historically specific politics underlying the naturalisation of female rivalry in the Freudian Oedipal triangle, and moving on to the work of Luce Irigaray and Mikhail Bakhtin, as well as considering studies of blood sister relationships. The following chapters will then explore the work of five women writers. 'Dialogue' is a crucial concept here. Conversation between women is a key motif in these novels, anticipating Irigaray's emphasis on women 'speaking together'. This is not necessarily an ideal – dialogue can be rivalrous as well as friendly and supportive. The novels themselves, in rewriting previous texts, including Freud, are part of an ongoing intertextual dialogue. They illustrate Bakhtin's point that any utterance is *only a moment in the continuous process of verbal communication* (1994, 59, original emphasis). Each word (or text) is reciprocal, both a response to previous utterances and anticipating a response in the future. Bearing this in mind, my own approach to theory has been to try to set up dialogues between different theoretical models of female rivalry and between the theory and the fiction itself. Above all, I have aimed to situate my discussion of both fiction and theory within the specificity of its historical context.

1
'An Age of Transition': Historical Context

The inter-war years were, as Winifred Holtby put it, an 'age of transition' (1934, 96), characterised by an acute sense of destabilised gender roles. Rosamond Lehmann conveys this sense retrospectively in *The Echoing Grove* (1953) when Dinah comments:

> I can't help thinking that it's particularly difficult to be a woman just at present. One feels so transitional and fluctuating...To [*sic*] I suppose do men. I believe we *are* all in flux – that the difference between our grandmothers and us is far deeper than we realise – much more fundamental than the obvious social economic one. Our so-called emancipation may be a symptom, not a cause.
>
> (EG 311–12)

Gender identity was a site of special conflict and anxiety, exacerbated by an anti-feminist backlash. 'There had been a rise of feminism', Holtby remarked, 'there is now a reaction against it' (1934, 151). According to Deirdre Beddoe in *Back to Home and Duty: Women Between the Wars 1918–1939*, 'the single most arresting feature of the inter-war years is the strength of the notion that women's place is in the home' (1989, 3). Fears that women were encroaching on traditionally male territory led to debates over women's education, work, appearance, sexuality, morality and so on. Holtby pin-points three key concerns – employment, the spinster, and motherhood:

> No popular magazine considers its appeal to public taste secure unless it advertises symposia on 'Are Women Blacklegs?'; 'Are Spinsters Superfluous?'; 'Is there a right to Motherhood?'[...] The Ibsen thesis that women are captives, the Strindberg thesis that women

are devils, the Barrie thesis that women are wistful little mothers, the Ethel M. Dell thesis that they are neurotic masochists yearning for the strong hand of a master – all these in different forms transform contemporary fiction.

(1934, 2)

In *Goodbye to All That* (1929) Robert Graves remarks that his wife, Nancy,

could not bear a newspaper in the house, for fear of reading some paragraph that would horrify her – about the necessity of keeping up the population; or about women's limited intelligence; or about the shameless, flat-chested girl; or anything at all about women written by clergymen.

(1960, 237)

Graves presents this as Nancy's neurosis but it indicates the mental battering women underwent from newspapers, magazines and novels. The 'theses' Holtby identifies were an attempt to stabilise a gender identity which was perceived to be dangerously free-floating.

This anxiety over women's changing role was part of a wider sense of social transition and division, of class as well as gender, within the period. The images which have come to characterise our sense of the inter-war years tend to fall into two extremes. Pictures of the carefree flappers of the 'Jazz Age' with their cocktails, cigarettes and new dances – the 'Charleston', the 'Turkey Trot' and the 'Black Bottom' – contrast with bleaker pictures of the General Strike of 1926, mass unemployment (reaching a peak of just under three million in the winter of 1932–3), bug-ridden slums in Liverpool, Glasgow, Manchester and East London, and the Jarrow Hunger Marchers.

In fact, there was a rise in the standard of living for many people as the new industries – engineering, cars, electricity and plastics – developed, cinema and wireless brought new forms of mass entertainment, and the suburbs spread. Over two-and-a-half million houses were built during the 1930s, two-thirds of which were for private purchase (Stevenson, 1977, 34). By 1939 two thirds of houses were wired for electricity (Stevenson, 1977, 17), and there were over three million motor vehicles on the road (ibid, 39) making day-tripping a new pastime. In this rapidly changing but divided nation, the middle-class woman, especially if she were married, might have a car, a new house, a wireless and other consumer goods. The working-class woman, however, especially if she were single or her husband unemployed, would see little of this.

In mapping out the historical factors which influence representations of female rivalry in inter-war novels, my contention is that male anxieties about women's changing role were displaced in the 1920s by media manipulation of women's fears about the man 'shortage', and in the 1930s by an ideology of domesticity which valorised marriage. Other women were presented as rivals for a limited supply of men rather than potential political comrades. Rivalry between women was encouraged and even manufactured within the dominant discourses as a way of distracting women's attention from the real competition – between men and women for political power and jobs.

In inter-war novels anger, guilt and hate are often directed at other women rather than men, especially women of different class, age, marital status or sexuality. In her ground-breaking study, *A Very Great Profession: The Woman's Novel 1914–39*, Nicola Beauman sees the inter-war 'woman's novel' as 'written by middle-class women for middle-class women' and 'permeated through and through with the certainty of like speaking to like' (1983, 3). Alison Light, however, in *Forever England: Femininity, Literature and Conservatism Between the Wars*, detects a tension between women in such novels, which she locates in the class struggle. She argues that the history of the 'private sphere' is 'one fraught with conflict between women, as well as between the sexes' and that feminism must 'confront the schism between women which separated them in the very heart of "private life"' (1991, 219). The relative freedom of the inter-war middle-class woman was predicated on the labour of other women: 'Clearly', Naomi Mitchison acknowledged, 'without domestic help I could not have had a family and been a successful writer' (1986, 27). The recurring 'servant trouble' in E. M. Delafield's *Diary of a Provincial Lady* (1930) or Jan Struther's *Mrs Miniver* (1939) or in Hermione Lee's biography of Virginia Woolf is one place where class tensions between women break through. The triangle novel, where the women are positioned as opposites, often in class terms, is another.

Light argues that the dominant mood of the inter-war period is a 'conservative modernity' – 'a conservatism itself in revolt against the past, trying to make room for the present' (1991, 11). While the authors I want to focus on are more politically radical than those Light considers, her analysis of class is extremely useful. Being 'middle class', she argues,

in fact depends on an extremely anxious production of endless discriminations between people who are constantly assessing each other's standing. The grocer's wife in Grantham, the female bank clerk in the metropolis, the retired memsahib in Surrey, were far more likely to be aware of their differences than their mutual attitudes.

(1991, 13)

These discriminations which establish difference from other women, particularly those of class, but also marital status or sexuality, are played out especially clearly within the triangle plot.

Clash (1929), written by the Labour MP Ellen Wilkinson, is a case in point. Set during the General Strike of 1926, this is one of the few novels to have a female protagonist who is not only working class but politically active. Joan's animosity towards the wife of Tony, the man she loves, is based partly on Helen's middle-class status, contrasted with Joan's work as trade union activist. Joan offers an interesting analysis of this triangle when she remarks to a friend: '[Helen] and I are the two people most nearly concerned. Tony, apparently, has become merely the prize for the victor. I suppose most men are that, though they don't know it' (1989, 172). Here the two women are the main players and the man is merely the 'prize'. The rivalry between the two women is defused when Joan comes to see Helen as a suffering human being not just a representative of the middle classes. It is women of Helen's class, however, who attack Joan during her final speech and who inspire her decision to 'stick with my crowd' (1989, 309). She finally marries Gerry Blain, a Labour supporter who will enable her activism. Ultimately, the tenuous personal understanding between the two women cannot bridge their class or political differences.

Class differences are an ongoing issue throughout this period, but five other specific factors encouraged divisions between women: the population imbalance; the war; the impact of the work of Freud and the sexologists; debates over women's education; and anxieties over a perceived 'crisis' in marriage. Not surprisingly, the divided nature of the inter-war feminist movement itself reflects these factors.

The 'surplus woman'

The population imbalance in Britain, caused mainly by male emigration to the colonies, dated from at least the 1840s (see Appendix 1) and concern over the 'superfluous', 'surplus' or 'redundant woman' began then (Vicinus, 1985, 1–46). The words 'surplus', 'superfluous' or 'redundant' indicated an 'excess' of women who were 'surplus' because they were unmarried. The problem 'was considered particularly vexing,' Jane Lewis comments, 'because [...] it affected middle class women most'

(1984, 4). Thus it is a concern which surfaces repeatedly in the inter-war 'woman's novel'.

Exacerbated by the casualties of the First World War, the imbalance peaked in the 1920s, coinciding with the campaign for the extension of the vote to women under 30, and with concern over rising unemployment, particularly as it affected returning soldiers. The 1921 census, which recorded nearly two million more women than men, generated almost hysterical anxiety in the media. An extreme example is A. M. Ludovici's anti-feminist *Woman: A Vindication* (1923), a *tour de force* of muddled misogyny, which argued that the spinster was not only 'abnormal' but a danger to the nation itself – a 'spiritual and material scourge' (1923, 278). Of particular concern to Ludovici was women's movement into the job market:

> The thousands of spinsters of all classes who are now achieving 'independence' both in commerce and industry – not to mention the professions – naturally only increase the acuteness of the economic difficulties which make their self-support a necessity; for, by competing with male labour they only aggravate the severity of the struggle, and increase ever further and further the age at which men can safely undertake matrimony.
>
> (1923, 263)

As this reveals, the hidden subtext of the concern about the 'surplus women' was the male fear of being outnumbered by newly-enfranchised women who were encroaching on hitherto exclusively masculine domains such as politics, education and the professions. One of Ludovici's suggestions for countering the problem was that parents should train their daughters for marriage more rigorously. Thus trained, women would pursue a husband with greater vigour, even to the extent of moving to the colonies (1923, 276–7). Focusing women's attention on the 'man shortage' and constructing other women as rivals rather than potential political allies was one way of controlling women and pushing them back into the home.

Newspapers were heavily implicated in this strategy. Between 1920 and 1939 the circulation of national dailies sprang from 5.4 million to 10.5 million (Curran and Seaton, 1985, 55). Billie Melman in *Women and the Popular Imagination in the Twenties* has shown how between 1918 and 1928 'the disenfranchised female haunted the popular imagination' (1988, 1). The debate over the 'flapper vote' was 'Orchestrated by the mass-circulation newspapers of the Harmsworth brothers' and reverberated in popular novels and pulp magazines (1988, 1). The unmarried female was described in the popular press as 'a menace to the country's economy and its social and political order' (1988, 20). On 26 June 1923 the *Daily Mail*, for instance, asserted: 'The superfluous women are a disaster to the human race [...] spinsters compete with men and aggravate the economic war' (quoted in Melman, 1988, 20).

When Curran and Seaton argue that 'The papers controlled by the press barons conjured up imaginary folk devils that served to strengthen commitment to dominant political norms and to unite the centre and the right against a common enemy' (1985, 66), they have in mind the treatment of Marxists, and Rothermere's brief flirtation with the British Union of Fascists in 1934. However, their remarks shed light on the papers' transformation of the 'surplus woman' into a similar sort of 'folk devil'. She was pursued with particular vigour in the *Daily Mail*, the first mass-readership popular daily and the first to cater for women and children. Its founder, Lord Northcliffe, advised his editors always to have a 'woman's story' in the headlines (Graves and Hodge, 1941, 59), and it regularly included opinion pieces on women.

The 1918 Representation of the People Act had enfranchised some 8 479 156 women (Pugh, 1992, 34) – 39.6 per cent of the total voters. Had all women been enfranchised instead of only those over 30 (subject to a property qualification) women voters would have outnumbered men, a possibility which generated intense anxiety. 'With the preponderance of women, if all spheres of political and intellectual activity are opened to women, what will be the result? Slowly, but insidiously, will she become the dominant sex?' asked one piece in the *Mail*. Reassuringly, the (woman) writer concluded:

> I think not [...] women care very little about politics or party, but they *do* care about the betterment of mankind, the abolition of war, the improvement of the marriage and divorce laws, and, most of all, the welfare of the race, in so far as it concerns the child [...] *It is here that woman will become the dominant sex.* She will protect the race, she will improve the laws concerning children [...].
>
> (*Daily Mail*, 22 January 1920, 6, original emphasis)

This essentialist ideal of women as apolitical housewives and mothers was increasingly held up to women as an ideal.

The population imbalance coincided with a decline in the birth rate – from 35 per 1000 in 1870 to 24 in 1913 (Pugh, 1992, 1) – which exacerbated the fear that the androgynous flapper was not 'womanly' enough to bear children. Pugh comments: 'Fears about a decline in both the mental and physical capacity of British women to fulfil their role as mothers was a characteristic of the inter-war period' (1992, 87). While the image of the housewife and mother was the 'only one desirable image [...] held up to women by all the mainstream media agencies' (Beddoe, 1989, 8) women were repeatedly confronted with the statistical improbability of their marrying.

In 1920 the *Mail* reported a lecture by Dr Murray Leslie at the Institute of Hygiene in London, which epitomised the media hysteria. Headed 'Million Women Too Many/ 1920 Husband Hunt/ Dr Murray Leslie on Girl Rebels/ Secret Love Affairs', it addressed the alleged breakdown in moral standards due to the fact that 'There are now more than a million excess females of reproductive age' in Britain. Dr Leslie reported:

> Never had there been so many unhappy marriages. Many married women were demanding divorce by mutual consent [...] while married men often sought happier relationships among the numerous unattached women.
>
> Speaking from his own medical experience he had no hesitation in saying that much of the existing unhappiness was traceable to the clandestine relations between young women and married men.
>
> (Daily Mail, 5 February 1920, 7)

Castigating the 'frivolous, scantily-clad "jazzing flapper"' as 'irresponsible and undisciplined', Leslie remarked that 'The type contained a large proportion of physically attractive girls with strong reproductive instincts and they were *ever vying and competing with each other for the scarce and elusive male*' (my emphasis). He advocated female emigration, a solution which was mooted repeatedly, though it never got as far as government policy.

It was not only the *Mail* which concerned itself with this issue. Following the 1921 census, a *Times* leader on the subject provoked a letter from Brittain to Holtby commenting: 'Personally I haven't the least objection to being superfluous so long as I am allowed to be useful, and though I shall be delighted for any work I may do to take me abroad, it will not be because I shall thereby be enabled the better to capture the *elusive male*' (TY 578, my emphasis).

The picture is more complicated than it at first appears. As Martin Pugh points out, the statistics do not corroborate the assumption that large numbers of women would not marry. He goes so far as to argue that:

the indelible impression caused by writers such as Vera Brittain about a whole generation of women suddenly deprived of husbands is a gross distortion of the facts. In fact the rate of marriage among women, which had been declining a little before 1914, was only slightly reduced during the 1920s.

(1992, 222)

For women in their late teens and twenties the marriage rate was actually *higher* than before 1914 and from 1930 a greater proportion of all women began to marry. We can now see, Pugh argues, 'that the 1930s marked the start of a significant long-term trend towards marriage'(1992, 222). Moreover, as Brittain observed, marriage itself was changing from the nineteenth-century 'master–servant relationship' to 'companionship between equals' (1953, 170). The problem was not so much that women were less likely to marry but that it was perceived to be far more important that they did marry. The exaggerated reports of the man 'shortage' became a powerful myth which generated an extraordinary amount of anxiety in women, who were thus encouraged to regard other women as rivals in the marriage market.

Anxiety over the 'surplus woman' reached hysteria level again in 1927, when the debate over the 'flapper vote' resurfaced. 'Flapper' was 'the popular press catchword for an adult woman worker aged 21 to 30, when it is a question of giving her a vote under the same conditions as men of the same age' (Graves and Hodge, 1941, 44). The *Mail* declared:

The proposal to add some 4 500 000 new voters – many of them quite irresponsible persons – to the enormous total of persons already franchised is thoroughly unpopular in the country and worthy of Bedlam. All the attempts to make a sex issue out of it have failed because most sensible women are entirely satisfied with present conditions, under which they have the vote at 30.

(*Daily Mail*, 31 March 1927, 10)

The supposedly flattering distinction between 'sensible' women and the 'irresponsible' flapper yet again encourages divisions among women. As the event became more imminent, the *Mail* ran a leader about the 'Flapper Revolution' which asserted:

The most extraordinary fact about this revolution is that practically no one wanted it [. . .] The women themselves never asked for it, and many of them have said that it was scarcely fair, at a time when the ranks of manhood are depleted by the terrific sacrifices of war, to make such a far reaching change.

(Daily Mail, 16 June 1928, 10)

In other words, 'irresponsible' and non-combatant women should not profit by the greater sacrifice of men. Under a week later the *Mail* launched a beauty competition for 'Pretty girls' with prizes totalling £3600 (*Daily Mail*, 22 June 1928, 11) – a perfect example of the media deflecting women's attention from competition with men for political power, and encouraging them in rivalry with each other.

After the 1928 Equal Franchise Act gave women over 18 the vote, the debate over gender roles shifted onto new ground. By the 1930s the population imbalance had started to even out, but the decline in the birth rate was causing increasing concern. It reached its lowest point in 1933, coinciding with the year of highest unemployment. As the inter-war 'ideology of maternalism' (Lewis, 1984, 32) intensified, the spinster was vilified not just as an irresponsible 'flapper' but as a sexually frustrated danger to society.

The spinster novels of the 1920s discussed by Maroula Joannou (1995, Chapter Three) clearly engage with this anxiety over the 'surplus woman'. Joannou argues that 'the meaning of spinsterhood became a site of contestation between those who wished to objectify the spinster and others who saw her as a person with needs, desires and potential of her own' (1995, 78). Some texts, like May Sinclair's *Life and Death of Harriett Frean* (1922), Radclyffe Hall's *The Unlit Lamp* (1924), F. M. Mayor's *The Third Miss Symons* (1913) or Katherine Mansfield's 'Miss Brill' (1922), sympathetically explore the frustration, waste and loneliness of the spinster's life. Others, like Mayor's *The Rector's Daughter* (1924) or Holtby's *The Crowded Street* (1924), assert the value of her life. Agatha Christie's Miss Marple, possibly the most famous of the inter-war 'surplus women', makes inspired use of the stereotypes which allow her abilities to pass undetected by others, as does Dorothy L. Sayers's Miss Climpson in *Unnatural Death* (1927). The spinster heroine of Sylvia Townsend Warner's *Lolly Willowes* (1926) finds her vocation and her freedom as a witch.

The popularity of the female–male–female triangle plot in both the 1920s and 1930s can also be attributed partly to the population imbalance and the supposed 'scarcity' of men. A comparison with the nineteenth-century novel of female adultery examined by Bill Overton in *The Novel of Female Adultery* (1996) is useful here. Used almost exclusively by men, the plot examined by Overton is one in which 'a married woman from the middle or upper classes is seduced by an unmarried man and comes to grief' (1996, vi). Again, Overton relates it to specific historical and cultural contexts. In contrast, there are few inter-war novels by women about female adultery – E. M. Delafield's *The Way Things Are* (1927), Margaret Kennedy's *The Ladies of Lyndon* (1923), and F. Tennyson Jesse's *A Pin to See the Peepshow* (1934) are relatively rare examples.

The female-centred triangle novel, on the other hand, is extremely common. The spinster novel often uses a triangle plot – the protagonists of *Life and Death of Harriett Frean*, *The Third Miss Symons*, *The Rector's Daughter* and *The Crowded Street* are unmarried because the only possible suitor marries someone else. When that someone else is a friend or a sister there is a particularly painful conflict of loyalties. In *The Rector's Daughter* Robert Herbert is on the point of proposing to Mary when he meets and marries the beautiful but vulgarly horse-mad Kathy. Mary's single moment of passion comes when, thinking his marriage a failure, Herbert kisses her. She finds herself, to her consternation, wishing for her rival's death. Instead, when a bungled operation destroys Kathy's beauty, she becomes Kathy's greatest support. Although to outward view Mary's life is a failure (even her poems remain unpublished), the novel asserts its value as a life of service to others: 'In a sense the whole village adored Mary, but quietly' (1987, 22). Even for her rival she sacrifices her own feelings and her support strengthens the Herberts' marriage. Traditional in form, *The Rector's Daughter* evokes *Jane Eyre* when, as a child, Mary falls in love 'with Mr Rochester, Hamlet and Dr Johnson' (1987, 14). Later, like Jane Eyre, she rejects the temptation of an adulterous love. Her father's remark, made in connection with George Eliot, that 'to indulge in love for a married man is always illicit' (1987, 199), raises the possibility of a different, more self-serving life, but the novel ultimately ratifies Mary's actions.

Dr Leslie's (unsubstantiated) assumption that the population imbalance led to affairs between married men and unmarried girls is interesting since the affair with a married man is a common plot (particularly in the 1930s) which I will examine in more detail below. E. Arnot Robertson's *Four Frightened People* (1931), for instance, is a self-conscious version of what is referred to in the text as the 'triangle drama' (1982, 22) of popular fiction, a comment which suggests its ubiquitousness. Moreover, several novelists – Rebecca West, Vera Brittain, Dorothy Richardson, Jean Rhys, Storm Jameson, Rosamond Lehmann, Ellen Wilkinson, Rose Macaulay, E. H. Young – did have important relationships with married men which are fictionalised in various ways in their novels.

The 'Great' War

While the war exacerbated the 'shortage' of men, it was also perceived as accelerating the destabilisation of gender roles as women undertook 'male' jobs and adopted more practical clothing:

> Skirts grew shorter and shorter, clothes grew more and more simple and convenient, and hair, that "crowning glory of a woman", was cut short. With one bound the young women of 1919 burst out from the hampering conventions, and with their cigarettes, their motor-cars, their latch-keys, and their athletics they astonished and scandalised their elders.
>
> (Strachey, 1978, 389)

Nostalgia for the lost Edwardian way of life and a more 'feminine' pre-war woman informs many inter-war texts.

In fact, as Claire Tylee shows in *The Great War and Women's Consciousness* (1990), the war reinforced the notion of separate male and female spheres and valorised the male soldier at the expense of women. It 'emphasised an essential difference between men and women. Women were not combatants. And they were not allowed near the firing line' (Tylee, 1990, 253). War became the ultimate signifier of gender difference. While men were fighting for their country, women's work was to 'fill subordinate roles in the Army auxiliary services or hurriedly raise sons to young husbands whose drastically shortened expectation of life left little opportunity for begetting children' (HE 347), entrenching further the ideology of maternalism. This was crucial to war propaganda because 'the fighters needed a concrete image of what they were fighting *for*' (Ouditt, 1994, 48) and this was provided by recruitment posters featuring images of loyal, waiting women and children. However, it was this sense that women were encouraging men to fight which produced the misogyny of texts like Richard Aldington's *Death of a Hero* (1929).

For the women left at home there was a 'humiliated sense of their own inferiority at being non-combatant burdens on the male part of the population' (Tylee, 1990, 253–4). In Rose Macaulay's *Non-Combatants and Others* (1916), Alix Sandomir's lameness symbolises her non-combatant status. The resentment against non-combatant women felt by the 'Fighting Forces' was intensified when returning soldiers found themselves unemployed because their jobs had been taken by women.

Folklore suggests that the war immediately provided women with greater employment and freedom. The picture is, however, more complex. Many middle-class girls found their war work was limited to knitting socks like the 'sister' in Macaulay's poem 'Many Sisters to Many Brothers' (*Poems of Today*, 1931, 23), making swabs like Joan Ogden in *The Unlit Lamp*, or 'dusting round carefully disinfected convalescents at the local hospitals' like Muriel in *The Crowded Street* (CS 127). For the sheltered middle-class girl who became a nurse, ambulance driver or Land Girl, there was a radical liberation. Woolf commented wryly that in 1914 'the daughters of educated men' would 'undertake any task however menial, exercise any fascination however fatal that enabled [them] to escape' the education of the private house (1986, 46). The almost erotic excitement felt by women who believed that they were at last participating in 'real life' is conveyed in Sinclair's *The Romantic* (1920), which sets out to prove that women could do war work as well as if not better than some men. As Holtby commented:

> One of the few good features of the war of 1914 was that it gave an opportunity for women to prove their individual capacity. Running hospitals, conducting operations, holding high positions in the Civil Service, working as farmers, engineers and bus conductors, driving lorries, making shells, cleaning windows, and finally replacing soldiers at the base in Queen Mary's Army Auxiliary Corps, they threw down a challenge to those who had hitherto relegated them to kitchen, nursery or drawing room.
>
> (Berry and Bishop, 1985, 94–5)

This, however, elides class differences. Women working in the Voluntary Aid Detachment (VADs) were recruited from middle-class women, who volunteered for patriotic reasons. In *Not So Quiet* (1930), Helen Zenna Smith's ambulance driver protagonist writes:

> It astounds me why the powers-that-be at the London headquarters stipulate that refined women of decent education are essential for this ambulance work. Why should they want this class to do the work of strong navvies, in addition to the work of scullery maids under conditions no professional scullery-maid would tolerate for a day?
>
> (1988, 50)

While the middle-class girls were 'doing their bit' for their country, most of the lower-class girls working as WAACS (Women's Army Auxiliary Corps) 'enlisted because of the pay' (Smith, 1988, 220).

This class division is confirmed by Gail Braybon and Penny Summerfield's comprehensive *Out of the Cage: Women's Experiences in Two World Wars* (1987) which shows that the typical woman war-worker was a young, working-class ex-domestic worker who went into a factory. Only about nine per cent of munition workers were upper- or middle-class volunteers, although the proportion was higher amongst VADs, the Land Army and the police volunteers (Braybon and Summerfield, 1987, 74–5). For the first year of the war women's employment actually *fell*. It was only after the establishment of the Ministry of Munitions and the Munitions Act of 1915 that women's employment started to rise and they were encouraged into 'men's jobs' in industry, commerce, transport, ship building and mining. After January 1916 their efforts made it possible for the government to introduce conscription for men. The figures are impressive:

> In July 1914, there were 3,276,000 women in industry (not including many homeworkers or those in small workshops), plus about 1,600,000 domestic servants. By April 1918, the total stood at 4,808,000. This meant there had been an increase of about $1\frac{1}{2}$ million women in the industrial labour force.
>
> (Braybon and Summerfield, 1987, 38–9)

Many of these women came from domestic service which lost 400 000 workers during the war (Braybon and Summerfield, 1987, 39).

After the war public opinion swung against women war workers. They were called 'parasites, blacklegs and limpets' (Strachey, 1978, 371), and 'represented as vampires who deprived men of their rightful jobs' (Graves and Hodge, 1941, 44) in order to force them back into the domestic sphere as wives or servants. Both Beddoe and Braybon and Summerfield provide evidence of working-class women's unwillingness to go into domestic service because of its low status, poor conditions and low pay compared to factory work, but women risked losing their unemployment benefit if they refused a job. By 1919 there were half-a-million women unemployed, and by 1921 domestic service was again the largest employer of women (Pugh, 1992, 82–3). Women's rate of employment in 1921 and 1931 was actually *lower* than it had been in 1911 (Beddoe, 1989, 4). To talk of women as emancipated by the war, then, is misrepresentative and erases class differences. It is even debatable whether it was their war work that gained women the vote in 1918. Certainly Sylvia Pankhurst attributed it to male fears of resumed suffragette activity (Pankhurst, 1977, 607).

The sense of sisterhood between women, developed by the suffrage campaigners and conveyed, for instance, in Elizabeth Robins's *The Convert* (1907), is lost at this point, as women constructed themselves instead as 'sisters' to their soldier 'brothers'. The need to defend Britain took precedence over the fight for the vote (although Anne Wiltsher estimates that half of the women in the movement opposed the war (1985, 1)) and the political alliances formed to fight for suffrage – the Women's Political and Social Union (WSPU), and the National Union of Women's Suffrage Societies (NUWSS) – were broken up.

Although the majority of women spent their day-to-day lives with other women, their hopes, energies and dreams were focused on the absent men. Two autobiographies particularly demonstrate this male-identification in women who worked as VAD nurses – Enid Bagnold's *A Diary Without Dates* (1918) and Vera Brittain's *Testament of Youth* (1933). Bagnold's *Diary* combines admiration for the British Tommy with 'an equally sincere contempt for women' (Tylee, 1990, 192). When a wounded soldier mistakenly addresses her as 'Sister', Bagnold thrills: 'How wonderful to be called Sister! Every time the uncommon name is used towards me I feel the glow of an implied relationship' (1978, 4). Crucially, the word 'Sister' is valued not as indicating Bagnold's place in a 'sisterhood' of nurses but as 'sister' to the soldier.

Similarly, Brittain records little interest in or respect for women until she meets Holtby. In *Testament of Youth* Brittain set out to write the 'epic of the women who went to war' (1953, 188) but she was also creating a memorial to the men who were killed, including her fiancé, Roland Leighton, and her brother, Edward. The tension between these two aims produces a text which valorises the men at the expense of women. At one point she even remarks that 'most women annoy me' (TY 85). Brittain nursed because it was the 'next best thing' to being a man (TY 213–4) but in the hierarchy of suffering nothing she, or any other woman, did could put them on a level with the soldiers.

This valorisation of the soldiers led women to internalise not only their own inferiority but that of other women, particularly those of a lower social class. Class differences were particularly obvious in hospitals where the middle-class VADs worked alongside lower-class professional nurses. *Testament of Youth* 'directly reproduces some of the less palatable ideologies that helped to make the VAD institution successful' (Ouditt, 1994, 3). Brittain disparages the professional nurses who were, she claims, driven 'almost frantic with jealousy and suspicion' (TY 309) by the VAD nurses they perceived as threatening their jobs. Such divisions enforce Brittain's sense of identification with the men of her own class. The lack of gender solidarity here is particularly surprising in a text written by a self-proclaimed feminist to publicise women's war work.

Macaulay's *Non-Combatants and Others* offers a more acute analysis of both how the war encouraged a male desire for traditional, comforting 'femininity', and how it altered women's loyalties to each other. The war-damaged Basil finds Alix 'too nervy', and wants instead a 'placid, indifferent, healthy sort of girl' (Macaulay, 1986, 73). The girl he turns to, appropriately named Evie, is a 'type' Basil would previously have resented and 'called [...] names, such as Woman' (1986, 98). Alix acts uncharacteristically when she deliberately destroys Evie's interest in Basil. 'It's the war [...] I shouldn't have done that before the war,' she thinks, 'I suppose I might do anything now' (1986, 128). This complicates Ouditt's contention that during the war 'Comradeship was a crucial element in women's new order of experience [...] A number developed close female friends and a concomitant sense of bonding and belonging' (1994, 31–2). This was true for some women, but it is not reflected in most accounts of the war which are characterised by a sense of divisions between women.

Helen Zenna Smith's *Not So Quiet* does document comradeship between women – Nell Smith's closest relationships are with her co-worker, Tosh, and her younger sister, Trix. But, despite this, the most scathing attacks in the book are not on male generals or politicians but on other women. Nell's anger is directed at the patriotic mothers who 'give' their children to the cause, women like the 'Little Mother' whose letter in *The Morning Post* attested her willingness to 'pass on the human ammunition of "only sons" to fill up the gaps' (Graves, 1960, 189). Nell fantasises about revealing the real horrors of the war to them:

> Look closely, Mother and Mrs Evans-Mawnington [...] These trays each contain something that was once a whole man [...] the heroes who have done their bit for King and country [...] Shut your eyes [...] lest their groans and heart-rending cries linger as long in your memory as in the memory of the daughter you sent out to help win the War.
>
> (1988, 90–1)

The few men in *Not So Quiet* are vulnerable victims in contrast to the portrayals of 'Mrs Bitch' who runs the ambulance corps, of cook – 'a fat, common, lazy, impertinent slut' (1988, 50), or of ward sisters who are 'Bitches – no other word' (199). *Not So Quiet*, like *Testament of Youth*, bears witness to women's internalisation of their inferiority as non-combatants and the projection of that internalisation onto other women.

Sharon Ouditt comments that after the war, 'The currency of romance [...] remained dominant, but it was undermined by the absence of its primary structuring force – the right man' (1994, 116). The myth that, as Brittain writes, 'the first-rate were gone from a whole generation' (TY 260) was one of the most enduring legacies of the war and powerfully affected women in two ways. Firstly, by stressing that the best of a generation had died in the trenches, it reinforced women's sense of inferiority. Not only had they not died for their country but they could not replace the men who had. Secondly, many women, including Vera Brittain and Rosamond Lehmann, felt they had been denied the men who should have been their husbands and lovers. Indeed, Brittain, who remarked that her post-war suitors 'hadn't the brains of an earwig' and 'simply provided one proof after another that the best of their sex had disappeared from a whole generation' (TY 608), was partially responsible for perpetuating this idea.

Anxiety about the changing role of women was fed by fears about masculinity. Men damaged physically or psychologically by the war are a recurring motif in inter-war novels right through into the 1930s – the amnesiac Chris Baldry in West's *The Return of the Soldier*, Septimus Warren Smith in Woolf's *Mrs Dalloway* (1925), the partially-paralysed Gerry Blain in Wilkinson's *Clash,* Sayers's shell-shocked Peter Wimsey, and the impotent William Gary in Storm Jameson's *Love in Winter* (1935). If the 'right man' is not killed he is often tied to an emotionally dead marriage, or so damaged that he turns either away from women or to a 'womanly' woman. The triangle plot is a double expression of anxiety about the lack of the 'right man' as well as the 'excess' of women.

Freud and the sexologists

When Virginia Woolf remarked that 'in or about December, 1910, human character changed' (1966–7, Vol. I, 320) it was largely, as her initial drafts show (Faulkner, 1977, 35), the impact of Sigmund Freud's work she had in mind. Selections of Freud's work were first published in Britain in 1909 and the first translation of a complete work, *Three Contributions to a Theory of Sex*, appeared in 1910, also the year in which Havelock Ellis's *Studies in the Psychology of Sex*, banned in Britain in 1897, was finally published in Britain in its entirety. This work brought sex out of the Victorian closet and opened up a new discourse. The key ideas of psychoanalysis – the unconscious, sublimation, repression and the 'Oedipus complex' – rapidly became common currency. Talking about sex became fashionable: 'the late war-intellectuals gabbled of Oedipus across the tea-cups or Soho cafe tables' (H. D., 1984, 8). But, as Graves and Hodge recorded, the 'Freudian gospel' that filtered down into people's minds through such popular discussion was that 'The first requirement for mental health is an uninhibited sex-life. To be well and happy, one must obey one's sexual urge' (1941, 103). This chimed with Ellis's emphasis on women's right to a fulfilled sex life.

As feminist theorists, particularly Sheila Jeffreys (1985) and Margaret Jackson (1994), have shown, it is not enough to regard this period simply as one of sexual liberation. The work of Freud and Ellis provided theorisations of gender which answered a specific historical need. By setting out an ideal of what women *ought* to be, Freud and Ellis offered a means of controlling them. Their construction of both lesbian and spinster as 'unnatural' and their pathologisation of female friendship forced another wedge between women.

Their acknowledgement of female sexuality ran hand-in-hand with an attempt to control it. Freud and Breuer's *Studies on Hysteria* (1893–5), as Elaine Showalter says, 'seemed to lay the ground work for a culturally aware therapy that took women's words and women's lives seriously, that respected the aspirations of New Women, and that allowed women to have a say in the management of hysterical symptoms' (1987, 158). As such, it attracted the interest of women writers such as May Sinclair, H. D., and Rebecca West. But, as Showalter shows, Freud became increasingly rigid in his treatment of hysteria. In 'Female Sexuality' (1931) and 'Femininity' (1932), the links between women's restricted lives and neurosis have been lost and his descriptions have become prescriptions. By the 1930s psychoanalysis had hardened into an attempt to establish and enforce a notion of 'normal femininity'. Similarly, the work of the sexologists reinforced the patriarchal model of female sexuality as 'natural', giving it 'scientific' validity (Jackson, 1994, 2–3).

This paradoxical mixture of liberation and control is reflected in the work of Marie Stopes. Her *Married Love* (1918), the first marriage manual, was heavily indebted to Ellis's work, and helped to disseminate it. The effect of her book on women's lives was practical and tangible, not least through her birth control clinics. Naomi Mitchison records the 'marked increase in happiness' in her married life after she and her husband read the book (1986, 69–70). However, Stopes did not advocate female sexual autonomy but female sexual health in the interests of the state: 'I am convinced,' she wrote in *Enduring Passion* (1928), 'that the more *happy*, child-bearing and *enduringly* passionate marriages there are in a State, the more firmly established is that State' (1934, xii–xiii, original emphasis).

Not only was contraception only to be available to married women, it was mainly middle-class women who benefited. Between 1910 and 1930 the number of middle-class people using birth control rose from nine per cent to forty per cent, while the number of working-class people rose from one per cent to twenty-eight per cent (Lewis, 1984, 18). In *Clash* a miner's wife bitterly castigates the vicar's wife: 'Your class keep us women in ignorance and then you treat us as though we had committed a crime when we have another baby that you won't tell us how to prevent' (1989, 247).

The new discourse endorsed women's 'natural' role as heterosexual wife and mother, but condemned as 'unnatural' behaviour (lesbianism or celibacy) which removed women from the control of men. By the 1930s chastity for women had become, Holtby remarked, a 'far worse crime than promiscuity' (Berry and Bishop, 1985, 91).

The lesbian was even more heavily stigmatised as 'unnatural' and dangerous to other women. Both Freud and Ellis theorised lesbianism in terms of masculinity. Freud's 'The Psychogenesis of a Case of Homosexuality in a Woman' (1920) argues that his patient, who is (tellingly) 'a feminist', has a 'masculinity complex' (Freud, 1991, 397). As Luce Irigaray (1985) has shown, Freud is unable to conceptualise female desire for another woman except as masculinity. Similarly, Ellis argued that 'The chief characteristic of the sexually inverted woman is a certain degree of masculinity' (1901a, 140), and she is attracted to 'more clinging feminine persons' (167), again enforcing a concept of homosexuality based on heterosexual models. While Freud's model of homosexuality is developmental, Ellis saw sexual inversion as 'based on congenital conditions' (1901a, 181). The implication of Ellis's distinction between 'congenital' and 'acquired' inversion was that heterosexual women could be seduced into lesbianism by 'true' lesbians. Moreover, Ellis classified as 'homosexual' 'precisely those forms of behaviour for which spinster feminists, the "New Women" of the 1890s, were criticised by anti-feminists' (Jeffreys, 1985, 100).

Both Lillian Faderman and Sheila Jeffreys cite the end of the First World War as the moment when 'openly expressed love between women ceased to be possible' (Faderman, 1985, 20). Faderman's *Surpassing the Love of Men* has been much criticised for her contention that pre-1900 'romantic friendships' were non-sexual. However, what Faderman usefully highlights is the political and economic implications of changes in the way that such relationships were *perceived*. It was not, she argues, simply that men condemned a female sexuality that they had only just discovered, 'It was rather that love between women, coupled with their emerging freedom, might conceivably bring about the overthrow of heterosexuality' (1985, 411). Lesbianism practised by women who had a vote, economic independence, and a name for what they were doing was a real threat. Hence, women 'were taught to see women *only as rivals* and men as their only possible love objects, or they were compelled to view themselves as "lesbian", which meant "twisted" either morally or emotionally' (1985, 412, my emphasis). Accusations of lesbianism, like the emphasis on the man shortage, were used to whip women back into the home.

An attempt to make lesbianism illegal in the 1921 Criminal Law Amendment Bill failed only because MPs were afraid that such a Bill would publicise lesbianism and give ideas to women who might not be aware that such a thing existed. The scandalous trial and banning of Radclyffe Hall's *The Well of Loneliness* in 1928, a text which, as Jean Radford (1986) has shown, uses the theories of both Ellis and Freud, provided exactly the kind of publicity MPs had tried to avoid. James Douglas, Editor of the *Sunday Express*, declared: 'I would rather give a healthy boy or a healthy girl a phial of prussic acid than this novel. Poison kills the body but a moral poison kills the soul' (Brittain, 1968, 16). The trial was a defining moment, after which social stigma increased dramatically. Anxiety about the issue can be traced in assertions during the 1930s that lesbianism among women was rising rapidly, a rise attributed by Graves and Hodge to the lack of men (1941, 101), and by the Jungian psychologist, M. Esther Harding, to the increased number of career women who reached their thirties to find 'all the men of their age already married' (1933, 132). Again, the issue here seems to be one of visibility, coupled with an anxiety about the incursion of 'surplus women' into the job market.

In *Between Men* Sedgwick argues that the continuum between homosocial and homosexual is less radically disrupted for women in our society than it is for men (1985, 2). However, it is precisely during this period, most explicitly during the *Well* trial, that we can see a radical disruption between the two being established and policed. This is reflected in contemporaneous fiction: 'What we see in 1920s novels is a process by which passionate friendship between women, which was still being written about as unexceptional in the early 1920s, is transformed by the intrusion of the lesbian stereotype' (Jeffreys, 1985, 121).

Not only did twentieth-century literature by heterosexuals usually show love between women as a disease, but lesbian women internalised these views and this 'was reflected in their own literature, which was full of self-doubts and self-loathing until the 1960s' (Faderman, 1985, 20). This view, however, does not allow for the fact that women could and did use the concept of the invert, as Hall did in *The Well of Loneliness*, as a political identity for their own ends.

The predatory, vampire lesbian is a recurrent figure in inter-war literature and frequently comes to a nasty end. She is usually an older, more experienced woman as in Clemence Dane's *Regiment of Women* (1917) and Rosamond Lehmann's *Dusty Answer* (1927). The 'congenital invert' of Ellis's theory, she represents the danger that heterosexual women would be seduced into lesbianism. One version of the triangle plot presents the 'true', and therefore 'unnatural', lesbian and a man as rivals for the 'feminine' woman. D. H. Lawrence's 'The Fox' (1922) is a particularly misogynous version where Bancroft is killed by Henry so that he can marry March, who despite her 'masculine' breeches and tunic, is the 'feminine' woman. In M. J. Farrell's *Devoted Ladies* (1934) the vampirish Jessica is again killed so that her friend, Jane, can marry. In Dorothy L. Sayers's *Unnatural Death* (1927), the 'unnatural' Mary Whittaker who plans to set up a chicken farm with another woman turns out to be the murderer. Elizabeth Bowen's *The Hotel* (1927) features an older women who, while a tease rather than a vampire, still wreaks emotional havoc.

When Stephen in *The Well of Loneliness* forces the woman she loves to marry a man it is a gesture of self-sacrifice which attempts to negate this stereotype of the predatory lesbian. Ironically, Stephen's gesture is the canonical one of exchange 'between men', where Stephen takes the place of one of the men and the feminine Mary is an object of exchange. Hall's use of this narrative pattern echoes her use of Ellis/Freud-inspired heterosexual models for the lesbian relationship. The 'masculine' Stephen desires Mary '*as a man*' (Irigaray, 1985, 194, original emphasis) would desire her. Hall's earlier *The Unlit Lamp* more skilfully destabilises the 'natural'/'unnatural' opposition. The 'rivals' here are Joan's mother and her former governess Elizabeth, while the man is almost irrelevant. It is the mother who is 'almost loverlike' (1981, 66), clinging to her daughter like an octopus. In contrast, the relationship between Joan and Elizabeth offers Joan a healthy 'natural' life.

Emma Donoghue suggests that eighteenth-century women writers 'often used a heterosexual plot as a framework for a safe discussion of women's love for each other' (1993, 138). After 1918 the sentimental friendships Donoghue discusses become suspect even within the romance plot. Instead, the strength of female bonding in the inter-war period is frequently explored, paradoxically, through female rivalry within the triangle plot. This becomes more understandable if we bear in mind Girard's point that the relationship between the two rivals can be more determining than that between either rival and the beloved. Several inter-war triangle novels, although apparently 'heterosexual', actually explore the strength of women's bonds. *Summer Will Show*, *Rebecca* (1938), and Mansfield's 'Bliss' (1920) although ostensibly about female rivalry, can be read as tracking lesbian desire. (See Hanscombe (1991) for a lesbian reading of 'Bliss', for instance.) In these novels the 'heterosexual' plot structure and the presence of the man act as a kind of alibi, under cover of which women writers can explore bonds between women. Desire for the other woman is mediated or displaced through the body of the man.

Bonds between sisters are, like those between mothers and daughters (as shown by Heather Ingman, 1998), a recurrent theme in inter-war fiction and are another way of exploring bonds between women. The rival sisters plot is used in Sinclair's *The Three Sisters* (1914), E. Arnot Robertson's *Ordinary Families* (1933), Kate O'Brien's *The Ante-Room* (1934) and Elizabeth Bowen's *Friends and Relations* (1931). The aunt and niece relationship in E. H. Young's *The Misses Mallett* (1922) is another version of this.

Finally, four texts based on Vita Sackville-West's elopement with Violet Trefusis illustrate another way of writing lesbian desire – by camouflaging it as 'heterosexual'. In Sackville-West's *Challenge* (1924) and Trefusis's *Broderie Anglaise* (1986; published in France in 1935) the Sackville-West character is fictionalised as a man. In both books lesbian desire surfaces in coded ways. In *Challenge* the affair between Julian and Eve is coded as incestuous (they are cousins), reflecting Sackville-West's fear of what she called her 'perverted nature' (Nicolson, 1990, 36). In *Broderie Anglaise* the primacy of woman-to-woman relationships surfaces through the movement of Alexa and Anne from the position of rivals over the man to that of 'colleagues, both on the same side' (1992, 95). In *Portrait of a Marriage* (1973) Sackville-West's autobiographical account of her affair with Trefusis is embedded within the 'portrait of a marriage', edited by her son, Nigel Nicolson, and thus presented as an temporary aberration. By camouflaging lesbian desire in this way, Sackville-West, Trefusis, and Nicolson, like Radclyffe Hall, all endorse heterosexual models as 'normal'. It is perhaps Woolf's version of the affair in the gender-bending *Orlando* (1928), where Orlando him/herself changes sex, which comes closest to writing about female desire without using the stereotypes of heterosexuality, although even here Woolf has to use the camouflage of fantasy.

'Autonomous women's worlds': women and education

Throughout the period, as both secondary school and university education for women expanded, there were ongoing debates about what kind of education was suitable for women; whether they should be given an education similar to boys, which might de-sex them, or whether they should be educated for marriage and motherhood. One particular concern was that, as Havelock Ellis argued, single sex girls' schools encouraged lesbianism. (Ellis's *Studies in the Psychology of Sex*, vol.I, included an appendix on 'The School-friendships of Girls', which investigated the phenomenon of the 'flame' in Italian schoolgirls.) These anxieties about women's education are reflected in 'gynaeceum novels' (Frith, 1988, Chapter Five, Part Three) like *Regiment of Women*, *Dusty Answer*, Brittain's *The Dark Tide* (1923), Sayers's *Gaudy Night* (1935) and 'Olivia's' *Olivia* (1949), which have a school or university setting, and in which conflict between women, often rivalry over another woman, is a central theme.

These years saw the emergence of the university-educated female novelist together with the birth of the educated woman as a character in fiction. By 1914 women could take their degrees at the universities of London, Wales, Scotland, Manchester, Leeds and Liverpool, while Oxford awarded degrees to women in 1920 and Cambridge in 1948. Out of my five central novelists, three were university educated: Lehmann went to Girton College, Cambridge, while Holtby and Brittain went to Somerville College, Oxford. The other 'Somerville novelists' numbered in an article by Brittain included Rose Macaulay, Dorothy L. Sayers, Margaret Kennedy, Hilda Reid, Muriel Jaeger and Sylvia Thompson (Berry and Bishop, 1985, 320–5), while Storm Jameson went to Leeds and London.

University education provided these women with the skills and confidence to pursue careers and to write. Yet this confidence was hard-won. The education system of the inter-war years was riddled with class and gender divisions. The Education Act of 1870 had established elementary schools for both sexes, thus increasing jobs for women teachers. In 1902 local authorities began setting up high schools for girls. The Education ('Fisher') Act of 1918 then raised the school leaving age from 12 to 14, providing elementary education for all children up to the age of 14 (although cuts in education spending in 1922 blunted the effects of this). Since all secondary education was fee-paying, however, only 14 per cent of children went on to it, half of those on scholarships (Beddoe, 1989, 34). For working-class children the chances of going to university were slim.

Girls' education in all classes was affected by the belief that it was unnecessary and might even be a disadvantage in married life. The educated woman in inter-war fiction is accompanied by her shadow, the woman denied that education. Poignant examples include Muriel in *The Crowded Street,* who is told by her headmistress that astronomy is not a necessary subject for girls – ' "How will it help you, dear, when you, in your future life, have, as I hope, a house to look after?"' (CS, 29) – and Joan Ogden in *The Unlit Lamp,* whose mother will not allow her to go to university.

The inter-war period did see a huge increase in the numbers of girls attending secondary school, from 185 000 in 1920 to 500 000 in 1936, although this was far outstripped by the number of boys (Beddoe, 1989, 40). Girls attending the single sex public and grant-maintained county secondary schools followed a curriculum based on that of boys' education. Such schools provided a space which validated female identity, rewarded intelligence and independence, and within which female friendships could flourish. Beddoe comments: 'What singled out girls' secondary schools, and to a certain extent women's colleges, was that they were autonomous women's worlds. Nowhere else did women have as much power' (1989, 43). This autonomy came under increasing attack during the inter-war period. Having enforced domestic subjects for girls in elementary schools as preparation for wife and motherhood, as well as domestic service, the Board of Education made a concerted effort to impose different curricula for boys and girls in secondary schools. Beddoe suggests that they failed only because of lack of evidence that girls and boys were psychologically different (1989, 41).

Particularly damaging were the attacks which used the discourses of 'perverse' sexuality made available by Ellis and Freud in order to stigmatise spinster teachers as sexually frustrated or deviant. Since the marriage bar, introduced in 1922 and only lifted by the London Council in 1935, forced women teachers to give up their jobs on marriage female teachers were, of necessity, single. They were attacked, Alison Oram suggests, not only 'as sexually independent spinsters and as feminists, but also as economically powerful women who challenged men's authority by demanding equal opportunities in the profession' (1989, 107). Women teachers were not only vocal in demanding equal pay with male teachers – they were paid four-fifths of the male rate (Beddoe, 1989, 80) – they also had a high profile in other feminist campaigns (Oram, 1989, 108). The widening awareness of lesbianism provided a discourse which could be used to control such women by threatening them with the stigma of perversion. The impact of these discourses can be traced in the schoolgirl story as written by Angela Brazil, Elsie Oxenham and Elinor Brent-Dyer. Rosemary Auchmuty shows that while Oxenham's early texts explore 'women's struggle to relate to each other in a mature, loving and non-possessive way' (1989, 128), her later texts focus on heterosexual love and marriage.

In fact, the anxiety over friendships between girls seems to have been less acute than concern over the potential influence of the spinster teacher. Oram quotes a newspaper report on a conference where a Dr Williams castigated spinster teachers, declaring: 'The women who have the responsibility of teaching these girls are, many of them themselves embittered, sexless, or homosexual hoydens who try to mould the girls into their own pattern' (1989, 105). The girls' school was increasingly seen as 'unnatural' but, also, conversely, as encouraging women's 'natural' tendency to be rivalrous and catty. Winifred Holtby records a man's comment on Roedean: 'Awful [...] Imagine a place like that. All those women, cooped up together, scratching each other's eyes out. Women weren't intended for that sort of thing' (1934, 1). Girls' schools were seen as sexual hothouses, forcing illicit, unhealthy emotions between women. Deprived of more 'normal' objects for their desire, their 'natural' rivalry was supposedly channelled into competition for other women, specifically teachers, rather than 'healthy' competition over men.

Clemence Dane's *Regiment of Women* replicates such fears and 'signal[s] the destructive impact of the sexologists' (Frith, 1988, 285). The over-crowded warren-like girls' school is seen as breeding 'unnatural' passions between women, in direct contrast with the co-educational school with its 'sunlight and fresh air and space' (Dane, 1995, 220). Clare Hartill is a text-book vampire lesbian who preys on her younger colleague, Alwynne Durand, and causes the death of one of their pupils. The novel uses a three-women triangle formation, and the rivalry or 'duel' (1995, 70) is between Clare and Alwynne's aunt, Elspeth, who has brought up the motherless Alwynne. However, Elspeth cedes her corner of the triangle to Roger, who woos Alwynne into the 'healthy' heterosexuality of marriage. The thesis of the book is articulated by Elspeth: 'After all, feminine friendship is all very well, very delightful [...] but when it is a question of Marriage – Oh, Miss Hartill, surely you see what I mean? [...] We both know that an unmated woman – she's a failure –

she's unfulfilled.' (1995, 334–5) As Alison Hennegan notes, *Regiment of Women* 'established a pattern and a cast of characters which would exert a powerful influence over lesbian fiction for the next half-century' (Dane, 1995, xiii), including Lehmann's *Dusty Answer*. Winifred Holtby's Sarah Burton in *South Riding* (1936) is an important and conscious corrective to it.

It was by no means an accepted move even for girls from the public and county secondary schools to go to university. While her brother's university entry was automatic, Brittain details the long battle to get her parents to allow her to go, and records 'one lugubrious lady' asking her mother: 'How *can* you send your daughter to college, Mrs Brittain! [...] Don't you want her ever to get *married*' (TY 73, original emphasis). Under a quarter of English university students in the mid-1920s were women (Stevenson, 1990, 257–8). They faced, as Susan Leonardi documents in *Dangerous by Degrees* (1989), hostility from both male undergraduates and the authorities. Women were mocked for their appearance, their diligence, and even for the spartan conditions they endured, so memorably recorded in Woolf's description of the meagre dinner at 'Fernham' in *A Room of One's Own*.

Brittain gives a moving account of watching the first women to receive degrees at Oxford in 1920:

> Even the unchanging passivity of Oxford beneath the hand of the centuries must surely, I thought, be a little stirred by the sight of the women's gowns and caps – those soft, black pseudo-mortar-boards with their deplorable habit of slipping over one eye – which were nevertheless the visible signs of a profound revolution.
>
> (TY 508)

Those 'pseudo-mortar-boards' epitomise the ambivalent plight of the educated woman, never quite equal to men and marked by her internalisation of the view that education equalled loss of femininity.

This anxiety is clear in Margaret Kennedy's best-selling *The Constant Nymph* (1924). As in *Regiment of Women*, an opposition is set up between the 'natural' woman, in this case the 'nymph', Tessa, and the 'unnatural' woman, her older cousin and guardian, Florence. While Florence is presented as corrupted by her school, Cleeve, which is, her father suspects, full of 'earnest cultivated women who read Robert Browning and wanted degrees. A dreadful type!' (Kennedy, 1924, 235), Tessa is linked to a pre-war Edenic Europe where, we assume, women were not educated. Tessa's attraction for Lewis Dodd, the composer husband of Florence, and, undoubtedly, for the inter-war male reader, lies in nostalgia for her 'innocent' (i.e. uneducated) youth and her status as an object for male use. Florence's father reflects that Tessa 'seemed almost like Lewis's belonging' (1924, 238). Florence is castigated for her sexual jealousy and, indeed, for desiring Lewis at all. Tessa dies, however, before she and Lewis spend their first night together, thus neatly evading the issues of both underage sex and adultery.

Reading this as an expression of anxiety about the educated woman, we can see how this anxiety was deflected into sexual rivalry between women. Lewis's comment to Florence that 'I feel that the worst thing I've done is that somehow I've put you and Tessa against each other. Because you ought to love each other' (1924, 288) indicates how the presence of the male constructs the two women as sexual rivals and cancels out any friendship between them. Claud Cockburn in *Bestseller: The Books that Everyone Read 1900–1939* argues that 'The bestsellers really are a mirror of "the mind and face" of an age' (1972, 7). That is, they reflect the prevailing ideology. *The Constant Nymph* not only reflects the dominant ideology, but has an almost schizophrenic feel as if Kennedy, herself educated at Cheltenham and Somerville, is not quite in control of her material.

Dorothy L. Sayers offers a more astute analysis of the divisive nature of this anxiety in her detective novel, *Gaudy Night*, which, despite its status as 'popular fiction', contests rather than reinforces the dominant ideology. Returning to her Oxford college to try to identify the writer of a series of poison pen letters, Harriet Vane finds herself accepting the stereotypes which suggest that the writer must be one of the celibate, and therefore 'repressed' female dons:

> The warped and repressed mind is apt enough to turn and wound itself. 'Soured virginity' – 'unnatural life' – 'semi-demented spinsters' – 'starved appetite and suppressed impulses' – 'unwholesome atmosphere' – [Harriet] could think of whole sets of epithets, ready minted for circulation.
>
> (Sayers, 1981, 74)

It's a piece of bad scholarship on Harriet's part to accept as 'truth' what her own experience should show her are easy stereotypes.

The force of the dominant ideology is such that the dons begin to suspect one another, nearly destroying their own community. As the Dean worries: 'I suppose it might even be one of ourselves. That's what's so horrible. Yes, I know – elderly virgins, and all that [...].' (1981, 76). In fact, the poison pen writer turns out to be the widowed scout, Annie, acting out the 'usual masculine spite against academic woman' (1981, 99). This spite can be traced to the male fear that independent women threatened male jobs and power – Annie's husband had lost his job and degree after Miss Hillyard, one of the dons, reported his academic malpractice. The female community is joyfully vindicated when, in *Busman's Honeymoon* (1937), Harriet is married from college with the dons as 'bridesmaids' and the Head to give her away. Despite the fact that it is Wimsey who solves the crime, *Gaudy Night* is one of the strongest fictional affirmations in this period of women's equal right to the world of academic excellence.

The 'Present Crisis in Marriage'

Despite women's movement into education and the professions, the ever-strengthening notion that women's place was in the home reinforced the demographic trend towards marriage in the 1930s. Alongside this ideology of marriage and domesticity, however, was a growing sense that there was, as a wireless series put it, a 'Present Crisis in Marriage' (Malinowski and Briffault, 1931, 7–8). This was attributed partly to the rising number of divorces following the 1923 Matrimonial Causes Act but also to women's changing expectations. The campaign for a further liberalisation of the law which culminated in A. P. Herbert's Matrimonial Causes Bill in 1937 provoked much debate. The abdication of Edward VIII in 1936 in order to marry the twice-divorced Wallis Simpson demonstrates both the increasing emphasis given to the need for a companionate marriage and the stigma against divorce.

The 'cult of domesticity' Martin Pugh identifies in the 1930s (1992, Chapter Seven) was particularly explicit in the new magazines for women – *Woman's Own* (1932) and *Woman* (1936) – which were dedicated to promoting the image of woman as happy homemaker. The business of running a home was lauded as a highly skilled job, indeed, as one writer put it, 'the most highly skilled job I know except, perhaps, the doctor's work' (*Woman's Own*, 28 April 1934, vol. 4, no. 81, 69). Sandwiched between the fashion tips and cookery hints, however, were articles offering advice on how to manage a marriage – and a husband – which suggest suppressed anxieties which are at odds with the otherwise highly idealised vision presented in these magazines.

The emphasis on female rivalry takes on a new flavour here as the wife is warned against 'vamps' (unscrupulously flirtatious women) who have designs on her husband. Barbara Hedworth's series 'Hold Your Man!' (see frontispiece), for instance, offered the following advice:

You have seen all the films and plays in which a married man is lured from his home by the charms of another woman, often not as attractive as his wife. [...] There is no reason why married women should not be able to hold their own against these vamps who exist, unfortunately, just as much in real life as they do in the screen or stage. You can vamp your own husband throughout your life if only you will take the trouble to understand him, and in this series of articles I am going to try to help you by showing how different types of men react to different types of treatment.

(*Woman's Own*, 20 January 1934, vol. 3. no. 67, 437)

The same year Leonora Eyles advised readers that 'No woman need lose her man if she will not let herself get mentally lazy or peevish' (*Woman's Own*, 18 August 1934, vol. 4, no. 97, 565). Clearly, the onus was on women to prevent their husbands from straying by maintaining their homes, their children and themselves in peak condition, while the men themselves were regarded as childlike beings to be tactfully supervised and guided. Not only that but one article even advised any wife whose husband strayed to 'Make Friends with the "Other Woman"' in an effort to learn from her rival how best to please her man (*Woman's Own*, 1 February 1936, vol. 7, no. 173, 641).

Holtby satirised such articles in a radio piece called 'The Native Women', a mock taxonomy of British women, where she writes of the 'Perfect Wives':

They are constantly greeted by home-coming husbands enraptured by the success of culinary experiments, unless by some chance they have omitted to take adequate care of their appearance, in which case the husband too frequently becomes unfaithful and is led away by a Vampire Type.

(1935, 947)

The man-hunting 'flapper' of the 1920s has undergone a change of name but in her new incarnation as the 'vamp' (close cousin to the vampire lesbian) she is still presented as a rival to other women. This stereotype that women will always and only see other women as sexual competitors comes from the assumption that men's interests are general while women are interested primarily in men.

The magazine fiction of the period tends to accept this assumption uncritically. In Mollie Seymour's 'Can Marriage Be Like That?' (*Woman's Own*, 4 January 1936, vol. 7, no. 169, 515) for instance, Patricia's husband Brian is seduced into infidelity by his 'slick-looking' secretary. In a plot with *Jane Eyre* overtones Patricia becomes governess to the children of the widowed Major Jonathan Grange, falls in love with him and, after Brian has conveniently died a drunk in Chile, is able to marry Jonathan without even having to go through the divorce courts. Fascinatingly, Patricia actually has the same name as Jonathan's first wife, suggesting that the two women are at some level interchangeable. However, Patricia's relationship with Jonathan is so all-encompassing that the other women are never developed beyond the stereotypes of perfect wife or vampish-rival.

The novels of the period, however, give the lie to this assumption because they so often demonstrate that women are interested in, even fascinated by, other women. If fiction were simply a direct reflection of the dominant ideology what one would expect in the 1930s would be a rash of novels about marriages threatened by vampish women. While the spinster novel prevailed in the 1920s, in the 1930s, as I have shown elsewhere, there is a shift in focus as women's novels examine the institution of marriage (Wallace, 1999). The wife and mistress triangle (perhaps the most obvious version of the erotic triangle) is common throughout the inter-war period but it is in forms which problematise the stereotypes. Point of view (or focalisation) is a key issue here. Barbara Hedworth's advice in *Woman's Own* directly addresses the *wife* ('you') as reading subject while the 'vamp' is constructed as '*other*'. Texts which are focalised through the wife are rarer and more complex than this would imply. In Katherine Mansfield's 'Bliss' (1920), for instance, Bertha's discovery that her husband is having an affair with Pearl Fulton is complicated by her own attraction to Miss Fulton, symbolised by the pear tree they both admire. That attraction awakens Bertha's desire for her husband for the first time but the ending of the story is left open. Reading it against *Summer Will Show*, also focalised through the wife, one possible answer to Bertha's final question, 'what is going to happen now?' (Mansfield, 1945, 105) might be love between wife and mistress.

H. D.'s *roman-à-clef Bid Me to Live*, written in 1927 and set during the war, includes a bitter portrait of the 'other woman' from the point of view of the wife. After Julia Ashton (based on H. D.) has a still-born child, her soldier-husband, Rafe (Richard Aldington), starts an affair with Bella Carter (Dorothy 'Arabella' Yorke), who lives upstairs. 'It's perfectly clear', he tells Julia, 'I love you, I desire *l'autre*' (H. D., 1984, 56). His attempt to impose this 'mind'/'body' opposition on the two women is rejected by Julia: 'But Bella was not a harlot, Julia was not a saint' (1984, 8). In a central conversation with Bella, Julia moves from the thought that

Bella 'looked *vampire-ish*, the stage type of mistress' (1984, 103, my emphasis), to the recognition that, 'She and Bella were simply abstractions, were women of the period, were WOMAN of the period, the same one' (103). Even here there is the recognition that Bella is not just '*l'autre*' (the 'other'), but that she is in some sense 'a mirror, another self' (1984, 103). H. D. is one of several writers – Mansfield, Woolf, Richardson, Sackville-West – who combined marriage with passionate relationships with women and their texts reflect this tension.

Two later texts focalised through the wife present the 'other woman' as a kind of chimera, less dangerous than internal fractures in the marriage. In E. H. Young's *Celia* (1937) the eponymous protagonist is forced to recognise that the husband she has contemptuously tolerated has his own internal life. Although Celia's vague suspicions are unfounded – Gerald's mysterious Maudie was his feeble-minded sister – Celia has to face the fact that he has been inspired into his best work as an architect by another woman who has commissioned him to build her a house. She is not a sexual threat but Celia is 'humbled by the necessity of building [her marriage] on another woman's foundations' (1990, 414). Likewise in Margaret Kennedy's *Together and Apart* (1936) Betsy and Alec's marriage crumbles not because of Alec's desultory, long-term adultery, or even his casual kissing of the youthful (and far from vamp-ish) governess, but because of Betsy's vague dissatisfactions, exacerbated by interfering relatives. Kennedy's novel, inspired by an 'epidemic of divorce' (1981b, viii) among her acquaintance, is a counterblast to what Marie Stopes earlier called the 'cynical "modern" novels, plays or short stories, so prevalent today, [where] one reads that the married couple separated for some trivial thing' (1934, 21), and a plea for couples to work at marriage. Both partners make unsatisfactory second marriages (Alec to the governess) and their children are emotionally damaged. Like *The Constant Nymph*, *Together and Apart* reflects the prevailing ideology, specifically fears that the new divorce bill would make divorce too easy.

At the opposite end of the political spectrum is the attempt at a socialist open marriage in Naomi Mitchison's *We Have Been Warned* (1935) where Dione selflessly encourages her husband to have an affair with a young Russian girl. Based loosely on Mitchison's own marriage, this reflects contemporaneous attempts to re-make marriage in a more flexible form.

It is more common for the triangle novel to be focalised through the mistress figure. Again, she figures less as a vamp than as a victim. Jean Rhys's *Quartet* (1928) offers an extreme of this where Marya is a pawn in a cruel marital game played by Lois and H. J. Heidler. As Marya finally comes to realise, 'it wasn't a love affair. It was a fight. A ruthless, three-cornered fight'(1969, 117), and it is a fight which she can only lose.

More often the protagonist is a victim only in the sense that she is prevented from the fulfilment of marriage by the existence of the first wife and the taboos against divorce, particularly the feeling that it was dishonourable for a man to initiate divorce. Examples include Ellen Wilkinson's *Clash*, Rose Macaulay's *Told By an Idiot* (1923), E. Arnot Robertson's *Four Frightened People* (1931), E.H. Young's *The Misses Mallett*, Storm Jameson's *Love in Winter* (1935), Rosamond Lehmann's *The Weather in the Streets* (1936) and Winifred Holtby's *South Riding* (1936). In these texts the first wife is often estranged from the man, and frequently presented as inadequate or even unbalanced (echoing *Jane Eyre*). Divorce was not only legally difficult to obtain but also required evidence of adultery. The sordid 'legal mummery' this often involved, using hotel chambermaids as witnesses, is described in Storm Jameson's *Love in Winter* (1984, 392) where both Hervey Russell and her lover Nicholas have to disentangle themselves from hasty, war-damaged marriages. In contrast, in *Four Frightened People* the problem of male 'honour' is solved when Arnold's wife decides to divorce him (the fact that Judy, a doctor, will lose her job if named as co-respondent is side-stepped by ending the novel before the divorce).

Several texts deal with the affair that never quite happens, thus evading these issues. Death or illness frequently intervene to prevent consummation of adulterous loves. In Rose Macaulay's *Told by an Idiot* Mr Jayne, whose wife refuses to divorce him, is stabbed just as Rome is about to tell him whether she will elope with him. The reader never knows what her decision would have been. Similarly, Carne's heart attack in Holtby's *South Riding* prevents Sarah Burton from sleeping with him. Loyalty to a sister prevents adultery with a brother-in-law in both Elizabeth Bowen's *Friends and Relations* (1931) and Kate O'Brien's *The Ante-Room* (1934). In the latter, as in Bowen's *The House in Paris* (1935) the man in the triangle commits suicide.

Such male deaths suggest that to occupy the subjugated position 'between women' can lead to a more final erasure than merely slipping out of the narrative as Frederick does in *Summer Will Show*. Although Max is engaged rather than married to Naomi in *The House in Paris*, his consummated affair with Naomi's friend, Karen, has devastating effects. The triangle is complicated by the fact that Naomi's mother, Mme Fisher, an arch-manipulator, is also in love with Max. Confronted by Mme Fisher and caught 'between women', Max cuts his own wrist to escape.

A widower or divorced man during this period was three times as likely as his female counterpart to remarry, partly due to the population imbalance (Lewis, 1984, 4). The second wife novel, such as Elizabeth von Arnim's *Vera* (1921) or Daphne du Maurier's *Rebecca* (1938), can be read as a reflection of women's fears that they could only achieve marriage at the expense (possibly death) of another woman. West's *The Return of the Soldier* is a version of this theme. E.H. Young's *Miss Mole* (1930) wonderfully subverts it by setting up what appears to be a classic *Jane Eyre* plot where the housekeeper, Miss Mole, will marry her widowed rector employer, but then marrying her to the delightfully unromantic Mr Blenkinsop.

'Feminism Divided'

In an era characterised by divisions between women it is not surprising that there were divisions in the feminist movement itself. As Holtby asked: 'Why, in 1934, are women themselves often the first to repudiate the movements of the past hundred and fifty years, which have gained for them at least the foundations of political, economic, educational and moral equality?' (1934, 96). One explanation was that after the 1928 Equal Franchise Act gave the vote to women over 21, there was a sense that the battle had been won. Hence, the first histories of the women's movements begin to appear at this point: Ray Strachey's *The Cause* (1928), Sylvia Pankhurst's *The Suffragette Movement* (1931) and Winifred Holtby's *Women* (1934), as well as many newspaper and journal articles. In novels such as Macaulay's *Told by an Idiot*, Brittain's *Honourable Estate* (1936) and Woolf's *The Years* (1937) women consciously attempted to write a female history of the years of 'transition'.

However, the generation gap between the old campaigners and their post-war successors was itself a problem. The elder women, possibly influenced by the media campaign against the 'irresponsible' flapper, felt that younger women were mis-using their freedom, a phenomenon Strachey felt was 'more a sign of the reaction after the war strain than of anything to do with the Women's Movement' (1978, 390). Meanwhile, the younger generation reacted against elders whom they saw as responsible for the war. Added to this was a change in sexual morality which meant that older feminists found themselves regarded by younger women as strait-laced and prudish spinsters. Whereas the older generation of feminists were often unmarried (63 per cent of WSPU members in

1913 were single (Jeffreys, 1985, 89)), younger feminists like Vera Brittain, Dora Russell, or Naomi Mitchison combined marriage and career. The divisions within feminism thus mirrored those divisions in society at large – age, marital status and class.

The struggle for the vote had been, as Brittain noted, a 'clear-cut issue, which was popular in the sense that it was easily understood' (Berry and Bishop, 1985, 101), and which united all classes. In contrast, post-war feminism was fighting for 'half a dozen things' which could only be summed up rather uninspiringly as an 'equal humanity' (Berry and Bishop, 1985, 101). The move from 'women' to 'humanity' is illustrated by the transformation of the NUWSS in 1919 into the 'National Union of Societies for Equal Citizenship' (NUSEC).

The diversity of issues tackled by the inter-war movement is reflected in the name of the 'Six Point Group' launched in 1921 by Lady Rhondda. It worked for satisfactory legislation on child assault, for the widowed mother, and for the unmarried mother and child, as well as equal rights for parental guardianship, equal pay for teachers, and equal opportunities for men and women in the Civil Services (Spender, 1984, 175). *Time and Tide*, the journal founded by Lady Rhondda to act as a voice for the Group, published writing by some of the best women writers of the period, including Holtby and West, both on its board of directors.

Such a wide field of action brought dispersal of energies and dissension over aims and tactics. Other feminist groups included the Women's Freedom League, the National Council of Women, the London and National Society for Women's Service (which became the Fawcett Society), while single issue groups, such as the National Council for the Unmarried Mother and her Child, the Housewives League, and the Married Women's Association were also set up. Women were increasingly active in the unions. The Women's Co-operative Guild (founded in 1883) and the Women's Institute (founded in 1915) expanded rapidly. Although both campaigned to improve women's lot they did so within the ideology of maternalism and domesticity. This fragmentation meant that there was no clear unity or voice and the diverse groups often did not co-operate. Although 36 women became MPs during this period, two of whom became Cabinet members – Margaret Bondfield as Minister for Labour and Ellen Wilkinson as Minister for Education – they were divided along party lines.

What is most striking about the period is a self-conscious division between 'Old Feminists' such as Lady Rhondda and Winifred Holtby, and 'New Feminists' such as Eleanor Rathbone, who became President of the NUSEC in 1919, and Dora Russell. The 'Old Feminists' emphasised equal rights and opposed any protective legislation based on women's 'special' needs. The 'New Feminists' argued that the majority of women were wives and mothers and that feminists should therefore lobby for protective legislation. In *The Disinherited Family* (1924) Rathbone argued strongly against the family wage system advocated by the trade unions and advocated a 'family allowance' paid directly to the mother. As Holtby, herself an 'Old Feminist', explained in an article entitled 'Feminism Divided': 'The New Feminism emphasises the importance of "women's point of view", the Old Feminism believes in the primary importance of the human being' (Berry and Bishop, 1985, 47–8). When in 1927 the NUSEC passed an amendment declaring their support for protective legislation, eleven members of the executive council resigned, and several went on to join the Six Point Group.

Again, this division reflects those of class, marital status and sexuality which were endemic to the era. While middle-class women saw the assertion of their 'right' to work as liberating and favoured 'Old Feminism', working-class women regarded the economic necessity to work as part of their oppression, and stood to gain from the protective legislation advocated by 'New Feminists'. This division is the key to much of the dissension. Carol Dyhouse argues that during this period 'feminists were ever more prone to attack each other on account of their class allegiances, real or otherwise' (1989, 193). Naomi Mitchison's criticism of Holtby's *Women* on the grounds that Holtby was writing 'too exclusively from the standpoint of the professional, middle-class woman' (1934, 93) is a case in point. Class loyalties frequently took precedence over gender loyalties, especially for socialists such as Margaret Bondfield.

'New Feminism' both reflected and reinforced the dominant ideology of maternalism. It 'only rarely questioned men's power in marriage and heterosexuality and did not generally include any positive vision of the spinster's role in feminist action' (Oram, 1989, 112). Indeed, a number of feminists – Vera Brittain, Dora Russell, Dora Marsden (editor of *The Freewoman*), Ellen Wilkinson – attacked the spinster in terms which replicated those of the sexologists. Both the demand for birth control and the campaign against the marriage bar involved many feminists in rhetoric which valued the 'wider' experience of the married woman at the expense of reinforcing the stereotype of the 'frustrated' spinster.

Although the 1920s was a productive period in terms of legislation for women the 1930s saw a tailing off (see Appendix 2). This was partly because many aims had been achieved and partly because women were channelling their energy into fighting unemployment or Fascism. But it was also the result of a society which increasingly pushed women back into the home and the domestic. Certainly the climate of the 1930s was not one that encouraged women to form political alliances. Holtby presciently links the idealisation of domesticity to the rise of Fascism in Europe – the ideology of 'Kinder, Küche, Kirche' (1934, 154) in Germany and the 'cult of the cradle' (166) in Italy. Virginia Woolf was to draw similar conclusions in *Three Guineas* (1938). In 1939, as in 1918, the feminist movement was again subsumed by world war.

Ultimately, the popularity of the female-identified triangle plot in its different forms during these years is closely linked to historically specific anxieties about shifting gender roles. The literary history of this period has tended to operate around a broad chronological division between 'Modernism', which rejected the nineteenth-century conventions of realist narrative and peaked in the 1920s, and 'the 1930s' which are associated with a return to more traditional and realist forms, reflecting an engagement with social and political issues such as unemployment and the Spanish Civil War. With the exception of Virginia Woolf, the major writers associated with both 'Modernism' and 'the 1930s' have been male. Clearly, this periodisation is not only extremely broad – 'modernist' (not, in fact, a term which was in use during the period) texts were being produced into the 1940s while many writers, such as Winifred Holtby, had been writing in traditional forms throughout – but has worked to marginalise women writers whose work does not fit the general pattern.[1] The five writers I have chosen to concentrate on have all been marginalised in different ways, partly because their texts do not fit easily into traditional categories or periods (Rebecca West, for instance, is difficult to place because she works across such a range of genres) but also because of their focus on the bonds and powers of women.

Used by a wide range of women writers to examine these bonds and powers, the female-identified triangle plot crosses and destablises categories such as 'modernist'/'traditionalist', 'popular'/'highbrow', 'lesbian'/'heterosexual'. Tracing it across their texts allows connections to be made across the period. It also reveals the extent to which these texts are engaged with the events of their time and with ideology. The rival friends or sisters triangles, the lesbian triangle, the wife and mistress triangle, and the second wife triangle all both reflect and engage with specific anxieties during this period – especially the volatile combination of the population imbalance with women's increasing political, professional and personal freedom. In the dominant ideology of the period exaggerated scare stories about the man 'shortage' function, like the newly emergent theories of 'deviant' sexuality, to control women and to redirect their energies into competition in the heterosexual marriage market and away from competition with men in the job market. Any attempt to theorise fictional representations of rivalry between women must take account of this historical specificity.

2
Theorising Female Rivalry

From the psychoanalytic point of view the original erotic triangle is, of course, the Oedipal triangle which underpins all Freud's thinking, including the two influential essays on female development which he formulated during the inter-war period – 'Female Sexuality' (1931) and 'Femininity' (1932). The male-identified erotic triangle, particularly if the male rival is older, can be read, as René Girard reads it in *Deceit, Desire and the Novel*, in terms of the boy's desire for his mother and rivalry with his father. Reading the female-identified triangle in terms of the female Oedipal complex, however, is complicated by the girl's initial, pre-Oedipal attachment to her mother.

Freud famously presents this attachment in 'Female Sexuality' as a radical discovery: 'Our insight into this early, pre-Oedipus phase in girls came to us as a surprise, like the discovery in another field, of the Minoan–Mycenaean civilisation behind the civilisation of Greece' (1977, 372). The central problem here for Freud is that if the primary attachment in the pre-Oedipal stage for both sexes is to the mother, then the little girl has to transfer her attachment to a man, initially her father, in order to develop satisfactorily. Freud's model of development is both linear and prescriptive – the little girl '*should*'(1977, 375, my emphasis) transfer her attachment to the father. But he has trouble accounting for the motivation for this transferral, offering what seems an almost excessive number of possible motives:

> that [the mother] failed to provide the little girl with the only proper genital, that she did not feed her sufficiently, that she compelled her to share her mother's love with others, that she never fulfilled all the girl's expectations of love, and, finally, that she first aroused her sexual activity and then forbade it.
>
> (1977, 381–2)

Admitting that these factors seem 'insufficient to justify the girl's final hostility', Freud falls back rather lamely on suggesting that the attachment to the mother has to cease 'precisely because it was the first and was so intense' (1977, 382). Despite this, he stresses that 'The turning-way from her mother is an extremely important step in the course of the little girl's development' (1977, 387).

In 'Femininity' Freud opts for the 'castration complex' as the specific factor which accounts for the little girl's transfer to the father. The attachment to the mother ends in hate, he argues, and the hostility which the little girl already feels towards the mother who failed to give her either a penis or enough milk/love 'is now greatly intensified for *she becomes the girl's rival,* who receives from her father everything that she desires from him' (1973, 163, my emphasis). With the discovery of her 'castration' there are three possible developmental routes open to the girl: 'sexual inhibition or [. . . .] neurosis', a 'masculinity complex', or 'normal femininity' (1973, 160). There is an interesting slippage here as Freud's account of inhibition and neurosis slides almost imperceptibly into the account of 'normal femininity', which is itself, in fact, never fully explained.

Thus Freud sees rivalry with the mother as a necessary and important stage in the route to 'normal femininity', while bonding between women, especially lesbianism, is theorised as evidence of immaturity, as a 'masculinity complex'. Moreover, the discovery that the 'phallic' mother in fact lacks a penis leads to women being 'debased in value for girls just as they are for boys and later perhaps for men' (1973, 160–1). Freudian psychoanalysis therefore legitimates and normalises rivalry between mother and daughter as an essential stage on the route to 'normal femininity'. It also normalises an internalisation of female inferiority in both sexes.

The female attachment to the mother which Freud found so problematic has proved suggestive for feminist theorists. Nancy Chodorow's object relations theory of female identity in *The Reproduction of Mothering* (1978) has been particularly influential for theorists interested in relations between women. The crux of her argument is that, because women mother, women's primary bonds are with women rather than men. There is, therefore, a marked difference in their sense of self:

> growing girls come to define themselves and experience themselves as continuous with others; their experience of self contains more flexible or permeable ego boundaries. Boys come to define themselves as

more separate and distinct, with a greater sense of rigid ego boundaries and differentiation. The basic feminine sense of self is connected to the world, the basic masculine self is separate.

(1978, 169)

Thus men define themselves through opposition to others, women through relation to others. Men look for a return to the mother through adult heterosexual relationships, but because men cannot provide a similar kind of return to oneness, women recreate the primary mother–child relationship by having children themselves – 'reproducing' motherhood. Thus 'women's heterosexuality is *triangular* and requires a third person – a child – for its structural and emotional completion' (1978, 207, my emphasis).

As Adrienne Rich writes, 'on the basis of her own findings, Chodorow leads us implicitly to conclude that heterosexuality is *not* a "preference" for women' (1980, 636, original emphasis). To account for the transference of women's attachments to men, Chodorow resorts to the unsubstantiated and sweeping statement that 'most women are heterosexual' (1978, 200), and the bleak assertion that 'women's economic dependence on men pushes them anyway into heterosexual marriage' (1978, 208). In contrast, Rich's provocative essay 'Compulsory Heterosexuality and Lesbian Existence' uncovers the male power structures (from physical force to consciousness–control) which enforce the 'lie' of compulsory heterosexuality.

The assertion that women's primary bonds are with women is an important corrective to Freud's insistence on female rivalry as 'normal'. However, as Judith Kegan Gardiner points out, both Chodorow and Rich, despite their differences, 'describe gender difference in terms that imply that women are *nicer* than men' (1990, 134, my emphasis). To argue that women are 'nicer' than men – basically more capable of putting others before themselves because their sense of identity is relational – is, in fact, remarkably close to traditional stereotypes of 'femininity'. The idea that, if uncoerced by patriarchy, women are too 'nice' to indulge in rivalry buys into notions that women ought always to sacrifice their own needs for others and never assert their own desires. A more complex theorisation of the effects of women's primary bonds with each other, including problems as well as possibilities, is necessary.

Chodorow's emphasis on the positive aspects of women's 'flexible ego boundaries' has led to an idealisation of 'merging' between women. Elizabeth Abel's essay '(E)Merging Identities: The Dynamics of Female Friendship in Contemporary Fiction by Women' focuses on women's desire to merge with a similar other and theorises female friendship as a 'mode of relational self-definition' (1981, 414) where identity is clarified through relation to another women who both embodies and reflects part of the self. The crucial problem with Abel's essay is that in four of the five texts she examines one of the 'friends' is either absent, dead or dies. The other woman has to be negated ('killed'?), as in Freud's paradigm, before the process of self-identification can be completed. As Judith Gardiner comments, in these novels 'a living process of interaction between women, with its exhilarating fusions and frightening threats to autonomy, often yields to a safer relationship with an absent other who can be recreated in imagination and memory' (1981, 441). The fluid ego boundaries which Abel, like Chodorow and Rich, endorses have been seen as a weakness by other theorists, including Jessica Benjamin and Luce Irigaray. In addition, Abel's essay treats fictional characters as if they were psychoanalytical case studies, without considering the importance of narrative structure. It is because of this that I want to examine the 'living process of interaction' between Winifred Holtby and Vera Brittain in relation to their texts.

The relationship between writers is of special interest to literary critics and Sandra Gilbert and Susan Gubar use Freud's 'Female Sexuality' to theorise a 'female affiliation complex' (1988, Chapter Four). Faced with a choice of matrilineal and patrilineal literary inheritances, they argue, women writers can either turn to the father–daughter paradigm (Freud's 'normal femininity'), relinquish creativity altogether (the rejection of sexuality), or retain their attachment to the mother (the 'masculinity complex'). This use of Freud's model is not entirely successful because it is virtually impossible to shake off the values Freud gives to each outcome.

What it does usefully suggest is women writers' ambivalence towards their literary predecessors – a potent mixture of exploration, affiliation and rivalry. Given the erasure of their literary matrilineage from the canon, Gilbert and Gubar suggest, women writers have actively to seek out and choose their precursors. Rather than the 'anxiety of influence' male writers struggle with, female writers have to overcome first an 'anxiety of authorship'[1] and then the problems associated with the affiliation complex. The choice of an appropriate matrilineage (literary foremothers who are 'serious' not 'silly', but who will not engulf their followers) involves a process of *looking for* and *at* those earlier writers. In the early twentieth century this process can be traced in texts which allude to and/or parody earlier texts. The inter-war rewritings of *Jane Eyre*, and the numerous critical essays and books on the Brontës and

Gaskell, as well as those on suffrage leaders such as Emmeline Pankhurst and Millicent Fawcett, can all be seen in this context. Gilbert and Gubar's model allows for a tension between rivalry and affiliation but it offers no way of thinking about relations between writers who are contemporaries, such as Vera Brittain and Winifred Holtby, and who might more easily think of themselves as 'sisters' than 'mother' and 'daughter'.

A Freudian reading of the female-identified triangle text can theorise rivalry between women in terms of Oedipal mother–daughter rivalry. In Daphne du Maurier's *Rebecca* (1938), a revision of *Jane Eyre*, the unnamed protagonist marries an obvious father-figure in the older, richer Maxim, while his dead first wife, Rebecca, fills the place of the 'mother'. The protagonist's move from idealisation of Rebecca to a rejection of her corresponds to the little girl's move from attachment to the mother to rejection of her. She attains maturity ('normal femininity') when she finally takes Rebecca's place as 'Mrs de Winter'. Maxim, psychically 'castrated' by the loss of his house and position, becomes the protagonist's 'child'. As Freud suggested in 'Femininity': 'Even a marriage is not made secure until the wife has succeeded in making her husband her child as well and in acting as a mother to him' (1973, 168).

To complicate this reading, *Rebecca* derives much of its power from the protagonist's unacknowledged desire for Rebecca – the shadowy, pre-Oedipal attachment to the mother. In a sexually charged scene the protagonist takes Rebecca's nightdress out of its case and touches it to her face, smelling Rebecca's perfume, an unmistakable image of female desire. Indeed, it is the protagonist's desire to *be* Rebecca – 'Mrs de Winter' – which initiates her desire for Maxim. This accords with Girard's argument that the love-object is chosen precisely because she is already the choice of the rival. Thus, as Eve Sedgwick argues, she becomes a mediator between the subject and the rival who is really the object of his desire. However, in *Rebecca* this triangle has been radically reversed so that its *subject* is a woman who desires another woman, and uses a man as a mediator in that desire.

The attachment to Rebecca empowers the protagonist to take the place of the mother. But it also threatens her life. In three scenes – when she imagines being Rebecca on the telephone, when she wears Rebecca's ball costume, and in the bedroom scene – the protagonist almost merges with Rebecca. Tania Modleski argues that in the Hitchcock film version, where Mrs Danvers tries to persuade the protagonist to commit suicide, both the protagonist and the spectator 'are made to experience a kind of annihilation of the self, of individual identity, through a merger with another woman' (1988, 49). To avoid this loss of self the protagonist has to assert her difference from Rebecca, by rejecting and 'killing' the 'mother'.

Rivalry here is a 'vehicle of self-definition' but the protagonist's identity is asserted through her *difference* from Rebecca. At first Rebecca is an ideal the protagonist cannot live up to (she imagines everyone saying, 'She's so different from Rebecca' (1975, 129)). But finally, as in the classic romance, the protagonist's identity is ratified by Maxim's choice of her as different from Rebecca, who is 'vicious, damnable, rotten through and through' (1975, 283). In becoming 'Mrs de Winter' (taking the 'Name of the Father') her separate identity is lost. This merger with Maxim is socially sanctioned, however, and it is the man who can provide her with a secure identity. This brings us, though by a different route, back to the Freudian necessity for the woman to reject the 'mother' in order to establish an adult identity.

Such psychoanalytic readings are inherently ahistorical. As Luce Irigaray remarks, Freud takes no account of historical factors:

> he takes female sexuality as he sees it and accepts it as a *norm*. [. . . .] he interprets women's sufferings, their symptoms, their dissatisfactions, in terms of their individual histories, without questioning the relationship of their 'pathology' to a certain state of society, of culture.
>
> (1985, 70, original emphasis)

Reinserted into the historical context of rapidly changing gender roles in both Vienna and England throughout this period, psychoanalysis can be understood as a controlling mechanism generated in response to the threat of women's increasing independence.

Biographical details substantiate this view. Earlier, in 1883, Freud commented on John Stuart Mill's *The Subjection of Women* (which he had translated) in a letter to his wife-to-be, Martha: 'It seems a completely unrealistic notion to send women into the struggle for existence in the same way as men. *Am I to think of my delicate sweet girl as a competitor?* [. . . .] the position of woman cannot be other than what it is: to be an adored sweetheart in youth, and a beloved wife in maturity' (Freud, 1961, 91, my emphasis). Not only was Freud unable to conceptualise any role for women other than marriage, but his case histories frequently end with the marriage of the female patient, suggesting that his science is infected by the ideology of the romance plot. His work gave 'scientific' veracity to a notion of 'normal femininity' which reinforced that patriarchal ideal of woman as 'adored sweetheart' and 'beloved wife'.

His comment about seeing his wife as a 'competitor' raises other key issues. Freud's point is that women should not compete with men for work. Here he accepts the traditional middle-class stereotype of the 'feminine' woman which regards her as too 'nice' for the dirty competition of the work place, which is thus secured for men. However, competition with another woman over a man, starting with the Oedipal rivalry with the mother for the father, is seen a natural part of the development towards 'normal femininity'. We need not only to distinguish between these different types of rivalry and competition, but to consider the possibility that eschewing some types, for instance competition in the job market, might actually contribute to women's financial dependence on men. Rivalry between women cannot simply be accounted for by the Freudian model as an inevitable stage in the universal psychic development towards 'normal femininity'. But neither can it be dismissed as something women should not dirty their hands with. Instead, we need a model which can be historicised and for this I want to turn to Luce Irigaray.

Luce Irigaray: women as rival commodities

There are two main strands to Luce Irigaray's work.[2] The first is a deconstruction of the major male thinkers of Western culture, particularly Freud, to show how their discourse has been based on an objectification of woman as 'Other'. The second is a utopian attempt to find a space for a female subjectivity and a means by which women can relate to each other as equal subjects. Relations between women and female rivalry are thus central to her thinking, particularly in *This Sex Which is Not One* (1985). As she puts it (in a somewhat transhistorical mode):

> Whatever inequalities may exist among women, they all undergo, even without clearly realising it, the same oppression, the same exploitation of their body, the same denial of their desire.
>
> That is why it is very important for women to be able to join together and to join together 'among themselves' [....] In order to love each other, even though men have organised a *de facto* rivalry among women. [....] The first issue facing liberation movements is that of making each woman 'conscious' of the fact that what she has felt in her personal experience is a condition shared by all women, thus *allowing that experience to be politicised.*
>
> (1985, 164, original emphasis)

Two major ideas in her work suggest a model of rivalry which can encompass both gendered power relations and the issue of history. The first is her rethinking of the mother–daughter relationship and her insistence that women should not reject the mother. The second is her theorisation of women's position as rival commodities in a male-controlled economy.

The unrepresented/unsymbolised relationship with the mother is, Irigaray argues, echoing Freud, the ' "dark continent" par excellence' (1991, 35) which underpins our society. She suggests that western culture is founded not on parricide, as Freud hypothesised, but on matricide. In 'The Bodily Encounter with the Mother' Irigaray argues that behind Freud's Oedipal myth lies that of Clytemnestra's murder by her son, Orestes. This is the 'more archaic murder, that of the mother' (1991, 36), whereby the father takes on the role of creator and the mother becomes merely the receptacle for his seed. In 'Woman–Mothers, the Silent Substratum of the Social Order' she clarifies this further: 'the whole of our western culture is based upon the murder of the mother. The man–god–father killed the mother in order to take power' (1991, 47). Woman is thus excluded from representation and the symbolic order except as a lack – the 'hole' of her womb. The 'castration' of the Oedipus myth conceals an earlier loss: the severing of the umbilical cord, the link to the mother. It is the desire for the 'bodily encounter with the mother' which is forbidden by the law of the father.

Irigaray stresses that women must retain and value their attachment to the mother because losing it uproots them from their identity. Moreover, they must reclaim their mother's history as subjects rather than mothers: 'It is also necessary, if we are not to be accomplices in the murder of the mother, for us to assert that there is a genealogy of women. [. . . .] Let us try to situate ourselves within this female genealogy so as to conquer and keep our identity' (1991, 44). This concept of a 'female' or 'maternal genealogy', a network of vertical and horizontal connections, offers a more fluid way of looking at the connections between women writers than the Freudian model used by Gilbert and Gubar. In addition, it allows for the political need for women to 'situate' themselves within such a genealogy.

In contrast to Chodorow and Abel, Irigaray sees women's fluid ego boundaries as a problematic state resulting directly from women's unrepresented state outside the symbolic order. Her essay 'And the One Doesn't Stir Without the Other' (1981) is a dramatisation of a suffocating mother–daughter merger. Within patriarchal culture woman is always 'Trapped in a single function – mothering' (1981, 66). Lacking an identity herself, the mother cannot offer her daughter a place in the symbolic order and becomes an engulfing figure. By turning to the father, however, the daughter is buying into a symbolic order which will allow her in her turn only the identity of 'mother'. The result is a vicious circle whereby the two women become rivals for the single place of mother: 'When the one of us comes into the world the other goes underground. When the one carries life, the other dies' (1981, 67). Margaret Whitford glosses Irigaray's thinking thus: 'Every women then has to take the place of the mother in an aggressive rivalry that allows no possibility of the *with*. In this economy women are forced into substitution and hate for the mother' (1991, 182, original emphasis). The mother–daughter rivalry which Freud regarded as universal and 'normal' is thus exposed as the specific result of a patriarchal culture. Instead, Irigaray attempts to imagine a different relation where mother and daughter 'play together at being the same and different. You/I exchanging selves endlessly and each staying herself. Living mirrors' (1981, 61). It is a utopian image which encompasses both difference and similarity, connection and separateness.

To return to *Rebecca*, we can interpret the protagonist's near suicide as a version of this suffocating merging. Her rivalry with Rebecca can be read in terms of competition for the single 'place' of the 'mother' allowed within patriarchy. Maxim's murder of Rebecca is a re-enactment of the 'archaic murder of the mother'. Here a comparison with an earlier novel, Elizabeth von Arnim's *Vera* (1921), another rewriting of *Jane Eyre*, is illuminating. In *Vera* the orphaned Lucy marries the widower, Everard Wemyss, and becomes fascinated by the figure of Wemyss's first wife, Vera, who killed herself by leaping from a window. Looking into Vera's mirror Lucy fears a loss of identity through merger: 'Now what shall I do if when I look into this I don't see myself but Vera?' (von Arnim, 1983, 179). However, it is not Vera who threatens Lucy's identity but Wemyss. As he increasingly tyrannises Lucy, she seeks refuge and explanation in Vera's room: 'She would go to Vera's room, get as close to her mind as she could, – search, find something, some clue....' (1983, 189). Like Bluebeard's locked room, the secret Vera's room holds is that of male violence towards women and Lucy becomes aware that, whether or not he actually pushed her, Wemyss killed his wife.

Reading *Vera* against *Rebecca* foregrounds the fact that the empowerment of du Maurier's protagonist is achieved precisely through conniving at the literal murder of the other woman – she has become an 'accomplice [....] in the murder of the mother'. In contrast, *Vera* affirms the attachment to the 'mother', as represented not only by Vera, but by

Lucy's Aunt Dot. When Aunt Dot attempts to protect Lucy, Wemyss throws her out of the house, a physical separation of the 'mother' and 'daughter' which enforces the psychic separation Freud insisted on.

In *An Ethics of Sexual Difference* Irigaray maps out the conditions for female subjectivity and distinguishes between two modes of relation between women:

> This world of female ethics would continue to have two vertical and horizontal dimensions:
> – daughter-to-mother, mother-to-daughter;
> – among women, or among 'sisters.'
>
> (1993a, 108)

The two axes are different but interdependent. The currently unsymbol-ised mother–daughter relationship must be represented in the symbolic order before women can relate to each other as 'sisters' on the horizontal axis. Love between women on both axes, she argues, is imperative if women's objectification within patriarchy is to be overcome: 'This love is necessary if we are not to remain the servants of the phallic cult, objects to be used and exchanged between men, rival objects on the market' (1991, 44–5)

Irigaray's analysis of women's position as 'rival objects on the market' offers a useful way of understanding the inter-war media emphasis on women's rivalry over men as a way of masking concern over women's entry into the job market and diverting women into more 'feminine' forms of competition with each other. Women, Irigaray argues, 'as the stakes of private property [....] have always been put in a position of mutual rivalry' (1985, 160). Indeed, 'men have organised a *de facto* rivalry among women' (1985, 164) as a way of controlling them.

In 'Women on the Market' Irigaray engages with Lévi-Strauss's con-ception of kinship as based on an exchange of women in *The Elementary Structures of Kinship* (1949):

> The society we know, our own culture, is based upon the exchange of women. Without the exchange of women, we are told, we would fall back into the anarchy (?) of the natural world, the randomness (?) of the animal kingdom. The passage into the social order, into the sym-bolic order, into order as such, is assured by the fact that men, or groups of men, circulate women among themselves, according to a rule known as the incest taboo.
>
> (1985, 170)

As Sedgwick notes in *Between Men*, women are always conduits in this exchange, never partners. The unanswered questions here, as Irigaray makes clear, are: 'Why exchange women?' (1985, 170) and 'Why are men not objects of exchange among women?' (171).

Irigaray argues that it is precisely the fact that it is women who are exchanged which both reflects and ensures the continuation of patriarchal society:

> The use of and traffic in women subtend and uphold the reign of masculine hom(m)osexuality [....] Reigning everywhere, although prohibited in practice, hom(m)osexuality is played out through the bodies of women, matter, or sign, and heterosexuality has been up to now just an alibi for the smooth workings of man's relations with himself, or relations among men.
>
> (1985, 172)

The pun on 'Hom(m)osexual' – 'homme' (man) and 'homo' (the same) – indicates that it is the male love of 'the Same' which structures patriarchy. It is this analysis which Sedgwick uses for her theorisation of the erotic triangle, although she attempts to retain the element of male *sexual* desire in the 'homosocial' which, she argues, Irigaray elides (1985, 26). Sedgwick takes the 'alibi' function of the woman's body to its logical extreme as a 'cover' for male homosexual desire.

Following Simone de Beauvoir's contention that 'Woman is defined exclusively in her relation to men' (1983, 174), Irigaray argues that there are three basic 'roles' imposed on women in Western culture: *'mother, virgin, prostitute'* (1985, 186, original emphasis). All three are defined by their exchange value for and in relation to men. A woman's value as a commodity is measured in relation to 'a third term that remains external to her' (the man) which 'makes it possible to compare her with another woman' (1985, 176). That is, in a patriarchy relations between women are always triangular, because they are mediated through their relation to a man. In the romance triangle the two women are defined as opposites (virgin/whore) according to their relation with the man. In *Rebecca* the protagonist's 'value' is determined by her difference from Rebecca, in relation to Maxim. The protagonist's move from 'virgin' to 'mother' (of Maxim), is defined through opposition to Rebecca as whore or 'prostitute'.

Woman's position as man's 'Other' means that women cannot function as 'other' for themselves: *'for the commodity, there is no mirror which copies it so that it may be at once itself and its 'own' reflection. One* commodity cannot be mirrored in another, as man is mirrored in his fellow men' (Irigaray, 1985, 176, original emphasis). This image becomes clearer if it is compared to Woolf's famous comment that 'Women have served all these centuries as looking-glasses possessing the magic and delicious power of reflecting the figure of man at twice its natural size' (1977c, 35). Because women can only be 'a mirror of value of and for man' (1985, 177), Irigaray contends, they can 'no longer relate to each other except in terms of what they represent in men's desire' (1985, 188). They cannot relate as equal subjects.

Women's commodification on the Edwardian marriage market is explored in Margaret Kennedy's *The Ladies of Lyndon* (1923) in terms that confirm Irigaray's view. John regards his wife Agatha as a possession: '"I don't deny that having *decent things* about the place," he glanced over his *perfect lawns* and then at *his wife* [....] "...does make a difference to me"' (1981a, 82, my emphasis). Gerald, a Marxist in love with Agatha, recognises that women like her are 'symbols of an assured, unearned income' (1981a, 83). The lack of connection between the women in this book (it is the women who ostracise Agatha when she elopes with Gerald) is due to their commodification. Moreover, it is women who perpetuate their own commodification, as mothers orchestrate marriage proposals for their daughters. This trade in daughters confirms Irigaray's hypothesis in *Sexes and Genealogies* (1987) that if women are not allowed other forms of exchange 'the commodities that women *are forced to exchange would be their children* [....] in exchange for market status *for themselves'* (1993b, 84, original emphasis). Kennedy's book charts the last gasp of the Edwardian marriage market, but inter-war women's novels are still full of unfulfilled women who treat their daughters as objects of exchange.

The final question in 'Women on the market' – what would happen if women 'took part in elaborating and carrying out exchanges?' (1985, 191) – informs 'Commodities among Themselves' where Irigaray asks: '*how can relationships among women be accounted for in this* ['hom(m)osexual'] *system of exchange'* (1985, 194, original emphasis). Female to female desire is unthinkable because women's commodification constructs women as (heterosexual) rivals:

> Commodities can only enter into relationships under the watchful eyes of their 'guardians'. It is out of the question for them to go to 'market' on their own [....] *the interests of businessmen require that commodities relate to each other as rivals.*
>
> (1985, 196, my emphasis)

As I noted in Chapter One, it was precisely when women began to move into the job market after the 1914–18 war and their economic independence made it possible for them to choose relationships with other women – 'to go to "market" on their own' – that taboos against lesbianism were strengthened. Irigaray suggests that this female economy has always existed, albeit in a submerged form:

> But what if these 'commodities' refused to go to 'market'? What if they maintained 'another' kind of commerce, among themselves?
> [....] Utopia? Perhaps. Unless this mode of exchange has undermined the order of commerce from the beginning [....].
>
> (1985, 196–7, original emphasis)

This 'refusal' can be illustrated through one of Freud's own case studies. In 'Fragment of an analysis of a case of hysteria' (1905) Dora's hysteria is initiated by a kiss from Herr K., with whose wife her father is having an affair. Freud reports that Dora believed that 'she had been handed over to Herr K. as the price of his tolerating the relations between her father and his wife' (Freud, 1990, 66). Freud hints at the truth of this on an unconscious level: 'The two men had of course never made a *formal agreement* in which she was treated as an object for barter' (1990, 66, my emphasis). Dora's hysteria is her 'refusal' to be treated as an object of exchange between the two men. Her termination of the analysis is also her refusal to take part in the 'market' of psychoanalysis, the exchange between Freud and her father. Moreover, Dora's love for Frau K., whose 'adorable white body' Dora praises 'in accents more appropriate to a lover than to a defeated rival' (1990, 96–7) hints at 'another kind of commerce', an exchange of desire between women, which undermines the male-controlled economy.

Diana Fuss has argued that Irigaray's work elides male homosexuals who simultaneously occupy different places in the economy (as both powerful and powerless):

> What [Irigaray's] theory of a phallically organised economy does not recognise is that there is more than one market, that there are as many systems of commodification and exchange as there are sets of social relations. A subject can be located in several economies, in competing and perhaps even incompatible social orders, at the same time.
>
> (1989, 49)

In fact, I think that Irigaray is aware that there are many systems of exchange – her point is that it is the phallically organised one which is *dominant*. My own contention is that women, positioned as commodities within a 'male hom(m)osexual economy', can also operate within a 'female economy', within which men can be commodified and 'exchanged'.

Sylvia Townsend Warner's *Summer Will Show* explores the co-existence of and tensions between these two 'economies'. The two women – the English upper-class wife, Sophia, and the Bohemian Jewish mistress, Minna – are initially set up as opposites and Sophia, like du Maurier's protagonist, becomes obsessed with her rival. But Warner then destabilises the opposition 'wife'/'mistress' to expose the women's shared condition as commodities controlled by the husband, Frederick. When Sophia and Minna become allies, Frederick deprives Sophia of money, making it clear that her status, and her 'difference' from Minna, depend on her position as his wife. The diversion of female energy into rivalry is in male interests. 'What easier,' Sophia realises, than for Frederick to 'retire behind those petticoats, stroll off politely and leave the two women to fight it out and dry each other's tears' (1987, 144).

The two women's desire for each other overcomes their positioning as rivals and subverts their commodification. Minna becomes not Sophia's 'Other' but another self, symbolised in a scene where Sophia, looking in a mirror, sees not herself but Minna (1987, 301). This is not a merger, rather the two women 'mirror' each other as equal subjects, instead of 'reflecting' Frederick who is erased from the novel. As Terry Castle argues, the male-identified erotic triangle only remains stable as long as the woman is isolated from other women:

> Once two female terms are conjoined in space, however, an alternative structure comes into being, a female–male–female triangle in which one of the male terms from the original triangle now occupies the 'in between' or subjugated position of the mediator.
>
> (1992, 132–3)

In *Summer Will Show* Frederick comes to occupy the 'subjugated position' of mediator, but he still holds the *financial* power. And it is indirectly because of this that Minna is (probably) killed on the barricades of the 1848 Paris revolution.

Castle goes on to suggest that because the archetypal lesbian fiction documents a world in which men are 'between women' rather than vice versa, 'it often looks odd, fantastical, implausible, "not there" – utopian in aspiration if not design' (1992, 146–7). Warner's novel is certainly 'odd', corkscrewing away from traditional narrative conventions, and, by leaving Minna's death unconfirmed, refusing the reader the satisfaction of closure. The final image is of Sophia reading the famous opening of Marx and Engels's *Communist Manifesto*: 'A spectre is haunting Europe'. What this does is to place the 'spectre', or possibility, of an 'economy' of lesbian desire alongside Marx's 'spectre' of Communism. This makes it clear that, since capitalism is both dependent on and reinforces the male 'hom(m)osexual' economy, the utopian 'fantasy' of open love between women can only be fully realised (as opposed to being played out in the interstices of patriarchy) if there is a revolutionary alteration of the economic base.

While Castle's essay is explicitly concerned with lesbian fiction, my own contention is that the female-identified triangle is a pattern which is widely used in women's fiction in general (in the same way that the male–female–male pattern is central to men's fiction). As *Summer Will Show* demonstrates, the bonds of lesbian desire are strong enough to overturn the canonical triangle. But what of other bonds between women? How might they subvert, revise or upend the canonical triangle plot?

Women as sisters: sibling rivalry

As I noted in the introduction, the notion of sisterhood so central to feminism has been much criticised because of its tendency to mask differences of race, class and sexuality, and, at the same time, privilege women of a specific race, class or sexuality. Notions of sisterhood are, in fact, subject to change over time and, as Gill Frith writes, have 'continually been linked with specific understandings of what a woman *is* and *should* be' (1988, 17–18, original emphasis). They are, therefore, always bound up with the dominant ideologies.

The romanticisation of an all-embracing sisterhood has meant that relations between blood sisters have been comparatively neglected. Amy K. Levin argues that literary critics have blurred the distinction between biological and non-biological sisterhood, and thus ignored the experience of friction between biological sisters which is so much at odds with the feminist ideal (1992, 16). Attention to the sibling rivalry which is central to that friction, I would argue, actually *reveals* rather than masks issues of difference and power. It is here that attention to the complexity of lived blood sister relationships is so important.

One of Freud's earliest case histories indicates the potential trauma when love of a sister conflicts with the need for sexual fulfilment. Fraulein Elisabeth von R. developed hysterical pains in her legs which Freud traced to her repressed love for the husband of her much-loved sister. At her sister's deathbed Elisabeth had been horrified to discover herself thinking: 'Now he is free again and I can be his wife' (Freud and Breuer, 1991, 226). This conflict – between the primary nature of sister bonds and women's position as rival commodities – is the crux of women writers' treatment of the triangle plot.

Although Freud has little to say about siblings, Alfred Adler made them central to his *What Life Should Mean to You* (1932). He argued that birth order is a key issue in identity formation:

> The position in the family leaves an indelible stamp upon the style of life. Every difficulty of development is caused by rivalry and lack of co-operation in the family. If we look around at our social life and ask why rivalry and competition is its most obvious aspect – indeed, not only at our social life but at our whole world – then we must recognise that people are everywhere pursuing the goal of being conqueror, of overcoming and surpassing others. This goal is the result of training in early life, of the rivalries and competitive striving of children who have not felt themselves an equal part of their whole family.
>
> (1962, 115)

Sibling rivalry thus becomes the model for later rivalry. Adler also acknowledges the issue of gender, pointing out that boys are more valued in our society than girls.

May Sinclair, who knew Adler's early work, writes particularly percept-ively about the intersection of birth order and gender. In *Mary Olivier* (1919) Mary is, like Sinclair herself, the only girl and youngest child and suffers because her mother always favours her sons. In *Arnold Waterlow* (1924), however, Arnold's privileged gender status in relation to his sister Charlotte is over-ridden by her position as older sister. Competition between siblings, then, takes place in different competing 'economies' – gender, birth order and parental attitudes.

The relations between sisters are especially complicated not only because of their lack of gender status but also because of a complex play between sameness and difference. M. Esther Harding's *The Way of All Women* (1933) noted sisters' special difficulty in establishing separate identities since they may not only look but act alike: 'Their psycho-logical condition approaches complete identity, even in ways which are ordinarily considered to be determined by chance. They may seem to share a similar *fate'* (1933, 304, original emphasis), even, she suggests, to the extent of falling in love with the same man. One method of dealing with this is for each sister to take on a clearly defined role – the 'pretty one', the 'domestic one', the 'clever one' and so on.

Harding's contentions are supported by more recent studies of sisters. These show that the 'sister knot' (Fishel, 1994, 78) or 'dialectical dance' of sisterhood (Bank and Kahn, 1982, cited in McConville, 1985, 12) is not only a primary factor in identity formation but a 'lifelong' bond: 'Our sisters do fundamentally shape the kind of person we become,' concludes Brigid McConville (1985, 33). Sisters function as models to be rejected or followed: 'From birth to death, sisters model and pattern their scripts on each other's' (Fishel 1994, 93). A sister, Toni McNaron argues, is 'someone who is both ourselves and very much not ourselves – a special kind of double' (1985, 7). The key question in identity formation is one of similarity/difference: 'Will I be like her – or different?' (McConville, 1985, 33). Both the tensions and the strengths of the sister relationship come out of this sense of being at once the same and different. Fishel, McConville and McNaron all agree with Harding that sisters deal with the problem of fluid ego boundaries by developing strategies for emphasising difference, such as assigning each other specific 'roles'. Rivalry emerges as one way of dealing with such enmeshed or merged ego boundaries.

Although the rival sisters plot is common in literature, in reality rivalry over the same man is strongly tabooed. McConville contends that the 'spectre of sisterly jealousy over men' is 'little more than a spectre' but it is 'aided and abetted by a male-run media and much pulp fiction which glories in the image of women scrapping over a male' (1985, 123). Several of Fishel and McConville's interviewees said their bonds with their sisters were *stronger* than with male partners. Competition and jealousy may therefore be as much to do with the primary nature of the sister bond as the desire for a man. Both suggest that sister relationships are often repeated or mirrored in other relationships and a woman may look for a male lover or husband who is like her sister.

Moreover, it may not even be a man who is the object of rivalry. Toni McNaron suggests that 'our heterosexual myopia may have led us to overlook the possibility that sisters, when they are jealous over a parent, may well be jealous over their mother' (1985, 6). Similarly, Susie Orbach and Luise Eichenbaum suggest that sometimes female competition is for another woman's attention in an attempt to recreate the primary mother–child attachment (1994, 98–9). In this pattern the man figures as a mother–surrogate, or as a badge of social success worn to win the mother's approval.

It is not surprising, then, that notions of sisterhood should be caught between an ideal of primary closeness and a stereotype of rivalry over men. An example of the disjunction between idealised sisterhood and the reality of sibling rivalry can be found in the suffrage movement itself, in the complex relations between the Pankhursts – Emmeline, and her daughters Christabel, Sylvia and Adela – who were the driving force of the WSPU. Sylvia Pankhurst's *The Suffragette Movement* is scarred by the rivalry between her and Christabel, 'our mother's favourite' (1977, 99). The political differences between the socialist Sylvia, and the more conservative Christabel are entangled with memories of childhood ambivalence. Sylvia writes: 'I often considered her policy mistaken [....] but her speaking always delighted me [....] I admired her, and took pleasure in her, as I had done when we were children' (1977, 221). This almost erotic admiration allegedly met with repeated rejection from the elder sister, while Mrs Pankhurst preferred Christabel, both as daughter and as comrade-in-arms.

While estranged from her mother and undergoing forcible feeding in prison, Sylvia wrote to Mrs Pankhurst: 'I am fighting, fighting, fighting. I have four, five and six wardresses every day, as well as two doctors [....] I resist all the time' (1977, 447). Sylvia's biographer, Patricia Romero, comments: 'Was it to win the vote that Sylvia put herself through such torture? Or were her motivations mixed, including especially at this time, the need to top Christabel in her mother's affections?' (1990, 79). This volatile conjunction of biological and political sisterhood demonstrates two points. Firstly, that rivalry between sisters/women can be over the mother. Secondly, that rivalry, however emotionally destructive, can also be a considerable spur to achievement in whatever sphere.

One further biographical example is useful here. The lifelong sister bond between Virginia Woolf and Vanessa Bell, discussed in Jane Dunn's *A Very Close Conspiracy* (1990), was primary, formative and, at least in Woolf's letters, erotic. The tension between likeness/unlikeness, closeness/separation seems to have been particularly pronounced. Dunn notes that Woolf frequently emphasised their merged identity, writing to Bell: 'Do you think we have the same pair of eyes, only different spectacles? I rather think I'm more nearly attached to you than sisters should be' (1991, 4). Early sibling rivalry was dealt with by each sister claiming clearly defined areas: Vanessa was the artist, sexual woman and mother, while Virginia was the writer, intellectual and non-sexual woman.

One illuminating incident is the flirtation between Virginia and Vanessa's husband, Clive Bell, after Vanessa's marriage left Virginia feeling lonely and abandoned. The object of Virginia's desire was not, in fact, Clive but Vanessa. Clive's role as conduit is demonstrated by one of Virginia's letters to him which requests, 'Kiss her [Vanessa], most passionately, in all my private places – neck – and arm, and eye, and eyeball, and tell her – what new thing is there to tell her? how fond I am of her husband?' (quoted in Dunn, 1991, 115). '*My* private places' stakes Virginia's prior physical and emotional claim to her sister, but it is Clive with a husband's access to Vanessa's body who can act out Virginia's desire. Dunn suggests Clive's actions might have been motivated by a desire to moderate the intimacy between the two sisters: 'How better to weaken their solidarity than to woo both and set up a sexual rivalry, albeit covert, one sister against the other?' (1991, 114). This demonstrates not only the primary nature of the sister bond, but the threat it offers to male power. The bonds between women are celebrated and explored again and again in Woolf's writing. Elements of Vanessa appear in several of her female characters, including Helen Ambrose in *The Voyage Out* (1915), and both Mrs Ramsey and Lily Briscoe in *To the Lighthouse* (1927), while Woolf's own adoration of her sister is parodied through the figure of Elizabeth Barrett Browning's spaniel in *Flush* (1933).

As Woolf understood, there is a disjunction between literary scripts and 'real life'. Mythic sister plots, such as fairy tales (Cinderella, Beauty and the Beast), Greek myth (Psyche) and *King Lear*, Amy K. Levin notes, traditionally present sisters, usually three sisters, who are rivals for the father's affection. The sisters are polarised as opposites, their difference ratified by the man who chooses them as wife/favoured daughter. The plot movement is away from sister-identification towards assimilation into heterosexual marriage. These mythic patterns fit Freud's Oedipal paradigm. By emphasising rivalry over men they negate women's own bonds (the mother is frequently absent) and serve male interests.

Both the reality of sister relationships and their representation in texts by women are more complex. Jane Austen's juvenilia includes a 'novel' entitled 'The Three Sisters' (1792), which shows that on the marriage market sisters may be regarded as interchangeable commodities, both by their suitors and their parents. 'Merging' here is imposed. Austen's three sisters are courted by Mr Watts who maintains 'it is equally the same to me which I marry of the three' (1975, 64). To the sisters, however, it is a matter of huge importance. Catching a husband is the only way they can establish a separate identity. The twist in Austen's tale is that the two younger sisters scheme not to marry Mr Watts but to persuade Mary, the elder, to marry him and thus avoid him themselves. The women do have a relative autonomy in the marriage market and the suitor is himself commodified – Mary regards him as little more than the means to a chocolate-coloured carriage and various bits of jewellery. Even here the bonds between sisters enable them to disrupt and manipulate the running of the male economy.

In her discussion of the 'sororal model' of nineteenth-century female friendship Carol Lasser has shown how women used the language of an idealised blood sisterhood, positioning friends as 'fictive kin' (1988, 164), even though such relationships often existed alongside less than ideal relationship with blood sisters. This sororal model sometimes extended to a public level as women became 'sisters' by working together. After the First World War this idealisation of sisterhood disappears. The threat of being labelled 'lesbian' makes political alliances between women too dangerous to discuss even through the metaphor of sisterhood.

Within the fiction of the period, however, relations between blood sisters are a common theme. The conflict between sisters' primary bonds and their positioning as rival commodities was especially pronounced in a period when men were in short supply. This is painfully clear in F. M. Mayor's *The Third Miss Symons* where Henrietta Symons loses her chance of marriage when her elder sister, Louie, entices her suitor away, because she does not want Henrietta married before her, but then refuses his proposal. Henrietta remains a spinster whose closest relationship is with her younger sister, Evelyn, who has, in fact, little time for Henrietta.

Two decades later E. Arnot Robertson's *Ordinary Families* (1933) charts a world where women still marry rather than work. Robertson's novel anticipates Martin's comment in Woolf's *The Years* (1937): 'It was an abominable system [. . . .] family life' (Woolf, 1968, 180). Lallie, the third of the four Rush children, is acutely aware of 'the cross-currents' (Robertson, 1962, 118) under the surface of family life, including her ambivalent relationship with Margaret, the youngest and most beautiful child: 'my feeling for Margaret, who remained enchanting to me however often, trying to get in touch with that rare something which I believed must lie behind such loveliness, I came up against the blank wall of an alien mind' (1962, 119). Enchantment is mixed with jealousy because Margaret's beauty ensured her superior appeal to adults and then men.

As Fishel and McConville indicate, sexuality is a key issue in sisters' construction of identity in relation to each other. Lallie's awakening sexuality is contrasted with Margaret's earlier, more casual experiences and the final moment of the novel records Lallie's devastation over a fleeting moment of attraction between her husband Gordon and Margaret: 'Even this she must have: all I really had' (1962, 288). The adult Lallie is marked by her experience of sibling rivalry, and her attempt to carve out a place in the 'abominable system' of family life. There is no dialogue between the sisters and Margaret's 'otherness' is never penetrated in the text.

While Robertson's novel presents this as the difficulties of a specific and individual family, Woolf's *The Years,* through an analysis of Victorian family life, provides an historical context through which we can reinterpret this silence between the sisters as a residue of the earlier system. The 'cross-currents' in the Pargiter family – Delia and Milly's competition over their father's attention, Milly's jealousy over Eleanor's affection for Morris – are the result of a family system which values the male above the female. This is clearer in Woolf's first draft, *The Pargiters.* Here she remarks explicitly that the repression of female sexuality 'aroused a certain hostility' between the sisters: 'Delia felt that Milly, Milly that Delia, was a rival who would intercept this excitement, this stimulus' (Woolf, 1978, 35). The *silencing* of female desire intensifies this rivalry. Lying to their parents about what they do, Milly and Delia also lie to each other about what they feel when they watch an unknown young man in the street.

In contrast, it is the love between two sisters which dominates Kate O'Brien's *The Ante-Room* (1934), set in 1880 in Catholic Ireland. Loving her brother-in-law, Vincent, Agnes refuses to elope with him, not because it is a sin but because of her love for her sister, Marie-Rose. O'Brien makes it explicit that Vincent in his relations with both Marie-Rose and Agnes is seeking a replacement for his dead mother, while their own mother, dying of cancer, makes her preference for her syphilitic son, to the exclusion of even her husband, painfully obvious. This chimes with Chodorow's contention that women look for a re-enactment of the mother–child dyad through their children, while men look for it through heterosexual relationships. In both cases the close mother–son relationship prevents the son attaining a separate adulthood. The novel ends with Vincent's suicide, but, tellingly, as he presses the trigger he is thinking of his mother. His death is an attempt to return to a pre-oedipal unity with her.

The bond between the two sisters is the 'only unifying thread' (1988, 9) in Agnes's life. As seen by the men, they appear both 'complementary beauties' (1988, 97) and to move 'almost as one person' (98) –

simultaneously the same and different. Agnes, although younger, provides for Marie-Rose the mothering both failed to receive from their mother. Indeed, both Marie-Rose and Vincent turn to Agnes for mothering and he especially resents Marie-Rose's prior claim to Agnes's attention – and to her bed.

In all these novels the mother is either inadequate or dead. Both Henrietta and Lallie are neglected middle siblings in large families. I am not suggesting that all sister relationships, or all woman-to-woman relationships, necessarily echo the mother–daughter dyad. But the inadequate mothering which Irigaray attributes to women's unrepresented position in patriarchy appears to be a key element in sisterly rivalry.

Within the triangle the rivalry can flow in (at least) two directions. It can be either between the two sisters for the attention of the man. Or it can be between one sister and the man for the attention of the other sister. *The Ante-Room* plays with the possibilities of both 'economies'. To return to Castle's argument, *The Ante-Room* provides an example of a novel where the bonds between women, although constituted by kinship not sexual desire, work to eliminate the male from the triangle.

However, the female bonds in O'Brien's triangle do not threaten but support religious and legal taboos against adultery, including the Deceased Wife's Sister Act. This act, which forbade a man to marry the sister of his deceased wife on the grounds that this was incest, was repealed in 1907 after a lengthy campaign. This was seen as being done in women's interests, in view of the man 'shortage' – in 1871 one MP remarked that women had special interest in a bill to repeal the Deceased Wife's Sister Act (Lewis, 1987, 72), while a year later Lydia E. Becker cited the bill as a particular example of women's need for a vote to represent their interests in Parliament (Lewis, 1987, 124). However, it is worth bearing in mind, especially in view of what Fishel calls the male fantasy of 'making love to sisters' (1994, 191), that this repeal might have served *male* interests, not only because it allowed access to a woman previously taboo but because it reinforced the idea that a sister was a sexual rival. The debates over the bill undoubtedly brought the issues involved to the public consciousness and this is reflected in fiction.

In Irigaray's female or maternal genealogy, sisters occupy the crucial point of intersection between the horizontal and vertical axes. Woolf's *The Years* explores the possibility of an alternative family system, constructed through the shared maternal genealogy of siblings. The novel uses Sophocles's *Antigone* as an intertext to explore how brothers as well as sisters are connected through their mother. Antigone, Irigaray suggests, defies the male-controlled law in order to bury her brother not because she has no respect for the law but because she respects a different law – the maternal ancestry which links her to her sibling (1994, 68). Woolf's emphasis on such sibling relationships also connects the aunt (the mother's sister) to her nieces and nephews within this maternal genealogy.

As E. H. Young's *The Misses Mallett* demonstrates, a female genealogy can be established even when the blood relationship goes through the male line. The four 'Misses Mallett', sisters Caroline and Sophia, their stepsister Rose, and niece Henrietta, are related through their father and brother, but make up a female household where it is the sister and aunt/ niece bonds which are important. Another rewriting of *Jane Eyre*, the text begins with Rose's rejection of the Rochester-like Francis Sales. Marrying a woman who becomes an invalid after a riding accident, Sales then pursues Henrietta. In each of these triangles Young subverts the stereo- types of female rivalry which we expect. Rose actively tries to bolster the marriage between Sales and Christobel, and then tries to protect Hen- rietta from Sales.

The central aunt–niece relationship between Rose and Henrietta oscil- lates between a sister model – Francis Sales remarks that they 'might be sisters' (Young, 1984a, 104) – and a mother–daughter model. Ultimately it is female ties which bind. Rose cares 'more passionately' (1984a, 187) for Henrietta than for Francis, and when she finally marries him it is primarily to save Henrietta from him. Equally, Henrietta's attempts to regard Rose as a 'rival adventurer' (1984a, 212) fail, and she comes to recognise that it is Rose's love which she desires: 'if only she and Aunt Rose were friends, what a conspiracy they could enjoy together! [....] How they might play into each other's hands with Francis Sales for the bewildered ball' (1984a, 236–7). This image of exchange between women, literally objectifying the man, reverses the Girard/Sedgwick triangle.

Sister bonds, then, like those of lesbian desire, introduce the possibility of other kinds of 'exchange' between women. The novels discussed here offer a range of such 'exchanges' where a man may be used as an object (a 'ball'), a mediator or conduit, erased or even 'killed' – suggesting that, at least within the pages of fiction, women can and do 'exchange' men.

'Speaking together': women in dialogue

Mikhail Bakhtin's dialogic theory, particularly as appropriated by Lynne Pearce for feminist criticism in *Reading Dialogics* (1994), offers a model of subjectivity which can encompass a more fluid notion of interaction between women.[3] As Pearce points out in a statement which brings together several of my own concerns:

> Dialogue is a concept which touches the heart of what it means to be a feminist: a concept evocative of sisterhood, of the perpetual negotiation of sameness and difference, of our dealings with men and patriarchal institutions, of our relationship to a language which simultaneously is, and is not, our own.
>
> (1994, 100)

My own interest in dialogue started when I noticed how many key scenes in the novels I was looking at simply showed women talking to each other. Put this bluntly it sounds banal – a point Woolf makes in *The Years*: 'All talk would be nonsense, I suppose, if it were written down,' remarks Rose, adding, 'But it's the only way we have of knowing each other' (1968, 139). In these dialogues female subjectivity is reconstructed in relation to an/other woman.

Bakhtin theorises language as a function of interaction between two participants:

> *word is a two-sided act.* It is determined equally by *whose* word it is and for whom it is meant. As word it is precisely *the product of the reciprocal relationship between speaker and listener, addresser and addressee.* [....] A word is a bridge thrown between myself and another. If one end of the bridge belongs to me, then the other depends on my addressee. A word is territory shared by both addresser and addressee, by the speaker and his interlocutor...
>
> (Bakhtin, 1994, 58, original emphasis)

Hence, '*Any utterance*, no matter how weighty and complete in and of itself, *is only a moment in the continuous process of verbal communication*' (Bakhtin, 1994, 59, original emphasis). Meaning is a *process* of interaction which looks both backwards to previous utterances and forwards, anticipating a response. It is always 'dialogic' and always in relation to an other.

Since meaning is always produced within a specific social and historical context the specificity of the addressee is crucial:

> *The word is orientated towards an addressee*, toward *who* that addressee might be: a fellow member or not of the same social group, of higher or lower standing [....] someone connected with the speaker by close

social ties (father, brother, husband and so on) or not. There can be no such thing as an abstract addressee [. . . .].

(Bakhtin, 1994, 58, original emphasis)

This power dynamic is inflected by the relations of nationality, class, race, family and education between the interlocutors. Although Bakhtin's work itself is gender-blind it can, as Pearce shows, encompass gender as one of these factors. These factors, I would suggest, are the varying and competing 'economies' within which the subject functions.

In contrast to the Freudian model of universal and linear stages of development, Bakhtin's dialogic offers us a model of human subjectivity as constructed through language and in relation to others. Whereas Chodorow, whose model of subjectivity is also relational, stresses sameness, Bakhtin emphasises difference – a sense of separation from others is necessary for the dialogic relation to exist at all.

One of psychoanalysis's 'most consistent errors,' according to Jane Gallop, 'is to reduce everything to a family paradigm', to the extent that 'Class conflict and revolution are understood as a repetition of parent–child relations' (1982, 144). Bakhtin's work shifts the emphasis away from the tight-knit family circle to place the subject in a web of connections. Thus Eleanor imagines her 'life' in *The Years* as a series of connections:

Perhaps there's an 'I' at the middle of it, she thought; a knot; a centre; and again she saw herself sitting at her table drawing on the blotting paper, digging little holes from which spokes radiated.

[. . . .] My life's been other people's lives, Eleanor thought – my father's, Morris's; my friends' lives; Nicholas's . . .

(Woolf, 1968, 295)

Gendering Bakhtin's theory allows not only for models of linguistic exchange between men and woman, and between women, but also for a model of exchange which can encompass both reciprocity and rivalry. We must, Pearce suggests, go 'beyond an interpretation of the dialogic as a model of amicable exchange and reciprocity, and [. . . .] explore subjectivity in relation to the political/social/historical constraints and expectations present in Bakhtin's accounts of spoken and written dialogue' (1994, 100). A power dynamic, however shifting, is inevitable in any exchange: 'As feminists we can never forget that our dialogues rarely exist between equal partners' (1994, 102). Dialogue can even involve an attempt to silence the other. Indeed, Pearce notes that Dale Bauer has commandeered the dialogic principle as 'a model for the fraught and volatile relationship women (both actual and textual) have with the patriarchal communities which "fail" them' (1994, 102). Pearce wants to 'preserve the notion of "meaning" depending on reciprocity, while acknowledging that the interlocutors on which the "bridge" depends [. . . .] may be multiple, changing and [. . . .] *in competition with each other'* (1994, 207, original emphasis).

Bakhtin suggests that the ruling class will attempt to monologise meaning, refusing to recognise its responsibility as addressee. Woolf's *The Years* offers a way of understanding this in gendered terms. Peggy's conversation with an egocentric young poet is peppered with his 'I,I,I,' but he refuses to let her take up the position of subject and address him: 'The fire went out of his face when she said 'I'. That's done it – now he'll go, she thought. He can't be 'you' – he must be 'I'' (1968, 290).

Although 'dialogue' implies two people, the 'dialogic' can encompass a multiplicity of voices. Pearce points out that we often manipulate utterances to one person through a mediating other: 'our personal relations are rarely between two people only: there is nearly always someone else's ghost or shadow fracturing our address' (1994, 203). Another conversation in *The Years* between Lady Pargiter and her daughters, Sara and Maggie, which seems to promise dialogic interaction between female subjects, is fractured by the intrusion of Sir Digby (significantly imagined as wearing a sword 'between his legs' (1968, 290)). Within a patriarchal society, utterances between women are frequently fractured by the 'shadow' of a man. The female-identified erotic triangle offers a way of exploring this point of intersection between male/female and female/female economies.

Dialogue is also a key trope in Irigaray's texts. 'And the One Doesn't Stir Without the Other' derives its effect from the fact that it is a 'bridge' flung out but failing to become dialogic because the response from the mother craved by the daughter is denied. 'When Our Lips Speak Together' is Irigaray's attempt to imagine ' "another" kind of commerce' (1985, 196) among women speaking together as receptive and equal subjects: 'Between us, one is not the 'real' and the other her imitation; one is not the original and the other her copy' (216). Like Bakhtin, Irigaray insists on the difference between the two participants in the dialogue – they are not the 'Same'. It is their separateness, necessary to avoid the confusion, or merging, of their identities within patriarchy, which enables a dialogic relation. The figure Irigaray uses for this relation is that of the 'two lips', used for its opposition to the male phallus, and connoting both female sexuality and 'speaking'. The 'two lips' are an image of plurality and of contiguity – neither is privileged above the other, they are '*neither one nor two*' (1985, 26). Hence: 'Between our lips, yours and mine, several voices, several ways of speaking resound endlessly, back and forth. One is never separable from the other. You/I: we are always several at once' (1985, 209). Irigaray's essay is thus an attempt to define the feminine, Ann Herrmann suggests, not through its relation to the masculine – as the 'Other of the Same' – but through relation to 'An/Other woman' who is 'the other woman as "another" woman in the form of an addressee [. . . .] or woman as both "self" and "other"' (Herrmann, 1989, 3).

Sylvia Townsend Warner's *Summer Will Show* demonstrates how women can take up a position within the symbolic order as speaking subjects through dialogue with an/other woman. It is through dialogue that Sophia and Minna, a story-teller by profession, move from being rival 'commodities' – 'wife' and 'mistress' of Frederick – to being mirroring subjects. Sophia spends a day pouring out her own story to Minna. Arriving later, Frederick finds his wife and his mistress seated together on the pink sofa, 'knit into this fathomless intimacy, and turning from it to entertain him with an identical patient politeness' (1987, 157). Again, the arrival of the male fractures the women's dialogue. A portrait of the two women seated on the pink sofa is tellingly given two names by its painter: '*Mes Odalisques*' and 'A Conversation between Two Women'. The two titles convey the women's simultaneous existence in two economies: both as '*Commodities* [. . . .] *a mirror of value of and for man*' (Irigaray, 1985, 177), and as female subjects in dialogue – 'living mirrors'.

Turning to the subject of literary production, Bakhtin made a distinction between 'monologic' texts, which subdue all voices in the text to the voice of the author, and 'dialogic' texts, which allow a range of voices to co-exist and refuse to privilege that of the author. Later he modified this view to suggest that all novels are inherently dialogic. Not only do they contain dialogic voices but they are both in dialogue with previous texts and anticipate a response (a reader). Herrmann shows how a woman's text can address either a male reader, conceived as an adversary, or a female reader conceived as an ally (1989, Chapter Two). In fact, it can do both at once. Pearce argues that different levels of positioning may co-exist in a text and that women writers have evolved a distinctive form of 'hidden dialogue' or 'hidden polemic' (1994, 108). Woolf's *A Room of One's Own*, for instance, ostensibly addressed to a female audience, is always conscious of the male listener behind the curtain.

This offers us an alternative to Gilbert and Gubar's 'affiliation complex' model of female literary tradition. Each of the texts I want to look at is *simultaneously* in dialogue both with the male literary tradition (the dominant discourse) and with texts by women. It is not so much a choice between the male or the female line of descent as Gilbert and Gubar suggest, but an ongoing engagement with both – a triangular paradigm. For instance, Warner's *Summer Will Show* engages not only with Flaubert's canonical *Sentimental Education*, but, as Janet Montefiore has noted, with Woolf's reworking of *Antony and Cleopatra*, Madame de Stael's *Corinne* and Brontë's *Villette* (1996, 169).

The novels I will be discussing enter a triangular dialogue with both the stereotypes of female rivalry in the dominant male discourse (sometimes through an explicit engagement with Freud, often through negotiations with traditional narrative structures, especially the romance plot), and with female-authored texts (for instance, the novels of the Brontës and Austen), which privilege female bonds.

These texts also engage with contemporaneous texts. I want to complete this section by looking again at the intertextual dialogue between Trefusis's *Broderie Anglaise,* Sackville-West's *Challenge* and Woolf's *Orlando*. This takes a rivalrous form in that it is a literary tussle over meaning – a *competitive* dialogue – as each writer aims to present the truth as she saw it. In her study of Woolf and Sackville-West, Suzanne Raitt sees the forging and exchange of such narratives as a key element in their relationship: 'Life stories are endlessly reworked in response to the narratives and the confessions of other woman' (1993, vii). In *Challenge*, Trefusis appears as the faithless Eve, who betrays Julian. In *Orlando*, Woolf portrays Trefusis as the bewitching Russian princess, Sasha, who again abandons Orlando. Both texts objectify the Trefusis character, presenting her as a mysterious, feminine 'other', with no voice in the text.

Trefusis enters this exchange with *Broderie Anglaise*, which is hidden polemic, in that its un-named addressees (Woolf and Sackville-West) can be inferred. It explores that 'othering' process, as well as the power of the writer to recreate their rival and/or beloved within their text. The discourse of Alexa, a novelist (Woolf), and her lover, John Shorne (Sackville-West), is always 'shadowed' by their imagined image of Anne (Trefusis), Shorne's former lover. At first she is a mysterious feminine 'other', an unattainable ideal like Rebecca or Vera. However, meeting the real Anne, Alexa discovers that not only is Anne not like the myth that she and John have created, but that John himself is 'as much the creation of one as of the other' (1992, 99).

The novel uses two key motifs which chime with Irigaray's work. Firstly, the image of two women 'speaking together'. It is an alliance formed between the two women during a conversation over tea and chocolate eclairs which empowers Alexa and enables her to rewrite the story of her relationship with John. Secondly, two mirror scenes depict the way in which the imagined Anne acts as a mirroring 'other' for Alexa and allows Alexa to reform her own identity. Before meeting Anne, Alexa sees herself in relation to her rival as too thin, lacking hair and colour – not a 'real woman'. After their conversation, she looks again in the mirror: 'Her face no longer wore the look of vagueness and indecision that had made her seem timorous and unnaturally young. What invisible artist had restored her features to their original serenity [....]?' (1992, 108–9). The 'artist' is Anne, who has herself been revised during the conversation. From the 'other woman' as the 'brilliant, volatile, artificial creature' (1992, 28) Alexa had imagined for her novel, Anne is transformed into an embodiment of femininity 'not necessarily more beautiful or more gifted than her sisters, but more womanly' (1992, 101). Seeing herself in relation to Anne as 'friend' or 'sister' rather than 'rival', Alexa accepts their 'difference'.

Such versions of the mirror ritual, where the heroine sees her mirrored reflection through the eyes of another woman, are, according to Gill Frith, a new development in early twentieth-century women's literature. In such rituals 'The "split" is not between "masculine" and "feminine" but between two kinds of femininity' (Frith, 1988, 13). The difference between 'two kinds of femininity' is what Irigaray is exploring in 'When Our Lips Speak Together', the ideal invoked by her figure of the two lips, as well as that of women as 'Living mirrors' for each other rather than for men. This mirroring process of exchange, an endless reconstruction of identity in relation to the other woman, is most clearly obvious in the intertextual dialogues of Vera Brittain and Winifred Holtby, where it takes place through a play of rivalry and friendship.

3
Rewriting the Victorians: May Sinclair's Transitional Modernism

May Sinclair's publishing career – from 1897 to 1927 – spans and exemplifies an important transitional moment in the shift from Victorian and Edwardian realist fiction to modernism. Although it was Sinclair who introduced the term 'stream of consciousness' (Sinclair, 1918, 58), her work has never become part of the modernist canon. Of her 25 novels only two are currently in print and there is remarkably little critical material on her work.[1] Yet her writing allows us to see the shift from 'Victorianism' to 'modernism' not as a radical break but as a process of evolution, and one in which gender issues played a central role.

Located in this transitional moment, Sinclair's work is dialogic in two key senses. Firstly, Sinclair located herself in an explicitly female tradition by engaging in an intertextual dialogue with Victorian women's fiction. Her work is an important link in a female literary genealogy which looks back to Victorian women novelists and forward to writers of the 1930s such as Rosamond Lehmann. One of the first novelists to engage with psychoanalysis, Sinclair's 'modernist' experimentation came out of her concern to find formal methods which could represent the 'reality' of female consciousness. Moreover, her writing is always informed by her commitment to feminism.

Secondly, Sinclair's practice was to take a theme or problem and rework it from different angles in several novels. She noted of *Life and Death of Harriett Frean* (1922), for instance, that 'I went with her over the road I had already gone with Mary Olivier [the protagonist of Sinclair's *Mary Olivier* (1919)] and put her to similar tests' (quoted in Boll, 1973, 143). *Arnold Waterlow* (1924) is a rewriting of *Mary Olivier* with a male protagonist, while *History of Anthony Waring* (1927) reworks *Harriett Frean*, as well as *Arnold Waterlow*. Sinclair's texts, therefore, are self-consciously in dialogue with each other. This may provide one

75

explanation for her neglect. It is only when her novels are read against each other that this intertextual dialogue becomes obvious, and the later novels can seen as part of a body of thinking around the issues of gender, sexuality, consciousness and creativity.

The female-centred erotic triangle is a pattern which Sinclair explored repeatedly throughout her career, sometimes two friends or sisters who love the same man, sometimes a woman in a relationship with a married man. It appears in *The Divine Fire* (1904), *The Creators* (1910), *The Three Sisters* (1914), *The Romantic* (1920), *Mr Waddington of Wyck* (1921), *Life and Death of Harriett Frean, Arnold Waterlow, Far End* (1926) and *History of Anthony Waring*, as well as the short stories 'Where Their Fire is Not Quenched' (1922) and 'Lena Wrace' (1930), and the long poem *The Dark Night* (1924). Both Tess Cosslett (1988, 3–4) and Gill Frith (1988, 75) have drawn attention to a pattern in nineteenth-century women's novels whereby when two friends loved the same man, one of the women would 'give' the man to the other woman, renouncing her own desires. Sinclair's texts engage with this pattern and the triangle becomes one of the matrices within which the transition from 'Victorian' to 'modern' is articulated most clearly in her work. This is especially clear in *The Three Sisters* and *Life and Death of Harriett Frean*, both of which use psychoanalysis to deconstruct Victorian notions of femininity and female sexuality.

One of the 'surplus women' of this era, Sinclair's own life was both exemplary and extraordinary and she writes especially perceptively about the plight of single women, particularly those in thrall to dominating mothers. Born in 1863, she was the sixth child and only daughter of William and Amelia Sinclair, who later separated, probably because of William Sinclair's alcoholism. Typically, she was given no formal education, except a brief year at Cheltenham Ladies College, but she read widely and taught herself French, German and Greek from her brothers' books. Her father died in 1881, and four of her brothers suffered early deaths, leaving Sinclair at home with her mother.

Her strongly-autobiographical novel *Mary Olivier* depicts the battle between Mary and her mother who, adoring her sons, tries to crush her daughter's sense of autonomy and force her into the mould of conventional femininity. In a rare moment of honesty 'Little Mamma' admits that: 'I was jealous of you, Mary. And I was afraid for my life you'd find it out' (MO 325). This suffocating, rivalrous mother–daughter relationship closely matches that depicted by Irigaray in 'And the One Doesn't Stir Without the Other'. Finally, Mary sacrifices her relationship with the man she loves in order to care for her mother, maintaining that:

'My body'll stay here and take care of her all her life, but my *self* will have got away' (MO 252, original emphasis).

After her mother's death in 1901, Sinclair went on to establish a successful career as a writer, becoming a well-known figure in the literary scene. Rebecca West remembered Sinclair as being 'extremely kind to young writers and particularly young women writers' (quoted in Boll, 1973, 158–9). She was an important enabler, introducing Ezra Pound, for one, to useful contacts. Charlotte Mew was another writer whose work Sinclair tried to place with editors, although their friendship was allegedly badly damaged when Sinclair rejected Mew's passionate advances (Boll, 1970; Fitzgerald, 1984). A 'web' of connections modelled on that drawn by Scott in *The Gender of Modernism* (1990) but focusing on Sinclair's links with women writers would connect her to Rebecca West, H.D.(she appears as 'Miss Kerr' in H.D.'s *Bid me to Live*), Dorothy Richardson, Katherine Mansfield, Virginia Woolf, G.B. Stern, Sheila Kaye-Smith, Rose Macaulay, Amy Lowell, Clemence Dane, Violet Hunt, as well as Vera Brittain and Rosamond Lehmann. Such connections not only link her to both female modernists and more 'traditional' writers, but also map a wider female genealogy. Vera Brittain, for instance, cites Sinclair's introduction to Elizabeth's Gaskell's *Life of Charlotte Brontë* (1857) in *Testament of Friendship*, using it to draw a parallel between Winifred Holtby and Brontë (TF 9–10).

Sinclair's reviews of other women writers, in themselves an important form of professional dialogue between women, were supportive and perceptive. Her delighted recognition of the 'startling "newness"' of Dorothy Richardson's *Pilgrimage* (1915–35) proved enabling for her own writing:

> To me these three novels show an art and method and form carried to punctilious perfection.[. . .] In this series there is no drama, no situation, no set scene. Nothing happens. It is just life going on and on. It is Miriam Henderson's stream of consciousness going on and on.
>
> (Sinclair, 1918, 57–8)

Sinclair had started to experiment with form as early as *The Divine Fire*, where she uses parentheses to indicate a character's unconscious thoughts. After reading *Pilgrimage* she developed the use of stream of consciousness in her own writing but this was not simply an imitation of Richardson's technique. Tightly controlled, shifting in and out of different characters' minds, and moving from third person 'she' to first person 'I' or second person 'you', Sinclair's 'stream is merely the *imitation* of a stream, not a stream at all' (Kaplan, 1975, 50, original emphasis), and makes inspired use of imagery and symbol. Sinclair did not, as Richardson did, regard hers as a specifically 'feminine' prose but used it equally to convey male and female consciousness. It is, however, in her use of these techniques to convey the complex, inner life of women who have narrow, constricted external lives – lives where 'Nothing happens' – that her fiction is most important.

Sinclair's status as a spinster during a period when attitudes to 'surplus women' ranged from pity to downright hostility undoubtedly militated against her being taken seriously by younger male writers such as D.H.Lawrence. Lawrence's projected novel, 'The Sisters', had to be renamed *Women in Love* partly because 'May Sinclair having had "three sisters", it won't do' (Lawrence, 1981, vol.2, 639). There are clear parallels between the two texts but Lawrence as high priest of sexual love was clearly not going to acknowledge this. Similarly, Richard Aldington's comment that pre-war London was 'a rather prissy milieu of some infernal bunshop full of English spinsters' (quoted in Benstock, 1987, 317) indicates a supposed opposition between the spinster and literary experimentation. Aldington was, in fact, one of the many young writers to whom Sinclair was kind. Even Rebecca West summed Sinclair up as 'an anachronistic figure [. . .] She was at once La Princess de Clèves, and the Brontës – and wished to be D. H. Lawrence' (quoted in Boll, 1973, 159).

Theophilus Boll speculates on the reasons for Sinclair's spinsterhood, recording West's assertion that Sinclair had been in love with a man, possibly a friend of her brother's, and might have married him but for ' "some very obscure grounds of scruple" ' (1973, 120). Obviously, this would provide a biographical explanation (however speculative) for Sinclair's interest in the motif of a woman who sacrifices her love for a man, usually because of another woman's prior claim to him. However, she also writes about the conflict between heterosexual love and a woman's desire for an independent self and work in a way that suggests she might herself have consciously chosen a single life. What is clear is that her work sympathetically articulates the conflicts faced by unmarried women in an era when marriage was still practically the only career open to women, but there was a perceived shortage of men.

Both Sinclair's commitment to feminism and her interest in psychoanalysis were central to her development of a modernist art. A member of both the Women's Freedom League and the Women Writers Suffrage League, her support was both active and public. Sylvia Pankhurst recalled Sinclair collecting money for the cause on street corners (1977,

279), while a photograph reprinted by Boll shows Sinclair outside the suffragist shop in Kensington.

Her pamphlet *Feminism*, published by the Women Writers Suffrage League in 1912, was in part a reply to a letter in *The Times* from the bacteriologist, Sir Almroth Wright, which denounced militant suffragettes as 'hysterics'. Wright attributed this 'hysteria' to sexual frustration, writing that 'the recruiting field for the militant suffragists is the half million of our excess female population – that half million which had better long ago have gone out to mate with its complement of men beyond the sea' (Wright, 1912, 7). Sinclair's reply neatly deconstructs Wright's '*pseudo-scientific*' argument (1912a, 8). She is especially clear on the economic facts, recognising that male hatred of feminism is 'as much a commercial as a sexual fear and hatred' (1912a, 36). Defending the need and right of women, especially single women, to work, she argues that:

> We are dealing less with a psychological portent than with a new sociological factor, the SOLIDARITY OF WOMAN. And there is only one other factor that can be compared with it for importance, and that is the SOLIDARITY OF THE WORKING-MAN.
> And these two solidarities are one.
>
> (1912a, 33–4, original emphasis)

Sinclair, then, not only regarded female solidarity as a political issue, but explicitly equated feminism with the class struggle.

It is this understanding which Sinclair brought to her use of psychoanalysis. In 1913 Sinclair became a founding member of the new Medico-Psychological Clinic in London, run by Sinclair's fellow suffragist Dr Jessie Margaret Murray (a student of Pierre Janet), and Julia Turner. It was the first clinic in England to use psychoanalytic methods, in combination with diet, exercise and medical treatment. Sinclair's financial support (a donation of £500) demonstrates commitment to a feminist use of psychoanalysis. Elaine Showalter, who offers a brief resume of the clinic's history in *The Female Malady*, sees its closure after the war as 'a striking illustration of the way that male professionalism could crush the early experimentation of women in psychoanalysis' (1987, 197).

Sinclair's fiction makes direct use of her wide reading in psychoanalysis through dreams, symbols, and the concepts of repression and sublimation. Contemporaneous criticism of Sinclair tended to bewail her use of psychoanalysis. Katherine Mansfield castigated *Mary Olivier* as merely a mass of undifferentiated surface impressions (Mansfield, 1990,

312). In fact, Sinclair uses psychoanalysis to analyse the patriarchal family as an institution which by repressing women's desires made them into hysterics. Her essay 'Symbolism and Sublimation' (1916), primarily a favourable review of Jung's *Psychology of the Unconscious,* although it also discusses Freud and Adler, lays out her argument for the value of sublimation. Sinclair's belief in sublimation allows her to show female sexual energy being redirected into artistic creation or philosophical thought, rather than necessarily (as Wright assumed) producing neurosis. Work and creativity are for Sinclair, as they would be for Winifred Holtby, satisfying alternatives to sexual fulfilment.

The Three Sisters (1914)

It is in *The Three Sisters* that Sinclair's interests in psychoanalysis and feminism come together with her passion for the Brontës to generate a critique of Victorian family and religious structures. She uses a double triangle – 'Three women to one man' (TS 184) – to explore the effect of a repression of female sexuality on women's relations with each other, and the triple conflict between the claims of sisterhood, the social pressure to get a husband, and the desire for sexual fulfilment.

The novel's title echoes that of Sinclair's critical study, *The Three Brontës* (1912), alerting the reader to the intertextual games she is playing. Between 1907 and 1914 Sinclair also provided introductions to the Everyman editions of the Brontës' novels, as well as Elizabeth Gaskell's *Life of Charlotte Brontë.* Gaskell's account of the Brontë sisters' evenings in Haworth parsonage is clearly the inspiration for the opening of *The Three Sisters* where the three Cartaret sisters – Mary, Gwendolen and Alice – wait in the dining room of a Yorkshire parsonage for their father, the Vicar of Garth, to read evening prayers. *The Three Sisters* is not a fictional biography of the Brontës. Rather, it is in dialogue with the over-romanticised Brontë myth created by Gaskell, problematising it to offer a more realistic picture of the possible relationships between three sisters similar to the Brontës but without their literary talents. While Sinclair's study defended the Brontës from the charges of frustrated spinsterhood, the novel delineates the effects of repression. The difference between the two texts demonstrates 'the contradictory need in early twentieth century feminists for rational analysis of women's psychological disabilities on the one hand and, on the other, for feminist heroines who would rise triumphant above them' (Stoneman, 1996, 70).

Sinclair's most radical move is to use psychoanalysis to expose the libidinous desires which the Brontës could only express obliquely, but

she also uses the insights of the Brontës' novels to reread early Freudian-
ism. This two-way dialogic is most obvious in Sinclair's engagement with
the nineteenth-century triangle plot where a woman sacrifices her interest in a man for a friend or sister. The genealogy of this plot can be traced
back to Harriet Martineau's *Deerbrook* (1839), a novel which influenced
Charlotte Brontë: *Jane Eyre* (1847), *Shirley* (1849) and *Villette* (1853) all
use variations on a triangle pattern – Jane/Rochester/ Bertha, Caroline/
Robert Moore/Shirley and Lucy/Dr John/Paulina. The neglect of *Deerbrook* within the critical canon (it is currently out of print, as is *The Three
Sisters*) supports my contention that the subject of female homosocial
bonds actively marks a text as uncanonical.[2]

In *Deerbrook* the doctor, Edward Hope, although in love with Margaret
Ibbotson, marries her sister, Hester, because he believes Margaret loves
Philip. The focus of the narrative, however, is on the sisters' relationship,
especially Hester's jealousy of Margaret's friendship with Maria Young,
a poor governess. Hester's jealousy of this is such that she even fails to
notice that her husband is in love with Margaret. Maria, in love with
Philip herself, cedes him to Margaret. In nineteenth-century women's
fiction, Gill Frith argues, this gesture of relinquishing the man, often
symbolised by the exchange of a book or gift, works to transform rivalry
into *voluntary* exchange. It offers, she suggests, a 'fantasised reversion' of
the exchange of women discussed by Sedgwick 'in which the sexual
contract is transformed into a collusion and exchange between
women' (1988, 76). Although such a 'collusion and exchange' can be
read as a subversive gesture of gender solidarity, a refusal to be positioned
as rivals, it also reinforces the nineteenth-century stereotypes of the ideal
woman as self-denying and untouched by sexual desire. What Sinclair
does is to use the psychoanalytic understanding of female sexuality to
show the psychological cost of such self-sacrifice.

In *The Three Brontës* Sinclair analyses in detail the silencing of female
sexual desire in the nineteenth century and the (unconscious) subterfuges to which women were reduced:

[Jane Eyre] sinned against the unwritten code that ordains that
a woman may lie till she is purple in the face, but she must not, as
a piece of gratuitous information, tell a man she loves him; not, that
is to say, in as many words. She may declare her passion unmistakably
in other ways. She may exhibit every ignominious and sickly sign of
it; her eyes may glow like hot coals; she may tremble; she may flush
and turn pale; she may do almost anything, provided she does not
speak the actual words. In mid-Victorian times an enormous licence

was allowed her. She might faint, with perfect propriety, in public; she might become anaemic and send for the doctor, and be ordered iron; [...] Everybody knew what that meant.

(1912b, 117–18)

In this passage are the seeds of *The Three Sisters*. Psychoanalysis provided Sinclair with a theory and a language in which to discuss this repression of female desire and its eruption in the form of hysteria.

It is Alice's failure to conceal her love for a man indifferent to her which causes the Cartarets' move from their old parish. Her father, regarding this as a disgrace reflecting on him, transfers his entire family to Garth. Isolated there, the sisters meet only one eligible man – the new doctor, Dr Steven Rowcliffe, whose name invokes *Dr* John Graham, *Ro*chester and Heath*cliff*, and possibly *Ro*bert Moore – ironically, because he is an unworthy romantic hero.

The use of three sisters, a common trope in myth and fairy tale, allows Sinclair to break away from a binary opposition between two women who are positioned as opposites – the romance heroine and her rival. Using three women allows Sinclair to explore three different kinds of femininity and differing reactions to female rivalry. A detailed description, which evokes Branwell's famous portrait of the Brontë sisters (used on the cover of the Virago edition), shows how, true to the 'sister knot', the sisters are the 'same' yet different. Mary, the eldest, is 'the one that had the colour' (TS 3). Alice, the youngest, 'departed in no way from her sister's type but that her body was slender and small boned, that her face was lightly finished' (TS 4). Gwenda is 'the tallest and the darkest of the three. Her face followed the type obscurely; and vividly and emphatically it left it' (TS 4).

Jean Radford suggests that Sinclair is using recognisable types: 'the steady, womanly elder sister, the independent "tomboy", the frail younger girl (almost the Meg, Jo and Beth-Amy of Louisa May Alcott's *Little Women)*' (TS ix). This accords with Adler's contention that birth order produces recognisable types. Mary, for instance, as the eldest takes seniority as 'Miss Cartaret', and expects to marry first. But the sisters also represent psychoanalytical types – the 'normal femininity', 'masculinity complex' and 'neurosis' which Freud outlined in 'Femininity' (1932). While this postdates Sinclair's text, these types are implicit in Freud's work earlier and Sinclair's use of them differs substantially from his. She explores them not as a norm and deviations from it, but as three reactions to the silencing of female desire within patriarchal culture.

Although Rowcliffe's coming energises all three sisters – 'life, secret and silent, stirred in their blood and nerves' (TS 9) – the key point is that they do not speak to each other about this. The 'unwritten code' of silence about female desire divides them from each other, making them unspoken rivals. Maria tells Margaret in *Deerbrook*: 'There are no bounds to the horror, disgust and astonishment expressed when a woman owns her love to its object unasked' (1983, 163). Thus every women conceals her desire and 'hopes that no one else has suffered as she did' (1983, 160–1). Irigaray's comment that the first issue facing feminism is 'that of making each woman "conscious" of the fact that what she has felt in her personal experience is a condition shared by all women' (1985, 164), is highly relevant here.

Unable to speak their desire, each of the sisters attempts to attract Rowcliffe in ways which accord with their psychoanalytic types: Mary by presenting herself as the 'womanly' woman; Gwenda by walking on the moors; and Alice by making herself ill. It is in her portrayal of Alice that Sinclair draws most obviously on psychoanalysis. Alice resorts to exactly the kinds of subterfuges Sinclair pin-pointed in her discussion of *Jane Eyre*. Sinclair makes explicit Alice's *unconscious* thoughts: 'Alice thought, "I will make myself ill. So ill that they'll *have* to send for him. I shall see him that way"' (TS 10, original emphasis). Her symptoms – she stops eating, becomes tired, anaemic, faints and has hysterical fits – are those of the hysteric as outlined in Freud and Breuer's *Studies on Hysteria*.

Although it is difficult to know exactly what Sinclair had read (she recorded first studying psychoanalysis in 1913 and read widely), *Studies on Hysteria*, translated into English in 1909, was certainly available to her. *Studies on Hysteria* linked hysteria, which included symptoms such as anorexia nervosa, depression, hallucinations, paralysis, fainting and mutism, to daydreaming (to which women were seen as especially prone because of occupations such as needlework), to sick nursing, to being in love, and to gifted adolescents, including 'girls who get out of bed at night so as secretly to carry on some study that their parents have forbidden' (Freud and Breuer, 1991, 321). The patients were often exceptionally intelligent women and their hysteria can now be seen as directly linked to the frustration and boredom of a restricted life, controlled by parents or husband.

Dr Rowcliffe's reading of Pierre Janet's *Etat mental des hystériques* (1894) signals his interests. He thinks of specialising in gynaecology or 'nervous diseases' because he is 'interested in women's cases' (TS 152) . As his contempt for Alice as a 'poor parson's hysterical daughter' (TS 80), indicates, however, he is one of number of 'experts' – Charcot, Janet and Freud – who make money and a professional reputation out of women's illnesses – another trade in women's bodies. His diagnosis of Alice's condition is textbook Freud – hysteria resulting from sexual frustration. Alice, Rowcliffe pronounces, 'isn't ill because she's been starving herself. She's been starving herself because she's ill. It's a symptom' (TS 77). 'Starved' emotionally, Alice reacts by 'starving' herself physically in order to attract attention. She would, Rowcliffe argues, be perfectly all right if she was married and had children. Mr Cartaret's refusal to accept this diagnosis and his talk of putting Alice 'under restraint' (TS 181) recall the fate of Brontë's Bertha.

Mr Cartaret deliberately manufactures rivalry between his daughters, telling Alice that Rowcliffe and Gwenda (with whom Rowcliffe is in love) have been walking together on the moors. Gwenda's reaction to Alice's subsequent relapse is the classic self-sacrifice of the nineteenth-century shared lover triangle plot. Told by Rowcliffe that Alice will die or go mad if she is not married, Gwenda leaves Garth in the hope that Rowcliffe will marry Alice, confiding in Mary: 'It's her one chance, Molly. I've got to give it her. How *can* I let her die, poor darling, or go mad? She'll be all right if he marries her' (TS 191, original emphasis). Her gesture is made out of sisterly love. But it is at this point that Sinclair disrupts the traditional paradigm of self-sacrifice, exposing it as 'monstrous, absurd, altogether futile' (TS 341), because it leaves the field for Mary.

Gwenda and Mary demonstrate two different reactions to the problem of female rivalry: self-sacrifice or manipulation. Mary's actions deny any kind of sisterhood, biological or ideological. Through Mary, Sinclair offers a critique of the Victorian 'Angel in the House', which predates Virginia Woolf's analysis in 'Professions for Women' (1931) by nearly two decades. Outwardly the embodiment of the Victorian ideal of the 'womanly woman' (even her name connotes ideal womanhood), Mary is, in fact, the strongest of the sisters, the best adapted to patriarchal society, because her 'womanly' facade masks not only ruthless manipulation but a total lack of gender loyalty. Here Sinclair fuses psychoanalytic theory with Austen's understanding of the economics of the romance novel. Like Mary in Austen's 'Three Sisters', Sinclair's Mary wants Rowcliffe for the status he can give her as a married woman, but will not acknowledge this, even to herself:

> Mary thought, '[...] On Wednesday I will go into the village and see all my sick people. Then I shall see [Rowcliffe]. And he will see me. He will see that I am kind and sweet and womanly.' She thought, 'That is

the sort of woman that a man wants.' *But she did not know what she was thinking.*

(TS 10, my emphasis)

The words 'sweet', 'good' and 'womanly' come to signify Mary's duplicity. Rowcliffe reflects that 'sweet and good women were not invariably intelligent. As for honesty, if they were always honest they would not always be sweet and good' (TS 74). Similarly, Woolf recognised that the 'Angel in the House' demanded that women must 'to put it bluntly – tell lies if they are to succeed' (1979, 60).

Sinclair makes it clear that 'normal femininity' as advocated by psychoanalysis was an extension of this Victorian ideal and thus not only involved repression but was itself was a form of neurosis. She uses parentheses to convey the gap between Mary's conscious and unconscious thoughts, as in Mary's deliberations over asking Rowcliffe to tea:

> It would look better if she were not in too great a hurry. (She said to herself it would look better on Ally's account.) The longer he was kept away (she said to herself, that he was kept away from Ally) the more he would be likely to want to come.

(TS 213)

Irigaray argues that to be a 'normal' woman in Freud's terms a woman has to enter a 'masquerade of femininity', and 'a system of values' that does not belong to women but which answers male desires (1985, 134). Mary thus enacts a 'masquerade of femininity' which answers Rowcliffe's desires. She plays the 'womanly' woman, feeding and cossetting him, and deliberately marking her difference from the independent Gwenda who strides the moors with Rowcliffe as an equal and challenges him intellectually.

There is a sense in the novel – evoked especially in the image of the sisters listening to Rowcliffe's approach while 'life' quivers in their blood and nerves 'like a hunting thing held on the leash' (TS 9) – of the women as hunters. We could see the man here as their prey, a commodity. But, as Sinclair's rewriting of the nineteenth-century paradigm makes very clear, Rowcliffe cannot be simply exchanged between Gwenda and Alice. Such an exchange is precisely, to reapply Frith's word, exposed as a '*fantasised*' one, that is, one only possible in the 'fantasy' of women's fiction. With both the economic power and the power to do the asking, to voice his desire, Rowcliffe makes his own decision. Even Mary, although she appears to do the choosing, can only put her goods on display, remaining an object in the market. It is Rowcliffe who does the ultimate buying. Although his choice is partly determined by his unconscious sexual desires, Rowcliffe's decision to marry Mary is a rejection of the alternative femininity Gwenda offers, in favour of the conventionally 'womanly'.

With both sisters married (Alice's hysteria disappears when she becomes pregnant by and then marries the farmer, Jim Greatorex), Gwenda's isolated spinsterhood, caring for her now invalid father, is made more bitter by Mary's flaunting of her married status and her children. But her second sacrifice, refusing to become Rowcliffe's mistress, is still made out of loyalty to Mary. It's worth noting at this point that even had Mary died, it would still have been legally impossible for Gwenda to marry Rowcliffe. Sinclair makes this clear early on when Mr Cartaret reads *The Spectator* 'to see what is had to say about the Deceased Wife's Sister Bill' (TS 23). This historical background is only hinted at but it makes the point that Gwenda's sacrifice is irrevocable, and it makes it impossible for Sinclair to manipulate a happy ending by engineering Mary's death.

Here it is worth comparing Gwenda's gesture with Charlotte Brontë's treatment of Caroline Helstone's similar sacrifice when she thinks Robert Moore loves Shirley. Shirley, who values woman-to-woman bonds, does not make a parallel sacrifice, neither does she take advantage of it, instead 'she reasserts the primacy of their female friendship, and attacks the "intrusion" of the male' (Cosslett, 1988, 131). But Brontë ultimately fudges the issue of female rivalry by introducing a convenient brother, Louis Moore, to marry Shirley. It's the narrative equivalent of cutting the man in half – a solution Sinclair refuses to take.

Gwenda's sacrifice is the central problem of *The Three Sisters*. Is it a monstrous waste or a laudable gesture of sisterly solidarity? Or something even more complex? Sinclair actually exposes Gwenda's gesture as unnecessary before she even undertakes it. Alice's 'secret and hidden kinship' (TS 193) with Gwenda allows her to understand Gwenda's intention and to refuse to take advantage of it. The novel is dialogic in that the contradictory viewpoints it offers are not finally subordinated to a single authorial interpretation.

Here the character of Mr Cartaret as a representative of the Victorian family and religious structures is particularly interesting. A highly sensual man who has had three wives, Mr Cartaret's main problem is the frustration of enforced celibacy. His first wife, mother of his three daughters, died giving birth to Alice. Gwenda states baldly, 'He killed Mother [...] He was told that Mother would die or go mad if she had another baby. And he let her have Ally' (TS 27–8). The second wife becomes a nervous invalid before dying of an obscure internal trouble which he has ignored. The third wife, Robina, runs away from Mr Cartaret after five years. Mr Cartaret has an unacknowledged but troubling vision of her in a divorce court explaining that she ran away from her husband because she was afraid of him: 'He could hear the question, "Why were you afraid?" and Robina's answer – but at that point he always reminded himself that it was as a churchman that he objected to divorce' (TS 21). Sinclair's depiction of a man whose profession has 'committed him to a pose' (or a masquerade) until he has 'become unconscious of his real thoughts, his real motives, his real likings and dislikings' (TS 21) is particularly good, laying bare the hypocrisy of his repression of his own and his daughters' sexual desire.

The fates of Mr Cartaret's wives can be related to Breuer's comment that hysteria could be caused by 'perverse demands made by the husband, unnatural practices etc' (Freud and Breuer, 1991, 328). Noting that the relevant case histories have had to be omitted from *Studies on Hysteria* (an interesting admission in itself), Breuer goes so far as to argue that *'the great majority of severe neuroses in women have their origin in the marriage bed'* (1974, 328, original emphasis). In *Feminism* Sinclair counters Wright's diagnosis of suffrage 'hysteria' as resulting from sexual frustration by drawing attention to 'hysteria and neurosis' in women which was the result not of sexual frustration, but of women's 'martyrdom' to the '"physiological emergencies" [a phrase used by Wright] of *men*' (Sinclair 1912a, 13, my emphasis). More plainly, women's vulnerability to the sexual demands made on them by men. In a footnote Sinclair singles out especially what women suffer from violent and drunken men (1912a, 14). Her analysis here is a radical one, far in advance of that offered by Freud, although Breuer moves some way toward it. Certainly, the marriage bed has proved literally lethal for two of Mr Cartaret's wives.

Mr Cartaret's 'killing' of his wives amounts to what Irigaray calls the 'murder [...] of the mother' (1991, 36), which leaves women without a sense of a 'female genealogy'. The three motherless sisters have no model of women-to-woman relationships, and no mother 'to sneak and scheme *for* [them]' (TS 27, original emphasis) in getting a husband. A comparison with the potentially rivalrous situation in Alcott's *Little Women* (1869), where there is initially one man to four sisters, is interesting here. Alcott situates her sisters in a matriarchal community, ruled by the benevolent Marmee, where sisterhood is valued and rivalry defused. In contrast, the Cartaret sisters' rivalry can be traced to the fact that their sense of identity is constructed within a patriarchal environment, which constructs them as rival commodities, most obviously through Mr Cartaret's manipulations. They are divided from each other by the code of silence.

Seen in this context, Gwenda's self-sacrifice is a positive affirmation of sister-love, and a subversion of male-manufactured female rivalry. Sinclair's other texts strongly affirm gender loyalty. Lucia in *The Divine Fire* is horrified when Rickman, despite his engagement to Flossie, writes love sonnets to her. In *The Creators* there is a series of interlocking triangles: Jane refuses to have an affair with Tanquerary out of loyalty to his wife, while Nina represses her love for both Tanquerary (out of loyalty to Jane) and Prothero (out of loyalty to Laura). In perhaps the most extraordinary example, in *Arnold Waterlow,* Effie literally dies so that Rosalind's prior claim to Arnold can be honoured.

However, a more complex reading is possible in view of Sinclair's advocacy of the option of sublimation. Freud suggested in *Three Essays on the Theory of Sexuality* (1905) that in sublimation 'we have one of the origins of artistic activity' (1977, 163). With this in mind, the single woman, particularly the single woman writer, can be seen not as merely sexually frustrated but as having made a positive choice to maximise her potential for creative endeavour. In 'Symbolism and Sublimation' Sinclair went on to endorse the value of sublimation:

> The psycho-analysts, Freud and Jung and their followers, have been abused like pickpockets, as if they offered us no alternative but licence or repression; as if the indestructible libido must either ramp outrageously in the open or burrow beneath us and undermine our sanity; as if Sublimation, the solution that they do offer, were not staring us in the face.
>
> (1916a, 120)

In the later *A Defence of Idealism* Sinclair defined sublimation as 'a turning or passing of desire from a less worthy or less fitting object to fix it on one more worthy and more fitting' (Sinclair, 1917, 9). However, in *The Three Sisters* she is more ambivalent.

Gwenda's unflinching self-knowledge in contrast to Mary and Alice is clear in, for instance, her reaction to Rowcliffe's appearance:

> 'I will go out on to the moor again. [. . .] He will see me when he drives back and he will wonder who is that wild, strong girl who walks by herself on the moor at night and isn't afraid.[. . .]' She thought *(for she*

knew what she was thinking), 'I shall do nothing of the sort. I don't care whether he sees me or not.'

(TS 10, my emphasis)

Having sacrificed the possibility of sexual fulfilment, she sublimates her desire into the study of philosophy and a semi-mystical feeling for the moors: 'Her woman's passion, forced inward, sustained her with an inward peace, and inward exaltation. And in this peace, this exaltation, it became one with her passion for the place' (TS 339). However, the ending of the novel with its bleak image of Gwenda 'mortally wounded' and trapped in a village which resembles hell with its houses 'naked and blackened as if fire had passed over them' (TS 387) suggests sterility. At this point Sinclair seems herself ambivalent about Gwenda's sacrifice and unable fully to endorse sublimation.

There is a further possibility – that Gwenda's sacrifice is, at a deeply unconscious level (possibly unconscious also to Sinclair?), as much an attempt to preserve her own integrity as to save Alice. Rowcliffe is not a worthy object for Gwenda's desire. In an early scene he fails to propose to Gwenda because he finds 'something inimical' in 'her absorption, her estranging ecstasy' (TS 157) in the moors and the moon, a symbol which links her to Artemis, the virgin huntress, and to Jane Eyre's vision of the moon as Mother. ' "Oh, look at the moon!" ' Gwenda cries, ' "[. . .] Something's calling her across the sky, but the mist holds her and the wind beats her back – look how she staggers and charges head-downward. She's fighting the wind" ' (TS 159). The moon, pulled between mist and wind, symbolises Gwenda herself, torn between her desire for Rowcliffe and her need to maintain an independence and integrity which would be lost in marriage with him.

In the 'Moony' chapter of Lawrence's *Women in Love* (1920), which clearly responds to this scene from the male point of view, Birkin's antagonism to the moon, again a female symbol, is such that he stones its reflection. This mirrors his attempt to subdue Ursula's independence: 'I want you to drop your assertive *will*' (Lawrence, 1982, 327), he tells her, and (a echo of Sinclair), 'I hate ecstasy' (328). Like Rowcliffe, Birkin is threatened by a woman who has a strong, independent sense of self.

Both Gwenda and Nina Lempriere in *The Creators* are modelled on Emily Brontë, and especially what Sinclair saw as Brontë's 'virginal nature' (1912b, 169) and 'passionate pantheism' (171). Nina believes that 'if any woman is to do anything stupendous it means virginity' (1910, 104):

Virginity – [Nina] had always seen it, not as a fragile, frustrate thing but as a joyous, triumphing energy, the cold, wild sister of mountain winds and leaping waters, subservient only to her genius, guarding the flame in its secret unsurrendered heart.

(1910, 313)

'Virginity' here is used, as it is used by Irigaray, to figure 'physical and moral integrity' (Irigaray, 1993c, 86), that is, a female identity which is not subject to male control or defined through relation to the male. Since marriage could mean literal death for women, as the fate of Gwenda's mother demonstrates, a subliminated celibacy can be seen as a positive and even subversive alternative.

Mary Olivier is a more sustained and positive study of sublimation. Having sublimated her sexual desire, Mary gains a knowledge of 'reality' which is the 'ultimate passion' (MO 379). Sinclair implies that, given the choice between this and Richard, Mary would not be able to give it up because it would mean 'losing, absolutely and for ever, my real self' (379). The integrity of self which comes from sublimation is placed above sexual fulfilment. The key difference between Gwenda and Mary Olivier, Nina Lempriere or Emily Brontë herself, however, is the capacity for creativity. Gwenda does nothing with her sublimated energies.

If the triangle plot dramatises the tension between women's loyalty to their primary bonds with their sisters and their need for sexual fulfilment, *The Three Sisters* articulates the moment of transition when the knowledge of the price paid for repressing sexual desire made it impossible for women to accept the repression demanded by the sacrifice of the nineteenth-century shared lover plot.

Life and Death of Harriett Frean (1922)

While *The Three Sisters* is ambivalent and *Mary Olivier* validates sublimation, *Life and Death of Harriett Frean* is an explicit study of repression. This is a monologic novel in the sense that it does away with the uncertainties of *The Three Sisters* and subordinates them to a single viewpoint, producing a parable or allegory on the theme of self-sacrifice. Technically, the novel is an advance on the earlier text. Sinclair's encounter with Richardson's work proved the catalyst she needed to develop a highly economical style, combining stream of consciousness with traditional omniscient narration. In contrast to Richardson's lengthy *Pilgrimage*, Sinclair's deceptively simple text is structured through a tightly controlled series of repeated and paralleled symbols and incidents.

Harriett Frean has much in common with Mayor's *The Third Miss Symons*, but whereas Henrietta Symons's problem is that she is not loveable because she has never been loved, Harriett is the only child of parents who love her too much. She is taught to repress her own desires in order that she should always 'behave beautifully'. The ideal of self-denying femininity she is to aim for is that delineated in Woolf's portrait of the 'Angel in the House':

> She sacrificed herself daily. If there was chicken, she took the leg; if there was a draught she sat in it – in short she was so constituted that she never had a mind or a wish of her own, but preferred to sympathise always with the minds and wishes of others.
>
> (Woolf, 1979, 59)

Taught this kind of sacrificial behaviour, Harriett never develops a mind or a wish of her own. At a children's party, for instance, her self-denial in going without food is approved by her mother: 'Well, I'm glad my little girl didn't snatch and push. It's better to go without than to take from other people. That's ugly' (HF 14–15). A succession of 'Angel in the House' type sacrifices made by Harriett to please her mother – having plain rather than breaded cutlets, living in Hampstead rather than Sidmouth – are pre-empted by her mother's parallel sacrifices for her daughter's sake. The result of Harriett's attempts to guess her mother's wishes is that each inadvertently deprives the other of her real preference.

As in *The Three Sisters*, Harriett's sacrifice of the man she loves provides the crux of the novel, but here her decision is the product of the education in self-renunciation given to the Victorian girl. When Robin, the fiancé of her friend, Priscilla, falls in love with her, Harriett convinces him that they must give each other up. Their anguished conversation in 'Black's Lane' re-enacts that between Maggie Tulliver and Stephen Guest (tacitly promised to Maggie's cousin Lucy) in the chapter 'In the Lane' in *The Mill on the Floss* (1860). Maggie's belief that 'I must not, cannot seek my own happiness by sacrificing others' (Eliot, 1979, 571) becomes Harriett's assertion that 'we've no right to get our happiness out of [Priscilla's] suffering' (HF 61). Harriett has, once again, 'behaved beautifully' and her parents approve her action, telling her 'you couldn't do anything else' (HF 62). The thought of this self-sacrifice gives meaning to her spinsterhood: 'At her worst she could still think with pleasure of the beauty of the act which had given Robin to Priscilla' (HF 116).

Rather than killing off her heroine as Eliot does, Sinclair delineates with chilling precision the psychological effects of Harriett's self-sacrifice on herself and the others involved over the next 50-odd years. Priscilla develops a mysterious paralysis which is, Harriett learns later, 'pure hysteria' (HF 133) developed to manipulate Robin. Nursing Priscilla turns Robin into a neurotic and selfish invalid (an interesting reversal of Freud's case histories where hysteria in women is linked to sickbed nursing), who, after Priscilla's death, marries and exploits his nurse, Beatrice.

The triangle motif is repeated in the next generation when Robin's niece, Mona Floyd, tells Harriett that she is about to marry a man who had been engaged to her friend. The representative of a generation no longer in thrall to the Victorian ideologies of female self-sacrifice, Mona justifies her action in a phrase which echoes Harriett's father's comment: 'We can't do anything else' (HF 144). The judgement of this new Freudian-influenced generation, as voiced by Mona, is that Harriett's earlier sacrifice simply made four people unhappy – Harriett, Robin, Priscilla and Beatrice. Moreover, Mona pin-points a selfishness behind the sacrifice. Harriett, she argues, had not thought of other people but of 'herself. Of her own moral beauty' (HF 144) and, even worse, Mona says, 'it wasn't even your own idea. You sacrificed him to somebody else's' (HF 145).

This is the key difference between Harriett and Gwenda. Harriett's sacrifice is the result of an internalisation of her parents' concepts of duty and self-sacrifice. The Victorian family life Harriett's parents represent is exposed as both sterile and damaging like the blue egg (a Jungian symbol of fertility) in their drawing room, which is not only hollow but contains scissors and a stiletto. In 'Symbolism and Sublimation' Sinclair had approved Jung's assertion of the need for conflict between mother and child:

> That conflict begins in childhood and is waged most fiercely on the threshold of adolescence. It must be fought to a finish, and the child must win it or remain forever immature. If the parent wins ten to one the child becomes neurotic.
>
> (Sinclair, 1916b, 144)

Mary Olivier is a dramatisation of that conflict where the child wins the fight. Similarly, Gwenda's sacrifice is a way of resisting her father's attempts to control her. In *Harriett Frean*, however, there is no conflict because Harriett's passion for her parents retards her development to the extent that she never develops a separate self. She remains forever immature and neurotic. Her identification with her mother culminates in her discovery that she has the same kind of cancer that her mother died from: 'With every stab she would live again in her mother' (HF 178). The final scenes in hospital bring her life full circle. The release of all that she has repressed in an anaesthetic-induced torrent which seems to resemble semiotic babble signals her return to childhood, and she greets her friend Connie with 'a sudden ecstatic wonder and recognition' as 'Mamma' (HF 184).

Harriett's inability to read serious literature is a telling indicator that she has repressed rather than sublimated her sexual energy. For several of Sinclair's characters – Gwenda, Mary Olivier, Arnold Waterlow – books, particularly those disapproved of by their parents, are a way of establishing a separate sense of self. They sublimate their sexual energy into their reading, and as compensation for their renunciation, they have moments of heightened awareness. Harriett, because she has never established a separate self, is incapable of sublimation. Again, Sinclair makes it clear that spinsterhood does not necessitate neurosis – Harriett's friend, Lizzie Pierce, although also a spinster, retains an active interest in literature.

Harriett's absorption in her parents prevents her from establishing relationships not only with men but also with her female friends. The silence between women on the subject of their desire which I noted in *The Three Sisters* is even more noticeable here. Lynne Pearce has suggested that in the 'dialogic model of sisterhood/subjecthood it is silence and not difference that is the great enemy [. . .] If we deny the other – by refusing to enter into dialogue with her – we also deny our own self' (1994, 171). Harriett not only fails to initiate a dialogue with Priscilla, but forms a conspiracy with Robin which both excludes Priscilla and denies her adult subjecthood. It is an 'insult' to Priscilla, as Mona says, '*handing her over* to a man who couldn't love her even with his body' (HF 146, my emphasis). In this exchange Harriett and Robin treat Priscilla like an object or a child. Harriett's sacrifice, far from being a bond or exchange between her and Priscilla, is a collusion and exchange with the man. This actually enables her to feel *superior and different* to Priscilla:

When she thought of Robin and how she had given him up she felt a thrill of pleasure in her beautiful behaviour, *and a thrill of pride in remembering that he had loved her more than Priscilla.*

(HF 67, my emphasis)

Harriett's unacknowledged satisfaction when Priscilla is paralysed, and the secret pleasure she gets from her pity for Robin's second wife are both in direct contrast to Gwenda's selflessness.

Sinclair's treatment of Harriett's failure to separate from her mother offers a corrective to Nancy Chodorow's theorisation of women's sense of self as connected to others. It makes explicit the connection between the Victorian prescriptions for ideal and self-sacrificing femininity and their demand that women sub/merge their sense of self in order to identify with the desires of others. Harriett merges herself so fully with her mother that she can no longer either separate herself from her mother or fully recognise her own desires. Rather than being replicated in her friendships with other women, this merger actively prevents such friendships developing.

The fiction of this period tends to advocate a model of female identity which depends on separation and autonomy rather than connection. Penny Brown has argued that many women writers felt that self-development was not compatible with commitment to another person: 'the demands made by any close relationship are seen to work against the development of individual freedom and autonomy' (1992, 223). Certainly this is the conclusion of *Mary Olivier*. Ironically, for Sinclair's *male* characters, fulfilment and a self-development come mainly through connection to others, a reversal of Chodorow's theorisation. In *Arnold Waterlow*, for instance, Arnold attains a similar fulfilment and philosophical insight to Mary Olivier's through the love he feels for Effie, rather than through maintaining a separate autonomy. In contrast to Nina's virginity in *The Creators*, Sinclair's male artists – Rickman in *The Divine Fire*, Tanquerery in *The Creators* and Christopher Vivart in *Far End* – all benefit from relationships with women which are necessary for their art to develop.

Two other texts in Sinclair's intertextual dialogue offer useful commentaries on *Harriett Frean*. A short story published in the same year, 'Where Their Fire is Not Quenched', has a protagonist called 'Harriott Leigh' (an obvious echo). Here Sinclair questions the notion that sexual relations in themselves are enough to prevent neurosis. Harriott has a purely sexual affair with a married man, Oscar Wade (probably a name intended to convey licentiousness), a relationship which gives her no spiritual satisfaction. After her death Harriott is condemned to a hell which consists of the repetition of their affair *ad infinitum*. Harriott's sin is not having had an affair with a married man, nor even the disloyalty to another woman this involved, but having had a sexual affair with a man she neither loved nor respected. The implication is that a single, and celibate, life would have been preferable because, like Mary Olivier's, it would have preserved the integrity of the self.

Sinclair's last novel, *History of Anthony Waring,* rewrites the *Harriett Frean* self-sacrifice theme with a male protagonist. Like Harriett, Tony gives up Jenny, the woman he loves, out of loyalty to her husband and to his own wife, Ellen. Despite his marriage and a fulfilling job, Tony's life is almost (although never quite) as barren as Harriett's. Here Sinclair analyses a certain type of masculinity as demanding its own repressions: 'A stern upright stroke was marked at each corner of his mouth, as if he had worn a bit, witness to his habit of holding himself in' (1927, 174). Both 'masculinity' and 'femininity', Sinclair's work suggests, are damaging constructions.

In the last 15 years of Sinclair's life Parkinson's disease left her in a twilight state. This in itself may have had a detrimental effect on her reputation – by her death in 1946 she had already been absent from the literary landscape for nearly two decades. She deserves reassessment, not least because her focus on the female-identified erotic triangle places the tension between women's need for sexual fulfilment and their primary bonds with other women at the centre of her work, and thus of a transitional moment in literary history. Her practice of rewriting this plot not only places her in dialogue with nineteenth-century women writers but also produces an internal dialogue which makes possible a variety of careful moral distinctions, balancing the needs of self and others. As Rebecca West indicates, Sinclair valued female friendship in her own life, and this is reflected in her texts where gender loyalty is both validated and problematised. Both through her work and as an example of a professional woman writer, she was an important influence on younger writers.

4
The 'Other Woman': Rebecca West's 'Difference of View'

Rebecca West's life was shadowed by her own role as the 'other woman' in a triangle drama. Her position as mistress of the married H.G. Wells not only dominated her life during the decade-long affair, necessitating tortuous cover-ups which included bringing up their son to call her 'Auntie Panther', but became an identity from which she was never able fully to escape. Indeed, 'Rebecca West', the pseudonym which the nineteen-year-old Cicily Fairfield borrowed from the heroine of Ibsen's *Rosmersholm*, the rebellious New Woman who loves the married Rosmer, now seems uncannily prescient. As Sinclair's literary identity was dominated by the label 'spinster', West's was overcast by that of the 'other woman' – the 'mistress', the 'unmarried mother'.

West's status as an important contributor to and commentator on modernism has only recently been recognised. Much early criticism focused on the relationship of her work to that of Wells, a focus which obscures not only West's modernism but her connections with women writers and her interest in relations between women.[1] Such criticism demonstrates, to borrow from Woolf, the tendency for a male critic to be puzzled and surprised by a woman writer's attempt to alter the 'current scale of values' and therefore to see in her writing not 'a difference of view but a view that is weak, or trivial, or sentimental' (Woolf, 1966–7, Vol. II, 146). Woolf herself recognised West's ability and used West as an exemplary modern woman writer in *A Room of One's Own*: 'Z, most humane, most modest of men, taking up some book by Rebecca West and reading a passage in it, exclaimed: "The arrant feminist! She says that men are snobs!".' (Woolf, 1977c, 35) West's writing, Woolf recognises, is a mirror where Z sees himself, not reflected at 'twice [his] natural size' (1977c, 35), but as 'other'. West understood that 'The woman who is acting the principal part in her own ambitious play is unlikely to weep because she is not playing the principal part in some man's no more ambitious play' (West, 1982, 84–5). Her own ambitious books give the 'principal parts' to women.

West provides an important connection between the 'modernist' writers of the period, such as Sinclair and Woolf, and more 'traditional' writers, such as Holtby and Brittain, not just on a personal level but as professional writers with a common commitment to feminism. West, like Holtby and Brittain, contributed to *Time and Tide*, and she knew them on a social level – it was at Brittain's house that West met her future husband, Henry Andrews. Brittain saw West as a symbol of feminism: 'the twentieth-century successor of Mary Wollstonecraft and Olive Schreiner' (TY 588). West also knew Rosamond Lehmann, to whom Woolf wrote that West is 'a very nice woman [...] She is rather fierce, and I expect has some bone she gnaws in secret, perhaps about having a child by Wells. But I couldn't ask her. Perhaps you know her' (Woolf, 1975–80, Vol. VI, 521). As this comment indicates, the identity of 'unmarried mother' acted as a barrier between West and other women.

At first glance West's writing seems primarily concerned with relations between the sexes. Bonnie Kime Scott remarks: 'Where West's women do bond, it is usually in the presence of, or for the sake of a man' (1987, 277). However, what West offers in her first two novels – *The Return of the Soldier* (1918) and *The Judge* (1922) – is precisely an exploration of relations between women which are 'for the sake of a man'. Her analysis of how women's commodification within Western culture isolates women, allowing them to relate to each other only in relation to that 'third term', a man, anticipates Irigaray.

Indeed, West's entire *oeuvre* can be read as an extended meditation on gender, an attempt to think through what Irigaray calls 'one of the major philosophical issues, if not *the* issue of our age' (1993a, 5), the issue of sexual difference. This difference is defined in *Black Lamb and Grey Falcon* (1941) where, noting that the word 'idiocy' comes from a Greek root meaning 'private person', West writes:

> Idiocy is the female defect: intent on their private lives women follow their fate through a darkness deep as that cast by malformed cells in the brain. It is no worse than the male defect, which is lunacy: they are so obsessed by public affairs that they see the world as by moonlight, which shows the outline of every object but not the details indicative of their nature.
>
> (1942, Vol. I, 3)

Asked if these were innate defects, West replied 'Oh, I really can't tell you that. [...] You can't imagine what maleness and femaleness would be if you got back to them in pure laboratory state, can you?' (Warner, 1988, 267). This is not an essentialist view of gender, but a critique of the crippling effects of separating the sexes into public and private spheres.

West's interrogation of binary oppositions, especially her interest in Manichaeanism and her gendering of what she called the 'the will to live and the will to die' (1928, 308) as female and male respectively, can be seen as a strategy for (borrowing Whitford's description of Irigaray) 'passing through essentialism' (Whitford, 1991, 103) in order to get beyond it. Like Irigaray, West is concerned to destabilise gender roles, at the same time as maintaining that we must 'symbolise' the feminine to counteract the overwhelming masculinity of Western thought. Thus she debunks the stereotype of the 'womanly woman'. She describes, for instance, meeting, while selling *Votes for Women* with her sister, 'a dear old lady in rustling black silk and a widow's bonnet' who 'raised her umbrella and brought it down on my sister's head, remarking: "Thank God I am a womanly woman!"' (1982, 162). In the short story 'Parthenhope' (1959) she pushes the stereotype of 'femininity' to an extreme to expose it for the 'idiocy' it is. The husbands of six of the seven sisters are at first attracted by what they see as their wives' 'feminine' silliness. Later, as it becomes clear that the sisters are mad – literally unable to function outside the private sphere – their husbands reject them. It is Parthenhope, who is, as her 'masculine' looks indicate, the only sister who is sane, who gives up her own life in order to protect them in a safe home hidden away from the world.

West often assigned 'masculine' qualities to women and 'feminine' qualities to men. Ironically, it was this which first drew Wells's attention to her. In a review of his novel, *Marriage,* West characterised him as 'the old maid among novelists' and castigated him for his 'sex obsession' (West, 1982, 64). 'Spinsterhood', she had asserted earlier, is 'the limitation of experience to one's own sex, and consequently the regard of the other sex from an idealist point of view' (1982, 48). She destablised the term by applying it to both men and women. Indeed, she cites May Sinclair as an example of a woman who, 'though an unmarried woman, is not [a spinster]' (1982, 48). Wells, then 46, already had a reputation for liaisons with literary women, including Dorothy Richardson (who miscarried his child), Violet Hunt, and Elizabeth von Arnim, which were tolerated by his wife, Jane. To call him an 'old maid' was like offering a red rag to a bull. He sought out West, then 19, and a year later, when his affair with von Arnim had foundered, they became lovers. West's accidental pregnancy followed swiftly. It's not surprising that this affair, which gave West bitter, first-hand experience of the precarious position of the 'other woman', has dominated accounts of her life and work.

Shifting the focus onto West's interest in relations between women, however, reveals her concern with the 'difference of view' between women, between different kinds of femininity, which destabilises the binary opposition male/female. West's own experience as one of three sisters cared for by their mother after their father abandoned them was a formative one, as evidenced by both her posthumously-published autobiographical *Family Memories* (1987), and the *Cousin Rosamund* trilogy of novels (*The Fountain Overflows* (1957), *This Real Night* (1984) and *Cousin Rosamund* (1985)). These texts explore how family life structures identity within the context of a matriarchal family structure. They centre on what West calls 'sibship', a Scottish word, she writes, which 'comes from the same root as "sibling" and signifies the bond between brothers and sisters, and so suggests emotions deeper and more variable than those implied by the term "kinship"' (1992, 54). In the trilogy West uses these bonds to structure a female-centred version of history.

Family Memories imaginatively reconstructs West's own 'maternal genealogy' and is dominated by portraits of women: West's widowed grandmother, Janet Mackenzie, and her sister Isabella; Janet's daughter, Isabella Fairfield (West's mother); and West's sisters, Letitia and Winifred. What is most extraordinary about this text is its uncontrolled hostility to her elder sister Letitia. Letitia is presented as a tyrannical elder sister who regarded West as 'a revolting intruder in her home' (1992, 201). West imaginatively reconstructs this sibling rivalry as the result of the humiliation suffered by Letitia, a stunningly pretty child who initially entranced their father, when Winifred, equally pretty, was born. Letitia's rivalrous attitude, as depicted by West, continued throughout their lives. West records a telephone call from Letitia after West was made a Dame which was allegedly 'a cry of undying hate' (1992, 202). In contrast, Winifred is presented as an idealised protector, a surrogate parent: 'she was glad to hold my hand and walk out with me, which was not the way of my eldest sister, the odious Lettie' (1992, 206).

It is, of course, impossible to know the truth of these relationships. Letitia Fairfield had a distinguished career as a doctor, and it was she who introduced West to feminism and socialism. West's biographer, Carl Rollyson, reports not only the affection with which the rest of the family held Lettie, but that her dying words to West were 'I have always loved you' (1995, 356). The fact that she felt it necessary to tell West this, however, perhaps indicates a desire to lay old tensions to rest. Conversely, during an illness Winifred, looking at West with intense hatred, told her ' "Oh yes, I am Anne Brontë" ' (Rollyson, 1995, 259). Here the Brontë myth is used as shorthand to convey Winifred's resentment of her sisters' success. Victoria Glendinning describes having lunch with West, then in her 80s, and Letitia, and feeling caught in the 'crossfire' between the sisters: 'The elder sister does not defer or refer – why should she, perhaps? – to the personal fame or professional achievement of the younger one, who is falling ever deeper into the well-rehearsed role of recalcitrant little sister' (Glendinning, 1988, 5). What is clear is the enduring nature of the roles sisters occupy in relation to each other.

Both Fishel and McConville argue that sister relationships provide a model for later relationships. West's depictions of 'Lettie' and 'Winnie' seem to act as models for her *fictional* women characters. (Interestingly, she herself noted the importance of Branwell Brontë as the model for the Brontës' 'Byronic' male characters (West, 1954, 260).) The *Cousin Rosamund* trilogy offers versions of three different types of women which recur throughout West's fiction, and which are clearly modelled on her family. Scott identifies two types: the 'perceiving woman' (1987, 283), represented here by Rose Aubery, the narrator, and the 'restorative woman' (280), represented by Rose's mother, Clare Aubrey, who holds the family together. While Rose is closest to West herself, Clare is clearly based on West's mother, Isabella Fairfield. A third type is the destructive, life-denying woman – represented by Cordelia in the trilogy and corresponding to West's version of 'Lettie'. The splitting of the ambivalence in the 'sister knot' is as important in defining these types as the splitting between good/bad mother. This difference between (at least) three types of women is one method West uses to destabilise the binary equation she sets up of male with evil/darkness and female with good/light.

The trilogy explores the bonds of family history as the matrix within which identity is formed. The Aubery family is 'fused' (1987, 162). Rose's relationships with her elder sister, Cordelia, and her twin, Mary, dramatise the tension of the 'sister knot' by splitting it and projecting different emotions onto different sisters. Rose and Mary, connected by their musical ability, are similar to the point of fusion ('rosemary', of course, conotes remembrance). Rose explains: 'I could not exactly love Mary, she was my twin and we were both pianists, we were nearly the same person' (1987, 24). Their relationship encompasses difference within similarity – the knowledge that Mary is the better musician does not create sibling competitiveness. The trilogy is, West said, about 'the difficulty of leading the artist's life' (1984, viii) and its narrative structure is driven not by the romance plot, but by Rose and Mary's quest to fulfil their identity as artists.

Their rejection of Cordelia, the bossy elder sister, is in part to do with the fact that she is a false artist. While her family see themselves as a 'fused' unit, Cordelia's competitiveness is driven by her need to separate from them: 'If I am not to be a famous violinist, how am I ever to get away from you all?' (1984, 382), she cries despairingly. Rose is later able to recognise and pity Cordelia's insecurity but the final volume reiterates the distance between them.

Ultimately, Rose, through her marriage, also has to separate from Mary, a move conveyed in a scene which epitomises the tension between separation/fusion in the 'sister knot'. A family friend points out that each sister is wearing a dress that would look better on the other, a long-standing habit according to their servant Kate: 'it was as if they were so close together that they mistook each other' (1988, 276). The two sisters act as mirrors for each other but the image they get is misleading. Changing the dresses enacts their separation – 'I was separate from my sister indeed' (1988, 278). Yet it is also an image of sameness – despite their physical differences they take the same size dress.

West's use of Rose as an unreliable narrator allows for an interpretation of the rejection of Cordelia as the result of Rose's resentment of their father's preference for Cordelia. Yet it is the link with her father which indicates Cordelia's positioning on the side of darkness/evil. Clare Aubery, cousin Rosamund and her mother, Constance, are 'restorative women' associated with the 'will to life', particularly Rosamund, 'the Rose of the World' (1987, 241). Rose feels that Rosamund is 'more truly our sister than Cordelia' (1988, 53) – 'sibship' here crosses the boundaries of 'kinship'.

In contrast, Piers Aubery and Cousin Jock (husband of Constance) represent the 'will to death', particularly Jock's links with the supernatural. This is not a simple gender divide, however, as male characters also nurture. The girls' adored younger brother, Richard Quin, has the gift of making people happy. Clare Aubery, Rosamund and Richard Quin are all 'by nature parents' (1988, 89). They are 'eternal [. . .] part of what keeps the stars from rushing away from each other' (1988, 92), that is, they represent the nurturing 'will to life'. Gender here crosses the Manichaean evil/good, dark/light binaries, rather than being simply mapped onto them.

Ultimately, the reader has to accept that Cordelia is intrinsically linked to the forces of darkness and evil, which is difficult in view of the identification of her with Letitia Fairfield. Letitia was, understandably, hurt by her portrayal as Cordelia and West denied the connection to her, although she admitted it in *Family Memories* (1992, 201). Glendinning records a note written by West which read: 'I know I have largely invented my sister Lettie' (1988, 54). What is worth noting here is the *power* of the writer as West, like Woolf and Trefusis, recreates her rival in her texts for her own ends.

A consideration of West's depictions of the problematic nature of maternal and sister relations helps to shift the focus away from her relations with men, especially Wells, and enables a rereading of her two earliest novels which recognises the centrality of their explorations of relations between women.

The Return of the Soldier (1918)

One of the earliest women's novels about the war, *The Return of the Soldier* is a study of its enhancement of the male–public/female–private binary. It is a detailed analysis of the role of class in the production of 'femininity' and in the differentiation of women as rival commodities, exploring the process whereby a woman's value as a commodity is measured in relation to 'a third term external [...] to herself' (a man) which 'makes it possible to compare her with another woman' (Irigaray, 1985, 176). It is the interaction between the three different women who love Chris Baldry – his wife, Kitty, his cousin, Jenny, and his youthful love, Margaret – mediated by this third term, the 'shadow' across their discourse, which is the focus of the book.

West centralises women's experience of the war. Her validation of this as an important subject is evident in her review of May Sinclair's *A Journal of Impressions in Belgium* (1915), which was, West thought, 'one of the few books of permanent value produced by the war' (1982, 305). Her work here has clear parallels with Jane Austen who has so often been criticised for writing about women rather than about the Napoleonic War. West's interest is in the suspended animation of the waiting women whose lives are dominated by the absent men: 'like most Englishwomen of my time' the narrator, Jenny, explains 'I was wishing for the return of a soldier' (RS 13). There is also an echo of *Jane Eyre* in the return of Margaret as Chris's first love, monstrous because she is poor and ugly, as well as sexual.

The Return of the Soldier is in dialogue not only with Freudian psychoanalysis, but with the stereotypes of women in two novels by influential male writers which West had reviewed – H. G. Wells's *Marriage* (1912) and Ford Madox Ford's *The Good Soldier* (1915) – and to which West offers a corrective female-centred vision.

Wells's *Marriage* is an Edwardian 'marriage problem' novel (Miller, 1994, 175), which depicts the New Woman but fails to give her a new narrative. It takes a young married couple, Trafford and Marjorie, to the wilderness of Labrador to reinforce essentialist notions of gender. Women are, Marjorie decides, 'half savages, half pets, unemployed things of greed and desire' (Wells, 1912, 508). On their return to London Marjorie will take up exactly the life as Trafford's helpmeet which bored her before, but which will supposedly now be sustained by her new insight. What attracted West's scorn was Wells's treatment of Marjorie's rampant consumerism: 'The horror of [the book]' she wrote, 'is that, confused by her clear eyes and copper hair, he accepts her scoundrelism as the normal condition of women' (1982, 65–6).

Marjorie is an example of what West calls a 'parasitic woman' (1982, 65). The 'parasite woman', a concept first outlined in Olive Schreiner's *Woman and Labour* (1911), is a recurring topic in West's early journalism. Such women are decorative commodities – 'the most expensive luxury the world has indulged in' (West, 1982, 130) – and their function as signifiers of their husband's wealth ensures the 'slavery of the working classes' (114). West refuses to accept Wells's generalisation from Marjorie's worthlessness to the worthlessness of all women and instead calls for women to have 'a chance of being sifted clean through the sieve of work' (1982, 69). Rather than generalising about 'all women', West's work analyses the class differences between the rich woman, 'the most idle human being that has ever secured the privilege of existence', and the poor woman, made 'ugly and clumsy' by hard work (1982, 130), and examines the effects of this division on relations between women. In 'The Quiet Women of the Country' (1913) she recalls seeing some MPs' womenfolk and three Jewish prostitutes watching, with enjoyment, while police brutally assaulted a suffragette. Both sets of women, West asserts, were 'hurtful parasites' (1982, 153), lacking gender loyalty. It is these analyses which inform *The Return of the Soldier*.

Formally and thematically, West's novel has similarities with Ford's *The Good Soldier*, suggesting that her text was a revision of his. West recognised its importance as a modernist text in her review, noting its use of an unreliable narrator slightly distanced from the action (1982, 300), a device she would use, like Ford, to explore unconscious desires. West's Chris Baldry is, like Ford's Edward Ashburnham, 'a large, fair person of the governing class' with a country house and 'a fatal touch of imagination' (West, 1982, 299). Both men are loved by three women but while Ford's women (Leonora, Edward's frigid wife; Nancy, the innocent girl; and Florence, the egotistical American) are stereotypes, West's (Kitty, Jenny and Margaret) are fully realised. Ford's Edward is a 'good soldier' whose ironised heroism lies in his steadfast resistance of his desire for Nancy, and thus his 'resistance' of the feminine. The narrator depicts Leonora and Nancy's joint victimisation of Edward:

> Those two women pursued that poor devil and flayed the skin off him as if they had done it with whips [...] I seem to see him stand, naked to the waist, his forearms shielding his eyes, and flesh hanging from him in rags. [...] It was as if Leonora and Nancy banded themselves together to do execution, for the sake of humanity, upon the body of a man who was at their disposal.
>
> (1972, 215)

In Wells's and Ford's texts women are always 'other'. Moreover, they assume that *all* women are the same, whether childlike pets or demonic savages.

By making her narrator a woman, West shifts the focus, making woman the subject and man the 'other'. By exploring difference between three kinds of femininity she destabilises the binary 'masculine'/'feminine'. The three women in her novel accord with the three 'types' I have outlined. Jenny is a 'perceiving' or 'thinking' woman, while Kitty is the destructive or 'parasite' woman, and Margaret, a 'restorative woman'. The assumption that Jenny articulates West's viewpoint, as well as the identification of Kitty with Wells's wife, Jane, has led to simplistic, biographical readings of this text.[2]   In fact, by using an unreliable narrator, West engages the reader in a process of 'psychoanalysing' Jenny, reading into the text what Jenny never acknowledges – her repressed desire for Chris.

Jenny undergoes a learning process, increasingly forced to reconstruct her own sense of self as she enters into a dialogue with the 'other woman' – Margaret. West's text analyses the anxious discriminations which produce female middle-class identity. Jenny and Kitty's status as upper-middle class depends on their difference from the working class Margaret, specifically delineated through their material appearance. The woman's body itself becomes a class signifier. Both Kitty and Jenny are parasite women, decorative objects within the fine house they have made for Chris on whom they are financially dependent. The nymph in the bowl in the hall is, Jenny believes, a little image of Chris's conception of women. Exquisite we were according to our equipment; unflushed by appetite or passion, even noble passion; our small white heads bent intently on the white flowers of luxury floating on the black waters of life; and he had known none other than us.

(RS 118)

Kitty and Jenny watch the flowers on the surface of 'the black waters of life' rather than plunging in. Their 'whole truth' is in their 'material seeming' (RS 137), but their 'femininity' necessitates a rejection of bodily passion.

Charming and pretty, Kitty is almost pure commodity – 'so like a girl on a magazine cover that one expected to find a large "7d" somewhere attached to her person' (RS 11). Like Sinclair, West deconstructs the 'angel in the house' to expose her as 'the falsest thing on earth' (RS 181). Jenny understands Kitty's *unconscious* conception of her function as a commodity to be bought by men:

Beautiful women of [Kitty's] type lose, in this matter of admiration alone, their otherwise tremendous sense of class distinction; they are obscurely aware that it is their civilising mission to flash the jewel of their beauty before all men, so that they shall desire it and work to get the wealth to buy it, and thus be seduced by a present appetite to a tilling of the earth that serves the future. There is, you know, really room for all of us; we each have our peculiar use.

(RS 154)

Placed in the context of West's journalism, I think that we have to read this as bitter irony on Jenny's part.

It is precisely Margaret's bodily drabness, 'repulsively furred with neglect and poverty' (RS 25), as a signifier of her lower-class status which initially makes Jenny and Kitty certain that Chris could never have loved her. If Kitty and Jenny with their tasteful clothes, soft skin and manicured nails represent 'femininity', then Margaret, with her cheap raincoat, her deplorable umbrella and seamed, red hands, is barely a 'woman' at all – 'not so much a person as an implication of dreary poverty' (RS 141). The vocabulary of physical disgust Jenny uses to describe her conveys deep-seated class-hatred: 'I [...] hated her as the rich hate the poor, as insect things that will struggle out of the crannies that are their decent home, and introduce ugliness to the light of day' (RS 32).

To even admit that Margaret might be a rival for Chris's love threatens Kitty and Jenny's sense of superior identity because it makes it clear that their class status is contingent on the male. Chris is the third term external to the woman which 'makes it possible to compare her with another woman' (Irigaray, 1985, 176). Like the MPs' womenfolk, Kitty and Jenny's status depends on maintaining their difference from the 'unfeminine' woman, from the working-class woman and the suffragette whose work or political activism take them into the masculine public world. To admit their similarity, their shared oppressed status, with the suffragette or the working-class woman, would be to relinquish the power and protection they gain from their class status as 'ladies'. Yet, Kitty and Jenny are themselves connected only tenuously by their love of Chris. To Kitty, Jenny, a 'surplus' woman, is always a potential rival, as Jenny realises: 'A sharp movement of Kitty's body confirmed my deep, old suspicion that she hated me' (RS 167).

Yet there is more than one economy, or system of commodification, here and Chris is himself commodified by the women – to the point of death. His primary function is to provide for them and his other female relatives. His lack of freedom is compensated for by the gracious life they arrange for him. But although the house is designed as a setting for him, and his labour maintains it, his bodily presence is not necessary. Though Jenny wishes for his return, Kitty is barely disturbed because they have not heard from him for a fortnight. Chris is as trapped within the social structures as the two women who live like parasites off him. Kitty's possessive '*our* Chris' – 'If he could send that telegram he isn't *ours* any longer' (RS 39, my emphasis) – clearly indicates ownership. Baldry Court is not a symbol of his happiness but a 'prison' (RS 55). The 'flowers of luxury' float on 'the black waters of life', as the conscious social self floats on the surface of the unconscious.

The Return of the Soldier was one of the earliest novels about shell-shock (Macaulay's *Non-Combatants and Others* preceded it) and, like Sinclair, West uses her fiction to re-read psychoanalysis. Dr Gilbert Anderson, the Freudian doctor, may initially appear no more than a fashionable plot device – a kind of modernist *deus ex machina* – but it is in her treatment of Chris's war-induced amnesia or 'hysterical fugue' that West is most radical, using it to destabilise concepts of sanity, normality and gender.

Elaine Showalter argues in *The Female Malady* that West goes well beyond even the pioneering doctor W.H.R. Rivers in 'grasping the connections between male hysteria and a whole range of male social obligations' (1987, 191). Shell-shock undermined the categories of sexual difference which constructed hysteria as a 'female malady'. Conscription and trench warfare, as Showalter has shown, imposed on men a power-lessness and passivity which paralleled that of the Victorian woman hysteric and produced similar symptoms. The story which haunts Jenny of the soldiers unable to help each other because they lack arms and legs (RS 14) takes this passivity to an extreme, a kind of embryo state. Shell-shock 'feminised' men in the sense that it made them victims of irrational emotion, undermining the ideals of the 'masculine' and 'heroic' as emotionally controlled – the 'stiff upper lip' of the 'good soldier'.

Dr Anderson himself acknowledges the truth of Margaret's comment that 'You can't cure [Chris]. All you can do is make him ordinary' (RS 168). Within the parameters of the novel Chris's amnesia is 'saner than sanity' (RS 133). It is the war itself which is insane, a manifestation of male 'lunacy' – the 'will to death'. The dreadful irony of the final sen-tence of the book – Kitty's 'He's cured' (RS 188) – is that Chris's return to 'sanity' ensures his return to the insanity of the war and 'to that flooded trench in Flanders under that sky more full of flying death than clouds, to that No Man's Land where bullets fall like rain on the rotting faces of the dead....' (RS 187) The final ellipsis suggests the nothingness to which Chris himself will come.

Both Jenny and Margaret acquiesce in the need to bring back Chris's memory because without it 'He would not be quite a man' (RS 183). In order to be a 'man' – husband, landowner, 'good soldier' – the wishes of Chris's 'essential self' have had to be suppressed by his 'superficial self' (RS 164). His loss of memory is the resurfacing of his repressed 'feminine' side, including the sexuality he has only ever been able to express in his youthful love for Margaret.

The 'will to life' is represented by the maternal sensuality of Margaret, a reversal of Ford's association of female sexuality with destruction. But this is not a simple male/female binary. The 'will to death' represented by the war is also embodied in Kitty. Significantly, as West's 1916 account of a visit to a munitions factory notes, 'kitty' was the name given to the mixture of beeswax, resin and tallow poured on top of the lyddite in the making of a shell (1982, 388).

West's use of the shabby lower-class woman to represent a different, spiritual kind of femininity (it is Margaret's 'bleak habit [...] to cham-pion the soul against the body' (RS 135)) challenges class-based stereo-types of femininity. When Jenny finds Margaret sitting protectively next to the sleeping Chris in the woods, she sees this as the loveliest attitude in the world. It means that the woman has gathered the soul of the man into her soul and is keeping it warm in love and peace so that his body can rest quiet for a little time. That is a great thing for a woman to do.

(RS 143–4)

Like Cousin Rosamund, Margaret stands for what art is about – 'life' – and therefore needs no surface decoration. However, West comes perilously close to making Margaret another stereotype of femininity, a nurturing mother figure divorced from intellect and the public sphere. Ultimately, *The Return of the Soldier* offers Chris a choice between two kinds of 'death' which correspond to the division between male 'lunacy' and female 'idiocy'. Either a return to the insanity of No Man's Land, or a regression to infancy, to a pre-oedipal state – a failure to separate from the mother.

The hope of the book lies in Jenny, the 'thinking' woman, who moves from the status of decorative commodity which aligns her with Kitty to an alliance with Margaret. There are two sets of mediation or exchange going on in the text. Margaret is an 'intercessory' (RS 158), used by Jenny as a conduit to Chris: 'The only occasion when I could safely let the sense of him saturate me as it used to was when I met Margaret in the hall as she came or went' (RS 131). But in narrative terms Chris is the catalyst which brings Margaret and Jenny together: 'We kissed, not as women, but as lovers do; I think we each embraced that part of Chris the other had absorbed by her love' (RS 184). Sharon Ouditt suggests that this gesture 'has implications for a female solidarity which offers hope for the deconstruction of the male order' (1994, 116). Their shared love for Chris becomes a mediating force which offers the possibility of a female solidarity. But this mediation comes at the almost certain expense of Chris's death in the trenches.

The novel's ending is ambiguous. It's as if at this point (perhaps inevitably in 1918) West could see no clear answer to the irreconcilability of 'masculine' and 'feminine', the unending seesaw between the 'will to death' and the 'will to life'. The solution advocated in her pre-war review of *Marriage* – that women should be allowed the 'chance of being sifted clean through the sieve of work' (1982, 69) – is not explicit in the novel. But West's journalism tells another story of women's war experience. The courage and diligence of the working-class women workers in munitions factories is detailed in three 1916 pieces entitled 'Hands That War' (West, 1982, 380–90). These stress the appallingly volatile nature of the explosives and the fact that the women face more danger daily than any soldier on home defence. These women are

among the comfortingly significant features to emerge from the purposeless welter of war. They are assets to England, they introduce reason and sympathy into the snarling colloquy of labour and capital; and they mark that industry has at last recognised that women have brains as well as hands.

(1982, 386)

In contrast to Kitty and Jenny, here rivalry is not over men but channelled into 'an orgy of competitive industry' (1982, 382) which produces a huge increase in output. This not only enforces West's argument that the middle-class woman can only escape her parasite status through work, but also suggests that the entry of women into the workplace (on terms which recognise their 'brains as well as hands') offers the possibility of reforming capitalism itself.

The Judge (1922)

One reason for the critical neglect of *The Judge*, a powerful and perceptive novel, may be the centrality it gives not just to homosocial relations between women but to a specific relationship, the rivalry of mother and daughter-in-law, which is more usually treated as a joke than as a subject for canonical literature. With the exception of the Biblical Ruth and Naomi, there are few serious treatments of this subject.[3] West's flame-haired suffragette heroine, Ellen Melville, dislikes 'becoming so nearly the subject of a comic song as a woman who hates her mother-in-law' (*J* 201), but she and her potential mother-in-law, Marion Yaverland, thrown together by their love for Marion's illegitimate son, Richard, almost inevitably become the rivals of the traditional mother-in-law joke.

West uses this triangle to 'think the difference' between the sexes and between women using a series of binary parallels. This theme is figured in Ellen's final thoughts as she waits to conceive Richard's child before Richard is hanged for the murder of his half-brother, Roger:

though life at its beginning was lovely as a corn of wheat, it was ground down to flour that must make bitter bread between two human tendencies: the insane sexual caprice of men, the not less mad excessive steadfastness of women. Roger had died, Richard was

about to die, because of the grinding together of these male and
female faults – Harry and Marion ... Poppy and her sailor ... her own
father and mother. . . .

(J 429)

Through Ellen's probable re-enactment of Marion's unmarried motherhood, despite their differences (of age, class, nationality and politics),
West dramatises the fact that women 'all undergo [. . .] the same oppression, the same exploitation of their body, the same denial of their desire'
(Irigaray, 1985, 164). West's text both explores and enacts through its
structure a dialogue between the two women as equal subjects.

Early critical responses to the novel demonstrate the failure to recognise West's 'difference of view'. H.G. Wells disliked the novel. It was, he
reported, initially to be about a judge who collapses in a brothel with
a woman whose husband he sentenced for murder years before. But West
set the beginning of the book before husband and wife had met and
'never got to the Judge':

> At the end of an immense mass of unequal but often gorgeous writ-
> ing, she had reached no further than the murder, and there she
> wound up the book, still keeping the title of *The Judge*, because that
> had been announced by her publisher for two years.

(Wells, 1984, 101)

The impression (perpetuated by Glendinning (1988), who relies on
Wells's account) is of a disaster of a book, arbitrary in form, character,
theme and title.

Wells's judgement is partly due to the difference between the modernist and the Edwardian, but it is also a failure to recognise that the book is
consciously female-centred, that it is the *mother* who is the 'judge'. *The
Judge* fills in the lacunae in Wells's *Ann Veronica* (1909) by detailing the
social rejection faced by unmarried mothers: as a pregnant, unmarried
girl Marion is stoned down Roothing High Street. It must have confronted Wells not only with the pain of West's unmarried motherhood,
but that of Amber Reeves (the original of Ann Veronica), who married
after finding herself pregnant by Wells.

The Judge has been damned for its style, its use of Freud and its
structure.[4] To take the issue of style first, West's long, complex, fluid
sentences reflect her belief, expounded in *The Strange Necessity*, that the
sentence (not the word as James Joyce argued) was the foundation of
language and unconscious thought (West, 1928, 32–6). Her own

sentences build up, clause by clause, following the thought process as it connects idea to idea, in order to convey the consciousness of a character. Stylistically, as Scott has noted, West is often remarkably close to Woolf (1987, 276). The narrative of *The Judge* is always focalised through the consciousness of one of the characters – most extensively through Ellen and Marion.

With regard to Freud, *The Judge* is profoundly revisionist in its use of the Oedipal triangle. One of the first writers to engage with Freud, West later called him 'a great enemy of women' (quoted in Spender, 1983a, 643). Compared to Lawrence's case-history of male Oedipal desire in *Sons and Lovers* (1913), *The Judge* can be seen as giving a voice to the mother – to Jocasta herself. As Christiane Olivier (1989) has shown, the mother's desire for her son and its effect on him is a subject which has been underexplored. West broke radical new ground here. Marion's name, linking her to Christ's mother, also pregnant outside wedlock, signals her mythic mother status.

The Judge blatantly invites a Freudian reading, heavily foregrounding the incestuous relationship between Richard (the modern Oedipus) and Marion. Richard's murder of his half-brother, Roger, could be read as the killing of the father by proxy – Roger represents both Harry, Marion's lover who abandoned her, and Peacey, the man she was forced to marry, whose rape of her produces Roger. Richard's anticipated hanging is the ultimate castration for his contravening of the Law of the Father.

This traditionally Freudian reading, however, falsifies the novel. Firstly, it makes the man its subject, whereas West's revision of the Oedipal paradigm explores the desire between mother and son from the *mother's* point of view. Using Richard as a substitute for her faithless lover, Marion projects all her love onto him, despite knowing that it is 'too heavy a cloak for one child' (J 286). Feeling sensual pleasure in suckling him, she experiences them as 'fused' and cannot endure the thought of being 'quite separate from him' (J 285). To maintain that unity she attempts to make herself 'the most alluring mother that ever lived' (J 286). Her flirtatious relationship with Richard, which prevents him developing a mature relationship with Ellen, is a way of maintaining that fusion into adulthood. The lack of separation between Marion and Richard contradicts Chodorow's view that women experience themselves as less separate from their daughters than their sons. In contrast, Ellen and her mother, though they have a close, loving relationship, are distinct and separate. West makes the Oedipal story (which Freud posited as universal) specific, the result of Richard's illegitimate birth, and the social rejection which focuses all his mother's attention on him and gives him reason to hate his father.

Secondly, the Freudian reading ignores the first half of the novel, which shows Ellen as a suffragette in Edinburgh. West's 'sisterhood' with the Brontës and the Brontëan nature of West's novel in general are noted by Jane Marcus (J Introduction). *The Judge* has specific structural parallels with *Wuthering Heights* which offer a way of reading it in terms of a female genealogy. Both novels fall into two halves with a 'daughter' reliving/ rewriting her mother's story – Ellen replicates not only Marion's fate but also her own mother's. Hence the novel's epigraph: 'Every mother is a judge who sentences the children for the sins of the father.' In both novels a complex, polyphonic narrative is structured by parallel sets of binary oppositions. In *The Judge* these include the opposite sex couples – Harry/Marion, Mrs Melville/Mr Meville, Ellen/Richard, Poppy/Roger, as well as same-sex parallels – Ellen/Marion, Mrs Melville/Marion, Richard/ Roger, Harry/Mr Melville, Harry/Richard. Both novels use two contrasted locations – Wuthering Heights and Thrushcross Grange, Scotland and Essex. Like Brontë, West uses place as a projection of psychology. Richard sees the Pentland Hills as embodying Ellen's mind: 'Surely this country was not real, but an imagination of Ellen's mind' (J 106). Similarly, Ellen sees the wide, flat Essex landscape as 'curiously like Marion' (J 232).

There are other echoes. The opening of *The Judge* with Ellen gazing out of the window at a rainy Edinburgh echoes Cathy imprisoned in the Heights on a rainy Sunday, while Ellen's name links her to Nelly (Ellen) Dean. Richard is Heathcliff-like in his illegitimate origins and his fortune made in foreign lands, although his mother-obsession undercuts his status as Byronic romantic hero. His work with cordite links him to the armament business and, like Kitty, to the 'will to death' embodied in the coming war.

Reading *The Judge* against *Wuthering Heights* like this allows us to see its structure as carefully constructed and tragic in the Greek sense. West read *Wuthering Heights* as a 'new myth' in which

> the goddess who is the most potent embodiment of good [...] consorts with the embodiments of evil, loving it, for love does not disdain the evil. But evil cannot put an end to good, which has its own title to existence that cannot be invalidated. Miraculously, from the slain goddess there springs a new goddess, who is invulnerable, who cannot be slain but who slays evil without a weapon and releases all its victims from their chains.

(West, 1954, 266)

This female-centred myth underlies *The Judge* and offers a hope for the future which is not immediately obvious in the ending of West's novel. West gives her story two equal but different female subjects. This readjustment of the Oedipal triangle allows her to explore female subjectivity and rivalry from two sides of the triangle – 'mother' and 'daughter'. Dedicated to West's own mother, who died in 1921, the novel can be read as an attempt to re-establish a broken female genealogy. The separation of Marion and Ellen's stories into the two Books of the novel enacts the separation of mother and daughter within patriarchal society. Read in traditional Freudian terms as the rivalry between 'mother' and 'daughter' over the 'father', Marion's death could be seen as the 'killing' of the mother so that the daughter can attain adult female sexuality. If, as Irigaray suggests, there is only one place for women in this paradigm – the 'place of the mother' – Ellen can only occupy that place once Marion has been 'killed'. The two women, in Freudian theory, cannot co-exist.

But West's use of binary oppositions suggests a more complex reading, through a dramatisation of the ambivalence in the mother–child relationship. Ellen's comparisons of Mrs Melville and Marion suggest that they are embodiments of the 'good' and 'bad' mother. Mrs Melville is, Ellen thinks, 'how a mother ought to be, little, sweet, and moderate' (J 393). Their primary connection is conveyed through an unspoken dialogue as Mrs Melville is dying:

> The mother's flesh, touching the daughter's, remembered a faint pulse felt long ago and marvelled at this splendid sequel, and lost fear. [. . .] The daughter's flesh, touching the mother's, remembered life in the womb, that loving organ that by night and day does not cease to embrace its beloved, and was the stronger for tasting again that first best draught of love that the spirit has not yet excelled.
>
> (J 185)

The ideal mother nurtures but does not engulf her daughter.

In contrast, Marion is the powerful phallic mother, who fails to separate from her son and enters into direct sexual competition with her daughter-in-law. Feeling an 'insane regret that being [Richard's] mother she could not also be his wife' (J 256), she recognises the possibility that she might find herself hating Ellen. At the same time, she understands Ellen better than Richard, grieving when Richard proposes to give Ellen jewels rather than a dictionary of economic terms. Marion's own analysis of the situation seems textbook Freud: '[Richard] cannot love Ellen because he loves me too much! He has nothing left to love her with!'

(J 346). The scenes where Richard comforts his mother by embracing and kissing her in bed, however, convey not a universal incestuous desire but the specific inappropriateness of her encouraging him to protect her in his father's place. The Oedipal tragedy is neither as universal nor as inevitable as Freud suggests. Rather, Richard's hanging will be the result of the specificity of Marion's historical position within a patriarchal society.

Marion's suicide is a self-sacrificing attempt to cede Richard to Ellen, as her final scribblings reveal: 'This is the end. I must die. Give him to Ellen' (J 423). In contrast to *Sons and Lovers*, where the son kills the mother in order to live, here it is the mother who commits suicide for the 'daughter's' sake. The failure of this transaction suggests that women cannot, in this society, carry out such exchanges. The book illustrates Irigaray's thesis that if women are not allowed other forms of exchange 'the commodities women *are forced to exchange would be their children* [. . .] in exchange for a market status *for themselves*' (1993b, 84, original emphasis). Marion has attempted to use Richard in this way, living vicariously through his triumphs. Similarly, Ellen's mother, abandoned by her husband, has treated Ellen as the 'man of the house' (J 44). This produces a more complex reading of the epigraph – the mothers 'sentence' their children for the 'sins of the fathers' because they have no other form of power within the male economy.

My interpretation of this text so far has been along the psychoanalytic lines which the text invites, but a dialogic reading offers a more complex understanding. The achievement of West's novel is that she presents us with *two* fully-realised female consciousnesses – the two Books of the texts offer a dialogue between the two voices, each colouring the other. While the mother-in-law joke constructs the two women as natural rivals, West's text forces the reader to engage with both women and to hold their (equal) claims to our sympathy in some kind of equilibrium. They are not rivals for the place of heroine in the novel but equal subjects.

The motif of conversation between women is important here but the two women themselves do not reach a mutual understanding within the text because their discourse is always fractured by Richard's shadow. During their first meeting, from which he is strangely absent, Ellen pinpoints their failure to engage as equal subjects when she comments: 'We're awful reactionary, letting our whole lives revolve around a man' (J 238). Their common love for Richard does not bring intimacy, partly because Marion's suffering has made her evasive. In an internal monologue Marion reviews their similarities and differences:

I can see that you, my dear, are going to break the spell that, so much
against my will, I've thrown over my son.[. . .] You have all the qualities that he loves in me, but they are put together in such a different
mode from mine that *there cannot possibly be any question of competition
between us.*

(J 215, my emphasis)

But the important point is that Marion never speaks this to Ellen, and
thus tacitly refuses to enter into dialogue with her.

Ellen sees Marion as an 'economic parasite' (J 209) but her naive
endorsement of suffragette theory is problematised by the reality of
Marion's predicament. She is not, as Richard bitterly remarks, '*the*
unmarried mother [but] my mother, who was not married to my father'
(J 177, original emphasis). Although gentle fun is poked at Ellen's enthu-
siasm, the text endorses her values, while retaining sympathy for Marion. The two women mirror each other. In one scene Marion watches
Ellen's mirrored face while she is brushing Ellen's hair, and connects
Ellen's vulnerability while selling *Votes for Women* in the streets, to the
public stoning she herself underwent. In their final encounter, Ellen
looking through a glass door into the night, suddenly finds herself
looking into Marion's eyes. It is this mirror image which brings her
final understanding of Marion's suicide.

The Judge is dialogic in that it offers two narrative voices, two different
view points, which are reconciled not in the plot but in the mind of the
reader. This is, I think, why West presents us with Ellen's story first, out
of chronological sequence. Our sympathies are thus engaged by her
before we shift to Marion's story, which might otherwise overshadow
Ellen's. Scott notes that her students, by then committed to Ellen Melville, regularly 'resist' this striking narrative shift (Scott, 1995b, 134). The
duality which structures the novel becomes in Irigaray's terms an
attempt to think the difference between women through dialogue.
Only when the structure of the novel is taken into consideration is this
fully apparent.

West offers the possibility that through this exploration of the difference between women we can move beyond male–female dualities, the
grinding together of male and female faults which make such 'bitter
bread' (J 429). The hope of the text lies in the possibility that Ellen is
the 'new goddess' who is on 'the side of victory' (J 430). Situating the
novel historically, rather than as a purely psychological or mythical
drama, is illuminating here. Written in 1922, its setting is both pre-war
and pre-vote. The post-1922 reader knows that the vote Ellen craves will

be won in 1918 and this re-enforces the possibility that Ellen as the 'new goddess', a politicised suffragette, can rewrite the impending tragedy. This political reading avoids positing either Marion or Ellen as representing an essential feminine psychology but it also explicitly locates hope for the future, however tenuous, in women.

Critics seem to agree that one of the reasons that West has not been accorded a secure status as writer is that her *oeuvre* spans such a variety of genres – fiction, criticism, journalism, travelogue, trial reportage, biography – that, as she herself put it, her work 'could not fuse to make a picture of a writer' (West, 1978, xviii). Even her novels are widely different from each other. However, the thread which connects this extraordinary body of work, as with Sinclair, is her concern with gender and with how sexual difference not only affects relations between men and women but casts a shadow between women.

5
A 'Shared Working Existence' : Vera Brittain and Winifred Holtby

The friendship between Winifred Holtby and Vera Brittain offers an example, not so much of a rare relationship between women, but of one which has been unusually fully documented and discussed. Part of a new generation of professional, university-educated writers, their six-teen-year long friendship was based on the fact that each encouraged and enabled the other's work. Meeting at Somerville College, Oxford, they shared a flat while they established themselves as writers in London, and then, after Brittain's marriage to George Gordon Catlin, lived as a *ménage a trois* until Holtby's death.

This unconventional set-up enabled both writers to produce a body of work which is, as Jean Kennard says in *Vera Brittain and Winifred Holtby: A Working Partnership*, 'an ongoing dialogue' (1989, 17), where each rewrites the other's texts in their own. Kennard's study takes Chodorow's theorisation of mother–daughter relationships and Abel's definition of friendship as a 'vehicle of self-definition' as starting points in order to argue that 'The friend as a second self provides a way of separating from the mother without rejecting the female self-image she represented, for the friend is after all a similar image' (1989, 15). The phrase 'second self' echoes Brittain's assurances to Holtby that: 'Gordon will never be *quite* the same; never quite my second self in exactly the same and dependable way' (quoted in Kennard, 1989, xiv, original emphasis). The aim of their dialogue, Kennard argues, is 'to resolve differences because what is valued is thinking alike; strength is drawn from the image of sameness. They both empower and rewrite each other in an attempt to reach consensus' (1989, 17). That consensus, Kennard suggests, was reached through the reconciliation with the 'mother' in Holtby's final novel, *South Riding* (1936), and Brittain's *Honourable Estate* (1936).

I want to offer a rather different interpretation of the relationship by reading their intertextual dialogue as a *competitive* dialogic in the Bakhtinian sense. While this retains the notion of reciprocity, it allows for the constantly shifting power dynamics between the two women, as well as attempts to silence the other. Their textual struggle over the meaning of their friendship, and female friendship generally, is clearest in Brittain's biography of Holtby, *Testament of Friendship* (1940). Published after Holtby's death, it is the text in which Brittain takes final control of the representation of the relationship.

Brittain's phrase 'second self' needs closer interrogation. 'Second', as de Beauvoir's *The Second Sex* indicates, implies a *secondary* placing – something which is lesser, additional or inferior in importance or rank to the first. A copy rather than an original. That rivalry can also be a 'vehicle of self-definition' is reflected in Brittain's concern to *establish*, rather than resolve, difference between herself and Holtby by presenting Holtby as 'second' in the sense of lesser/inferior. This is especially obvious in the contrast between Brittain's status as a married woman and Holtby's as a spinster.

Rather than reading their relationship as a linear development towards a point of consensus I read it as an ongoing process of interaction in which the self is continually reconstructed through a dialogue with the other. Brittain and Holtby make use of a range of different discourses and positions – not only mother and daughter, or sisters, but also opposite-sex models, especially brother and sister. This indicates in part the lack of a language within which to think about female friendship. But it also suggests the lack of a language within which to think about rivalry between women – unless that rivalry is over a man. The romance plot which has so dominated women's fiction also shapes textual representations of women's rivalry. Reading Brittain's fiction against her non-fiction texts reveals how, in the process of transmuting fact into fiction, academic and professional rivalry between the two women is transformed, through the use of the triangle plot, into romantic rivalry. The romance plot shapes not only Brittain's fiction but her autobiography and even her biography of Holtby. Holtby's fiction, in contrast, is concerned to overturn the triangle plot by erasing the man and re-establishing connections between women.

As the relationship between Brittain and Holtby shows, rivalry and friendship are not mutually exclusive, they can co-exist in the same relationship, and within the same linguistic exchange. Moreover, their professional rivalry had a beneficial effect, since it spurred each on to greater achievement. It can, ironically, be seen as a part of their enabling of each other's work. Brittain's erasure of this rivalry in *Testament of Friendship* indicates how unacceptable it is in our society. A further erasure has taken place in feminist commentary on the relationship, which has become something of a icon of ideal female friendship.[1] The political need to valorise female friendships and to dispute what Brittain called the 'fiction of women's jealous inability to love and respect one another' (TF 118) has led to an idealisation, indeed, a sentimentalisation, of the friendship which obscures its actual complexity. Brittain was, as the much-quoted prologue to *Testament of Friendship* indicates, aware of the political importance of friendships between women, and herself presented the friendship as exemplary:

> From the days of Homer the friendships of men have enjoyed glory and acclamation, but the friendships of women, in spite of Ruth and Naomi, have usually been not merely unsung but mocked, belittled and falsely interpreted. I hope that Winifred's story may do something to destroy these tarnished interpretations, and show its readers that loyalty and affection between women is a noble relationship which, far from impoverishing, actually enhances the love of a girl for her lover, of a wife for her husband, of a mother for her children.
>
> (TF 2)

In *Testament of Friendship* and in her editing of the published correspondence (Brittain and Handley-Taylor, 1960), Brittain, as Marion Shaw has shown, smoothes away the stresses of the relationship and obscures the fact that it was 'intense, hungry and anxious in ways that Brittain did not want, or could not bring herself, to acknowledge' (Shaw, n.d., 38).

One of the stresses in the relationship is what Brittain refers to as the possibility of it being 'falsely interpreted' – that is, as a lesbian relationship. To avoid this she carefully positions female friendship within the context of heterosexuality. It '*enhances*' heterosexual love – it is not an alternative. Even the example she gives, that of Ruth and Naomi, is one which is socially sanctioned because, as in West's *The Judge*, it is mediated by the man to whom they are mother and wife. Brittain returns to the theme later:

> Other sceptics are roused by any record of affection between women to suspicions habitual among the over-sophisticated.
> 'Too, *too* Chelsea!' Winifred would comment amiably in after years

when some zealous friend related the newest legend current about us in the neighbourhood.

(TF 118, original emphasis)

This defends female friendship while distancing it from anything sexual. A note Brittain pencilled when she was dying again makes a careful distinction between heterosexual and homosocial love: 'I loved Winifred but I was not in love with her' (Berry and Bishop, 1985, 13).

Brittain's defensiveness is understandable in the context of the inter-war years when, as I have argued, the continuum between homosocial and homosexual was being radically disrupted, especially following the 1928 trial of *The Well of Loneliness*. Brittain had reviewed *The Well of Loneliness* on its first appearance, 'critically, but on the whole favourably' (Brittain, 1968, 10), and was a potential witness at the trial. Her book *Radclyffe Hall: A Case of Obscenity?* (1968) is a clear summary of the issues, but it has the tone of a tolerant outsider, sympathetic towards 'the biologically abnormal woman' (1968, 48), but not intimately engaged. It is precisely Brittain's careful distinction between 'friendship' and what is represented by a silence in *Testament of Friendship* (the word 'lesbian' is noticeably not said), which offers the most telling evidence of this disruption of the continuum.

Despite Brittain's denials (or because of them), the relationship has been the subject of speculation ever since. It has become a contested site, the subject of a kind of rivalry between those who claim it as an ideal friendship between two heterosexual women, and those who see it as a repressed or camouflaged lesbian relationship.[2] The definition of 'lesbian' is itself, of course, contested. Adrienne Rich's concept of the 'lesbian continuum' (1980) extends 'lesbianism' to include relationships which depend on primary emotional intensity rather than physical contact. In this sense Kennard concludes that: 'It is impossible to deny that the partnership between Holtby and Brittain was one of primary intensity, *whether or not one is willing to call it lesbian*' (1989, 8, my emphasis). The point, surely, is that Brittain herself was strongly antagonistic to the word 'lesbian'.

As Brittain's struggle to fix the meaning of the relationship indicates the anxieties of the historical period she was writing in, so the contemporary debate tells us as much about our own needs and anxieties as it does about Brittain's or Holtby's. Brittain's insistence on its impeccable heterosexuality indicates the strength of taboos against lesbianism which are still in force today. The identification of their relationship as 'lesbian' by critics such as Lillian Faderman indicates the political need for such relationships to be made visible as a part of a suppressed women's history. Ultimately, the insistence on either label can obscure the emotional complexity of their relationship and in both cases lead to an elision of its rivalry.

Both writers made extensive use of their own experience in their writing. Indeed, Brittain's reputation rests on her autobiographical best-seller *Testament of Youth* (1933). What I am interested in here is not a straight biographical reading of their fiction but the disjunctions between the texts, especially those which indicate the strains when biographical material is transmuted into fiction.

The two women who met in 1919 at Somerville where they shared a history tutorial did not, Brittain admits, 'to begin with, like each other at all' (TF 92). Both were returning to Oxford after war service and both wanted to be writers but in other ways they were very different. While Brittain, the daughter of a Staffordshire paper-manufacturer, had had to struggle to persuade her parents to let her go to university, Holtby, four years younger and the daughter of a farming family in Yorkshire, wrote that: 'I am one of the very few women I know who went to Oxford because my mother wished it' (Berry and Bishop, 1985, 273). Alice Holtby was a strong-willed matriarch who became the first woman alderman in the East Riding, while Edith Brittain was a conventional woman who admitted to Vera that she 'would much rather have an ordinary daughter – living and sleeping and dying and leaving no impress behind!' (Brittain, 1981, 51).

Brittain's war experience had been one of devastating personal losses – the deaths of her fiancé, Roland Leighton, her brother, Edward, and their two close friends, Victor and Geoffrey. When she returned to Oxford she was close to a nervous breakdown. In contrast, Holtby's time as a WAAC in France was a time of gain, including the development of a close friendship with Jean McWilliam. While Brittain saw herself as irretrievably damaged by her war experience, Holtby saw herself as one who owed a 'debt to life' (TF 113).

After graduating they shared a flat in London where they combined teaching, lecturing for the League of Nations Union, and journalism for a range of publications, including *Time and Tide* (of which Holtby became a director). Holtby was the first to publish her novel, *Anderby Wold* (1923), which was followed by Brittain's *The Dark Tide* (1923). This 'shared working existence' (TF 101) was disrupted when Brittain married and went to America with her husband, but re-established when she returned to England after a year, having failed to establish a career over there. Brittain and Catlin embarked on what she called a 'semi-detached marriage', where Brittain lived in London with Holtby, and later her children, John and Shirley, and Catlin spent half of each year with them and half in America. This continued until Holtby died of Bright's disease in 1935 at the tragically early age of 37.

In the version of Holtby's life presented by Brittain in *Testament of Friendship*, Holtby's spinsterhood was not chosen but was the result of the failure of her relationship with Harry Pearson, the son of a local bank manager in Yorkshire. Pearson, according to Brittain, was 'deeply, irretrievably wounded' (TF 54) when the eighteen-year-old Holtby tactlessly rejected his proffered love poems. After the war Pearson failed to settle to a job and flitted in and out of Holtby's life, often accepting her help, but only proposing marriage when she was dying.

There is no doubt that Brittain and Holtby enabled each other as writers. Holtby attributed her feminism to Brittain, writing in the copy of *Women* she gave to Brittain: 'For Vera, who taught me to be a feminist' (TF 133). Some of her last words to Brittain were: 'remember that I love you dearly... I'm intensely grateful to you – you're the person who's made me' (Brittain, 1986, 210). Brittain also saw their friendship as crucial to her own work and *Testament of Friendship* was her tribute to 'the best friend whom life has given me' (TF 4). In a 1926 letter to Holtby she wrote: 'You are more necessary to me than [Catlin] is, because you further my work' (quoted in Kennard, 1989, 8). But this enabling was the product of an ongoing process of negotiation over the roles and boundaries in the relationship. Brittain, four years older than Holtby, initially saw herself as the leader and when Holtby's career as a writer took off first their relationship had to be extensively re-negotiated.

Brittain's competitiveness can be traced back to her relationship with her younger brother, Edward. While Fishel and McConville argue that sister relationships are often repeated or mirrored in other relationships, here it is a brother–sister relationship which is mirrored in a later female friendship. The intersection of the different economies of birth order and gender is very clear in Brittain's relationship with Edward. Although it is suppressed in *Testament of Youth* where Edward is idealised, Brittain's diary records sibling rivalry co-existing with her obvious love for her brother. She had a strong sense of her intellectual superiority to Edward and records a revealing conversation with her father:

> I asked if it were not equally important that I should have a career. He answered very decidedly 'No, Edward was the one who must be given an occupation and the means to provide for himself.' The secondary sex again! It made me very angry that I, the more intellectual of the

two, should be regarded in this light because I happen not to be a man. But I will show them.

(Brittain, 1981, 287)

This frustration at being the 'secondary sex' was at the root of Brittain's feminism and fired her ambition.

The sibling model offers one alternative to the mother–daughter model. What West called 'sibship' can encompass both rivalry *and* supportiveness. Brittain not only treated Holtby as a younger sibling in terms of rivalry, but also actively identified her with Edward's supportive role, writing that Holtby represented in her life 'the same element of tender, undistressing permanence that Edward represented' (TY 658). Sadly, neither offered permanence. Holtby, according to Brittain, 'identified herself so closely in imagination with Edward and Roland that they almost seemed to be her dead as well as my own' (TY 521). She records Holtby listening to a concerto which Edward had often performed when 'the words "I am his deputy" came into her head' (TF 312). Holtby included these words in a poem addressed to Edward, which articulates a sense of the non-combatant's inadequacy in terms of her inability to 'hear as well as other men', as well as in a sense of her trespassing on 'loveliness [which] was never planned for me' (TF 313). This cross-gender identification with Edward seems to re-enforce her sense of her own inadequacy – she can only be a 'deputy', never fully take his place. However, it seems to have allowed her to take a 'male' role in relation to Brittain which was protective and companionable but not sexually threatening.

This identification is also significant in light of the fact that Brittain identified more with Edward and his friends than with other women. Her first published diary entry records her gratification at always having male partners at a dance where there were 'too many girls' (1981, 26). Later she writes:

I suppose it will be my lot to see Edward and his friends, who are as much or more to me than my own (as I really can't stand girls) going off to university, while I, having failed my exam, am left here once more to toil on drearily alone.

(1981, 81)

Yet she also passionately desired a female friend. Anticipating university, she writes: 'Surely now [...] I may begin to *live* and to find at least *one* human creature among my own sex whose spirit can have intercourse with mine' (1981, 16, original emphasis). It is striking, especially in view of its use in the nineteenth century, that she rarely uses a sister metaphor for her relations with Holtby. She does, however, favour a sibling rather than mother–daughter model here:

> The only person who could possibly have meant the same to me would have been a sister whom I loved as I loved Edward. As for a daughter, it would take at least 25 years from now before I could be as fond of her as I am of you!
>
> (Brittain and Handley-Taylor, 1960, 74)

Holtby's own experience of biological sisterhood with her elder sister, Grace, was problematic. Although more intellectually gifted, and possibly her mother's favourite, Holtby was always cast as the plain one in comparison to her pretty sister. This was re-enforced by their childhood recitation of a poem which ended 'One is for use, the other for show' during which Holtby always had to take the role of the one for 'use' (White, 1938, 29). When Grace was dying, Holtby recorded that, 'ironically true to our relationship, I irritated her even by going into the room, and her last words to me were [...] "Don't stare. You make me tired"' (Brittain and Handley-Taylor, 1960, 168). The friendship, then, repeats two established sibling patterns – Brittain's rivalry with Edward, and Holtby's positioning as the plain one in contrast to Grace.

The Brittain and Holtby dialogue offers a valuable record of how their academic and professional rivalry was negotiated within the friendship. The damaging nature of competition between academic women today has been explored by Evelyn Fox Keller and Helen Moglen (1987). They suggest problems frequently arise from the perceived necessity for avoiding competition as threatening sisterly bonding, and from the attempt to use mother–daughter or sister models of female relations which are inappropriate in a professional context. The problem seems to be that women have no scripts for the negotiation of rivalry in a professional (rather than romantic) context, and this is evident in the Holtby–Brittain relationship.

The publication of Holtby's *Anderby Wold* involved an almost total restructuring of the dynamics of their relationship. In *Testament of Youth* Brittain recorded her feelings of jealousy in the tones of an outpaced elder sibling:

> To me [...] this event was something of a psychological crisis; Winifred was considerably my junior, at Oxford she had followed

modestly in my wake, and it had simply never occurred to me that her work could be preferred and published before my own.

(TY 597)

Previously it had been Brittain offering advice and contacts. Now the power balance in the relationship had changed, as Brittain noted in a letter at this point: 'we are not equals any more' (Brittain and Handley-Taylor, 1960, 20). A few months later Brittain was still trying to re-negotiate their relationship, writing to Holtby in rather bitter tones:

As Vera Brittain, lecturer and speaker for the League of Nations, etc [...] I feel quite able to hold my own with Winifred Holtby – and to tell you the honest truth, I don't care a damn if I can't; I don't really care for anything but writing, and making up my mind to stop doing it would never prevent me from going on...

(TY 598)

Their relationship is constructed as a competition in which Brittain must 'hold her own', which she can only do by shifting the parameters of the competition to include lecturing. Significantly, it is not her affection for Holtby that enables her to say that she doesn't care a 'damn' but her own determined ambition.

These letters contrast with Holtby's generous reply to Brittain's first letter, which attempts to neutralise any competition by reasserting Brittain's superior position: 'You are perfectly right in saying that we are not equals. We never were and never will be. I have always known how much keener and clearer and finer your mind is than mine' (Brittain and Handley-Taylor, 1960, 20). While Holtby's generosity undoubtedly played a huge part in the re-negotiations, Brittain obviously worked hard at overcoming her insecurities.

Brittain's sense of superiority also led to attempts to direct Holtby's writing, recalled by Holtby in a 1925 letter to Catlin:

Knowing my very great faults as a writer, she tried to cure them by analysing and criticising my ideas before they became books... It nearly drove me crazy until I had to set a complete taboo upon her discussion of my work save after it was done.

(quoted in Shaw, 1999, 124)

This struggle for textual control is rather different from the idealised image of their relationship as a supportive dialogue. Brittain's attempts to shape Holtby's writing are attempts to make Holtby into her 'second self' in the sense of a lesser copy of Brittain herself. It is in the context of this competitive struggle for control of representation that I want to read the dialogue between Brittain's *The Dark Tide* and Holtby's second novel, *The Crowded Street*, both of which use a triangle plot which positions women as rivals over a man.

The Dark Tide (1923)

Brittain started planning *The Dark Tide* during her unhappy 1919 autumn term at Oxford but in 1920 she came close to a nervous break-down:

> no one, least of all myself, realised how near I had drifted to the borderland of craziness. I was ashamed, to the point of agony, of the sinister transformation which seemed, every time I looked in the glass, to be impending in my face, and I could not bring myself to mention it even to Winifred, who would probably have dispelled the illusion by the sane reassurance that I was neither developing a beard nor turning into a witch.
>
> (TY 496–7)

The five large mirrors in her room became an especial torment, as she feared that 'five identical witches' faces should suddenly stare at me from the cold, remorseless mirrors' (TY 500).

To someone as conscious as Brittain of her own 'chocolate-box pretti-ness' (TY 211) this fear of mirrors is particularly significant. The key factor is the loss of her sense of identity as an attractive, marriageable woman, which triggers the fear that she is becoming either a man or a witch. Brittain's brief, abortive engagement during this time is men-tioned in passing as an illustration of the 'follies' 'some of us' were driven into by the 'biological needs of that tense, turbulent year' (TY 499). It seems to have been Holtby's support which enabled her to end it. The following day Brittain wrote the bitter poem 'The Superfluous Woman', which asks 'But who will give me my children?' (TY 534). Brittain was trying to rebuild her sense of self in the light of the fact that she had, she believed at this point in her life, lost forever the chance of marriage and children.

Holtby's support was largely responsible for Brittain's recovery. Holtby offered a (single) mirror in which Brittain could see herself reflected, partly in contrast to the less stereotypically 'feminine' Holtby, as a whole and attractive, even elegant, woman. As Brittain acknowledged, the building of their friendship was Holtby's achievement not Brittain's, yet Brittain also desperately desired that friendship. *The Dark Tide* has to be read with an awareness of the nature of this identity crisis, and Brittain's resentment of her own emotional dependence on Holtby. Yet on the surface *The Dark Tide* contains none of this need. Instead, it gives us a cruel caricature of Holtby as the gauche, naive Daphne Lethbridge. Physically, the two main characters resemble Holtby and Brittain. Daphne, like Holtby, is tall, golden-haired, blue-eyed, and favours clothes in clashing primary colours. Virginia Dennison, like Vera, is small, dark and pretty, and immaculately dressed, usually in black or blue.

The first sections of *The Dark Tide* are a barely fictionalised account of Brittain's and Holtby's initial meetings at Oxford, which appear in both *Testament of Youth* and *Testament of Friendship*, but with interesting differences in presentation. In the novel they are told, as is most of the novel, from Daphne's point of view. Their first meeting is, as Holtby and Brittain's was, in their history tutorial, where Virginia has (like Brittain) done all the preliminary reading, while Daphne (like Holtby) has done none. The physical contrast between the two women is inflected by class difference. Virginia makes Daphne feel like a 'vulgar barmaid in her Sunday best' (DT 32) and she tries to reassert her own superiority by reminding herself that Virginia's father was 'only "Dennison's China"' (DT 32). In terms of academic ability, Virginia produces excellent essays, while Daphne is told that her style is 'laborious, her sentences involved, her subject matter confused, and her spelling abominable' (DT 42) – comments made about Holtby's work.

Despite their physical appearances the two characters both represent sides of Brittain herself. Virginia is a wish-fulfilment portrait of Brittain, while Daphne, with her class insecurity and desperate desire for heterosexual success, is Brittain as she feared she might be. This is particularly evident when the early scenes from *The Dark Tide* are compared with Brittain's other accounts. In *Testament of Youth* the emphasis is on Brittain's post-war loneliness and isolation. Told that Holtby's war experience will form a link with Brittain's, Brittain, like Daphne, feels 'unaccountably antagonistic' (TY 486). Her first impressions of Holtby are of youth and energy: 'Superbly tall and vigorous as the young Diana with her long straight limbs and her golden hair, her vitality smote with the effect of a blow upon my jaded nerves' (TY 487). Brittain is the one who feels old, insecure and envious here – and then triumphant because her essays are preferred to Holtby's.

In *Testament of Friendship* Brittain shifts the emphasis to foreground the bond of their war service, presenting it as a link not a cause for rivalry. The reader already knows that the two women will become friends so when Brittain writes 'We did not, to begin with, like each other at all' (TF 92) the statement has already moved forward to their later liking. Holtby is a 'radiant goddess' (TF 92) while her clashing clothes 'exaggerate both her impressive size and her glowing animation' (TF 93), rather than connoting class difference as they do in the novel. It is the contrast between Holtby's popularity and Brittain's isolated depression which provokes Brittain to 'barely concealed hostility' (TF 93). Again, it is Brittain who is insecure, isolated, competitive – and seeking the reader's sympathy.

The second incident drawn from life is the humiliating debate which Daphne sets up to persuade Virginia to 'make a fool of herself' (DT 43), based on one organised by Holtby. Virginia, as Brittain had done, argues that 'a life of travel is a better education than a life of academic experience' (DT 44). Daphne turns the debate into a personal attack and concludes, as Holtby had done, with Rosalind's words from *As You Like It*: 'I had rather have a fool to make me merry than experience to make me sad; and to travel for it too!' (DT 48).

The account of the debate in *Testament of Youth* is prefaced by the comment that Brittain has already given a 'substantially correct version' (TY 488) in *The Dark Tide*, thus endorsing that version. Brittain softens this by presenting it as an example of one of the 'misunderstandings' which 'embittered the relations of the War generation and its immediate juniors' (TY 488), particularly the 'antagonism' between those who suffered deeply from the war and those who had not. Holtby's part in the debate is described as 'witty' and 'trenchant' (TY 489) – a backward view informed by Holtby's later success as a lecturer. Perhaps most telling is Brittain's comment that 'For years I believed that [the debate] had been deliberately planned with a view to my humiliation' (TY 488).

The oddest thing about these statements is that, though Brittain held Holtby as the Debating Society secretary responsible for the debate, she implies that she has still never asked Holtby, now her closest friend, to explain. Even writing *Testament of Youth* in 1933 she only remarks that 'it seems to me *far more probable* that the whole situation developed spontaneously and unintentionally' (TY 488–9, my emphasis) – implying she has still not discussed it with Holtby. Finally, she positions herself and Holtby on opposite sides of the 'antagonism' between those who have suffered in the war and those who have not – despite arguing that their war experience drew them together. In *Testament of Friendship* the debate is treated even more briefly, merely noted as being 'at Winifred's instigation' (TF 93).

This textual manoeuvring is typical of much of Brittain's writing about their relationship, which continually positions Holtby as the same but lesser, and textually silences her. Although we get three versions from Brittain, the only hint she gives of Holtby's side is in *Testament of Youth* where Brittain records Holtby telling her long afterwards that their history tutor ' "put her off" ' because he looked like a colonel and she expected him to treat her as a WAAC – 'who weren't supposed to be ladies' (TY 487). Brittain follows this up by quoting Holtby's good-humoured 'boast' that as a Yorkshire farmer's daughter she had the advantage as a journalist over Brittain, who as 'a descendant of the Staffordshire *bourgeoisie*, was merely "genteel" ' (TY 487). The class antagonism between Daphne and Virginia has its roots in this bantering over the graduations of middle-class identity.

In fact Holtby did put her own side in a 1933 letter to Brittain while Brittain was writing *Testament of Youth*. She had thought of the debate as a ' "rag" – [. . .] to rub off what seemed to me something of your superiority towards all my fellow-students who had not been to the War', and added that she had seen war experience as such a 'fortunate privilege' that she thought any 'superiority based upon it an intolerable form of snobbery, until I heard your story' (quoted in Berry and Bostridge, 1995, 147–8). This appears in neither *Testament*.

The Dark Tide is the drama of Brittain's two selves (one having borrowed Holtby's appearance) rather than of her interaction with Holtby as 'other'. Daphne represents Brittain's insecurities about her intellect, her class, her popularity, her dependence on male admiration – and her rivalry with Holtby. While the later biographical texts smooth over these 'misunderstandings', foregrounding the similarity of shared experience, *The Dark Tide* is evidence of its initial bitterness.

In all three texts the initial rivalry between the two women is over their academic work, but in *The Dark Tide* Brittain diverts this into romantic rivalry over Sylvester, the rather unrealistic don with whom Daphne falls in love and who marries her only after Virginia has refused him. Academic rivalry between women, rather than competition on the marriage market, was a new area both in life and fiction. Although it was not the first (L. T. Meade's college novels were published in the 1890s), Brittain's novel was one of the earliest novels of women's university life. It is perhaps not surprising Brittain fell back on romance rivalry to provide a narrative structure for the novel.

Susan Leonardi has drawn attention to the way that Brittain's fiction 'repeats and reinforces the romance plot' (1989, 225). *The Dark Tide* articulates her ambivalence towards it, allowing her on one level doubly to reject it for herself, both through Virginia's refusal of Sylvester, and through the disaster of Daphne's marriage. After an affair with an opera singer who reminds him of Virginia, Sylvester has a violent quarrel with the pregnant Daphne, and abandons her to premature labour and a crippled child. Through this rather over-melodramatic scenario, Brittain rejects marriage and the conventional values espoused by her own mother.

The text articulates the contemporaneous anxieties around the figure of the educated woman. Daphne believes that Sylvester has chosen her because of her difference from Virginia, specifically because she is more 'feminine'. People like Virginia may be good at examinations, he tells Daphne, but 'they were not the sort of women that men wanted to live with' (DT 150). This is the opposition between the educated woman and the 'womanly' woman which underlies *The Constant Nymph*. Ironically, as the reader knows, Virginia was exactly the woman Sylvester wanted to live with. There is a clear disjunction between the romance clichés within which Daphne tries to interpret Sylvester's behaviour as a romantic lover, and his real motivation. She even suppresses the fact that his physical advances terrify her.

The text attempts to expose as an illusion Daphne's belief that she is to be privy to 'the great elemental secrets of love and marriage and birth' (DT 152). Ultimately, though, it endorses this through Virginia's words: 'why does this one thing [love and marriage] make all one's work and all one's achievement seem dust and ashes?' (DT 204). Despite Brittain's attempts to debunk the romance plot, the thrust of the text is that heterosexual marriage is the most fulfilling option for a woman. Ouditt's suggestion that in post-war novels romance 'was undermined by the absence of its primary structuring force – the right man' (1994, 116) is the key to *The Dark Tide* – the 'right man' is missing. For Virginia, who still treasures the last letter from her dead fiancé, he is dead, while Daphne makes a mis-identification. Brittain's work is haunted by the absence of the 'right man'. When he does appear – as he does in the novel for the young history don Patricia O'Neill – the risk of marriage is worth taking.

The alternative is an almost Victorian ethos of self-sacrifice and purification through suffering which is far bleaker than anything explored by Sinclair. Neither Daphne nor Virginia has work they enjoy for its own sake. Virginia sublimates even her intellectual desires into her nursing, while Daphne is encouraged not to ruin her husband's political career by divorcing him and to devote her life to her crippled son. This reflects not only the difficulty of denying the inter-war ideology of maternity but also Brittain's attempt to come to terms with the fact that, as a 'superfluous woman', she believed she had no choice but to sublimate her energies.

There is, however, a second reason for Brittain's use of the romance plot in this novel. If we read it as an attempt to rectify the power balance between Holtby and herself, then shifting the rivalry from the academic sphere to the romantic sphere achieves this function. Both Brittain and Holtby got Second Class degrees – but it was Holtby who nearly got a First. In the novel, Brittain shifts the academic balance to give Virginia a First, while Daphne gets a Third. The one area where Brittain seems to have been sure of her superiority over Holtby was that of heterosexual attractiveness. Brittain was the one whose fiancé had been killed (and who eventually married). Yet it was also her sense of herself as attractive which was most threatened by her breakdown. By rewriting her rivalry with Holtby as romantic rivalry, Brittain reasserted her sense of her own superior identity through a contrast with Holtby's lesser attractions.

Daphne's appearance (which resembles photographs of Holtby) is described in masculine terms: she has long legs, large hands, a 'slightly masculine element' in her nose, and a 'strongly moulded chin' (DT 23). While Daphne is patently not a success with men, Virginia finds dances satisfying because she is 'always such a success' (DT 95), echoing Brittain's own feelings. Sylvester's comparison of the two women during the wedding is significant:

> Virginia would have come to him all in white, filmy, soft, delicate, nothing solid about her [...] How Daphne's aggressive gold train caught the sunlight, and seemed to divert it from her face just when he needed her to look her very best!
>
> (DT 154–5)

Reversing Kennedy's schematisation in *The Constant Nymph*, here it is Virginia, despite her 'man's brain' (DT 89), who is truly womanly. Daphne fails both academically *and* as a woman. The text sets Virginia up as Sylvester's real choice, and therefore superior to Daphne, in a way which is uncomfortably reminiscent of the sense of superiority Harriett Frean gained from knowing that she was Robin's real choice.

The novel does attempt to validate female friendship through Virginia's support of Daphne after she is abandoned by Sylvester but this is so obviously second-best that it remains unconvincing. There is also a suggestion in the text that the two women are complementary doubles. Patricia thinks that they are 'each able to supply what the other lacked' (DT 78). Although this confirms the fact that they represent two aspects of Brittain, it is never fully explored in the text.

Holtby's letters show a remarkable generosity towards *The Dark Tide*, considering its unflattering portrait of herself, calling it 'a fine book' (Brittain and Handley-Taylor, 1960, 11). But it is from Holtby's rewriting of it in *The Crowded Street* that we can gauge her response to it. While Brittain uses the triangle plot to establish difference between women, Holtby undoes Brittain's romance plot in favour of a validation of female friendship.

The Crowded Street (1924)

One of the spinster novels of the 1920s, *The Crowded Street* not only rejects the romance plot but validates female friendship and work as an alternative to marriage. Where it moves on from *Life and Death of Harriett Frean* or *The Rector's Daughter* is that it presents spinsterhood as a positive choice. *The Crowded Street* ends with a marriage proposal but the protagonist, Muriel Hammond, refuses it because marriage would mean giving up 'every new thing that has made me a person' (CS 270). This refusal is not a self-sacrifice but an assertion of self and a rejection of her mother's values.

Holtby's rejection of the romance plot is explicit in Muriel's reflection that:

> All books are the same – about beautiful girls who get married or married women who fall in love with their husbands [...] Why doesn't somebody write a book about someone to whom nothing ever happens – like me?
>
> (CS 219)

This is, of course, exactly the book Holtby is writing. Significantly, she had trouble with its form, tearing up her first draft: 'It's like a jelly that won't "jell",' she wrote, 'cold, flabby, formless' (Holtby, 1937a, 190). In the Prologue the eleven-year-old Muriel goes to a party, where she commits the 'unforgivable sin' (CS 16) of having no partners and is then caught taking a sweet from the supper table. Holtby's formal problems can be related to the task of finding a narrative structure for a heroine who finds neither 'the Party' (CS 19) nor a partner, and to whom, therefore, in the eyes of the world, 'nothing happens'.

In her portraits of Muriel and Delia Vaughan, the vicar's daughter who becomes Muriel's friend, Holtby rewrites the characters of Daphne and Virginia, and thus both herself and Brittain. Brittain, who found the novel a failure, thought that Delia was 'a partial and less successful imaginary reconstruction of my war-time self' (TF 160), a comment which distances herself from the character. Muriel was, Holtby admitted, based on herself but 'part of me only – the stupid, frightened part' (Holtby, 1937a, 288). But Muriel is also a portrait of how Brittain might have been had she accepted the provincial ideals of her mother.

In contrast to Brittain's cruel portrayal of Daphne, Holtby sympathetically delineates the social structures which trap Muriel. Jean Kennard calls *The Crowded Street* the 'strongest political statement Holtby was to make in her fiction [. . .] a cutting indictment of society's oppression of women and of mothers as the primary agents of that oppression' (1989, 59). It is in this novel, Kennard claims, that Holtby 'affirms [. . .] the need to reject the mother's values' (1989, 59). However, it is the values of Brittain's mother rather than those of Alice Holtby which Holtby is rejecting in her portrait of Muriel's mother.

Mrs Hammond's maiden name, Bennet, recalls that other great matrimonial schemer – Jane Austen's Mrs Bennet in *Pride and Prejudice* (1813). Both illustrate Irigaray's argument that 'the commodities that women *are forced to exchange would be their children* [. . .] in exchange for a market status *for themselves*' (1993b, 84, original emphasis). Mrs Hammond's own marriage to a lower-class man has been 'her one act of spontaneous folly' (CS 260). The following thirty years are devoted to a minutely calculated campaign, an attempt to trade her daughters on the marriage market in exchange for her own increased social status. In Marshington, as Delia tells Muriel, the only thing that counts for a girl is 'sex-success' (CS 88), and such success also enhances the girl's mother's status. Mrs Hammond's antennae for the tiny nuances of class distinction are finely developed and she assesses each man in terms of the status he can give a woman, and each woman in terms of the husband she has or might get.

Like Brittain, Holtby uses the triangle plot but she undercuts the rivalry theme by splitting the rival function between Delia and Clare Duquesne, Muriel's glamorous, half-French schoolfriend. Displacing the romance narrative, Holtby makes Muriel's relationships with both of them more vivid than her feeling for the ostensible object of the rivalry, the local squire, Godfrey Neale. Delia is merely his friend, but Godfrey falls deeply for Clare and is briefly engaged to her. In looks, social position and genuine kindness, Godfrey appears the perfect romantic hero. Muriel's rejection of him is the more courageous because he is a far more realistic and sympathetic character than Brittain's Sylvester.

Holtby, more carefully than Brittain in her treatment of Daphne, maps out the disjunction between what Muriel thinks she ought to feel and what she really does feel. Realising that at some point Godfrey will propose to her simply because she is Clare's friend, Muriel believes she will accept him. Like Daphne, she tries to fit the facts into the romance narrative:

> 'I *have* loved him all my life,' said Muriel, and lay, waiting to feel the glow of love warming her coldness.
> 'This is not as it should be,' she felt. But nothing ever was as it should be in a world where the best conclusion was a compromise.
> (CS 119, original emphasis)

The 'glow of [heterosexual] love' never does warm Muriel.

The emotional centre of the novel, unlike that of *The Dark Tide*, lies in Muriel's relationships with women – with Clare, Delia, and her sister, Connie. Through the depiction of Clare, Holtby shows how the rivalry between women, organised by men and enforced by women, disrupts the potential for 'passionate friendship' between women. Muriel meets Clare at the school where she has been sent to cultivate suitable friendships. However, the headmistress actively discourages 'passionate friendships' since, 'if carried too far [they] even wrecked all hope of matrimony without offering any satisfaction in return' (CS 41). Clare does wreck Muriel's matrimonial prospects but by enticing away her prospective suitor rather than claiming her emotional loyalty. Mrs Hammond sees Clare not as a potential friend for Muriel but as her rival, sending her away when she realises that Godfrey has fallen for Clare. Muriel's fierce desire for Clare to stay is directly contrasted with her lukewarm feeling for Godfrey: 'Why care whom Godfrey looked at, whom he knew? Why did she feel this silent force of her mother's will coming between her and the most glorious friendship that she could ever know?' (CS 79).

Through the loss of her sister Muriel does experience very real suffering. Connie functions as a warning that in the Marshington marriage market to take what you want – whether it is a sweet or a man – is 'against the rules of the game' (CS 100). The melodrama of Connie's fate, her unwedded pregnancy, loveless marriage, and the death of herself and her unborn child, recalls Daphne, but is again treated with far more sympathy.

It is in her depiction of Delia, however, that Holtby most decisively rewrites *The Dark Tide*. A kinder, more generous version of Brittain than Virginia, she also has those qualities – a capacity for hard work and political commitment – which Brittain shared with Holtby. The motif of Muriel and Delia as alter egos is more carefully worked out and suggests again that both characters share something of both Brittain and Holtby:

> It was as though Delia in her London office, looking up from the work which her brilliant, courageous mind directed, might think of Muriel in Marshington, living her drab ineffectual life among tea-parties [. . .] and might say to herself, 'There, but for the grace of God, goes Delia Vaughan.' Most successful people, thought Muriel sadly, have a shadow somewhere, a personality sharing their desires and even part of their ability, but without just the one quality that makes success.
>
> (CS 102–3)

While education simply confuses the issue for Brittain's Daphne and, indeed, for Virginia, Holtby validates it through Delia.

What Delia offers Muriel is not an ethic of self-sacrifice but a sustaining, practical partnership. The image of the two women sharing a flat in London (as Holtby and Brittain did) is a far more positive valorisation of female friendship than *The Dark Tide*. Like Holtby and Brittain's friendship, it is based on mutual enablement and allows them to use, not suppress, their abilities. It differs from the Holtby–Brittain friendship in that Muriel's work initially consists of acting as a surrogate wife to Delia. However, there is a hint that she may move on to work in her own right.

Holtby separates the passionate, emotionally-intense feeling Muriel has for Clare from the practical friendship with Delia. This is obvious if the novel is compared to Radclyffe Hall's *The Unlit Lamp*, where the enabling friend and the love object are the same person. Although Hall's novel is more radical in its treatment of female desire, Holtby's is radical in its assertion that work can be as fulfilling for women as personal relationships. Although Muriel's love for Clare is the closest Holtby comes to depicting passion between women in her fiction, it is more to do with Clare's glamour and Muriel's loneliness than with sexual desire. In this, as well as its school setting, it is closer to Lehmann's *Dusty Answer* than *The Unlit Lamp*.

Delia does not reject marriage per se but 'marriage as [. . .] the ultimate goal of the female soul's development' (CS 230). Her choice of a mate, the stocky, untidy but kind and brilliant Martin Elliot, offers her the chance of combining work and marriage. Yet Holtby removes Martin from the text in an accidental death which is, as Leonardi says, 'gratuitous' (1989, 184). The loss of the 'right man' is not, as it is for Brittain, inevitable, but seems contrived in order to create Delia's need for Muriel.

Indeed, Holtby's 'romantic' heroes – Robert Carne in *South Riding*, David Rossitur in *Anderby Wold*, Teddy Leigh in *The Land of Green Ginger* (1927) – have a disturbing tendency to die. The only marriage ending Holtby depicts is that between Jean Stanbury and Maurice Durrant in *Mandoa, Mandoa!* (1933), problematic not least because Jean has married not the man she loves but his brother. There is only a hint that Eleanor will marry Roger Mortimer in *Poor Caroline* (1931). For Holtby, marriage frequently brings death or loss of self to women, as in Connie's case. Thus her rewriting of the triangle plot entails killing off the male in order to bring the women together and give them the space to exercise their abilities.

It is therefore significant that the only time that Muriel does feel love for Godfrey is when she thinks that he is about to be killed, and when she thinks he has been wounded and she is 'tortured [. . .] with his pain' (CS 167). The phrasing of this scene recalls an earlier one when Muriel, hearing of Martin's death, thinks: 'I would give all I possess to share [Delia's] tears if I could have her memories. I-I am hungry for her pain' (CS 143). It is not Godfrey's love which Muriel desires but any strong emotion. Her real suffering is 'the awfulness of a life where nothing ever happens; the shame of feeling half a woman because no man has loved you' (CS 233). This also echoes Holtby's 1920 poem 'The Dead Man', which concludes 'They long for easeful death, but I/ Am hungry for their pain' (TF 82). Here it is not the action of the combatant (as in other non-combatant poems such as Macaulay's 'Many Sisters to Many Brothers', or Sinclair's dedicatory poem in *A Journal of Impressions in Belgium*) which is envied, but the pain of the bereaved. The male persona is 'dead' because he cannot feel and thus envies other men who 'walk wild ways with love' (TF 82).

This connects with Holtby's sense of herself as one who 'can't even love as we usually speak of love' (Holtby, 1937a, 202). In her letters to Jean McWilliam Holtby several times mentions her lack of experience of 'love', by which she always means heterosexual love. Her main regret, however, is that this lack of love experience will affect her writing:

I really shall be disappointed if I go through life without once being properly in love. As a writer, I feel it is my duty to my work – but they are all so helpless, and such children. How can one feel thrilled?

(Holtby, 1937a, 325)

There is a distinction here between 'being *properly* in love' (with a man) as opposed to the love Holtby frequently expresses for both Brittain and McWilliam. Here she seems to accept the myth of the necessity of experiencing *heterosexual* passion in order to write well – the myth that a spinster (as with Sinclair) cannot know enough of the world to create art.

Brittain, on the contrary, had experienced sexual passion. Her public image as a woman who had lost her first love in the war was enhanced by *Testament of Youth* which presented her as representative of her war-bereaved generation. Muriel's jealousy of Delia because she has had 'The best of both worlds [...] Love to remember and work to do' (CS 233), probably reflects Holtby's own envy of Brittain in this area. An ignoble emotion, as Muriel recognises, but it reflects yet again the internalisation of inferiority by both non-combatant and single women. The crux of *The Crowded Street* is this feeling of never having felt 'real' emotion, of never finding 'the Party'. It is this which Muriel fears has 'cut me off from other women, made me different' (CS 233). But the important point is that Muriel wants to feel sexual passion not for its own sake, but because not having felt it sets her apart from other women. Similarly, Holtby wanted to feel it because it would supposedly make her a better writer and put her on a more equal footing with Brittain.

6

'My Second Self': Winifred Holtby and Vera Brittain

The friendship between Vera Brittain and Winifred Holtby epitomises the problematic differences between married and single women during the inter-war period. Brittain's marriage in 1925 required an even greater readjustment in their relationship than that caused by the publication of *Anderby Wold*. That difference had to be continually re-negotiated and it is at the heart of the intertextual dialogue between Holtby's final novel, *South Riding* (1936), and Brittain's *Honourable Estate* (1936). Brittain was writing *Honourable Estate* as she corrected the proofs for *South Riding* after Holtby's death, commenting: 'What a strange experience of communion with [Holtby's] spirit this proof-correcting is! In her book, all the time, she says the things that we both thought and said to one another' (1986, 239). That 'we', suggesting that the women think as one, obscures the radical differences between the books. While Brittain's novel sets up the ideal of 'semi-detached marriage' (redefining the 'honourable estate' of matrimony), Holtby's offers a vision of female community based on shared work. Competition is still evident, however, in Brittain's reflection that: 'I shall never do anything to equal this!' (1986, 228).

In both novels the friendship between women is centred in the protagonist's connection, mediated by a man, with an older woman: Sarah Burton and Mrs Beddows, and Ruth Allendyne and her mother-in-law, Janet Rutherston. Thus, Kennard argues, both novels provide reconciliation with 'mothers or substitute mothers' and 'a vindication of the mother's life and work' (1989, 161–2). The model of the female friend as a surrogate mother or daughter is a seductive one. Certainly, both novels assert the importance of situating the female subject in a maternal genealogy, and of acknowledging the mother's identity as a separate subject. However, the linearity of this model with its movement towards

138

consensus is over-schematic, obscuring the endlessly fluid process of interaction in a living relationship. Friendships need ongoing maintenance, particularly during changes in career, marital status or location. What the Brittain–Holtby relationship demonstrates is how friends take up a range of different subject positions in relation to those changes. Holtby acted as mother, brother, colleague and/or lover to Brittain in response to Brittain's needs. Although Brittain's occupation of the positions of daughter, sister, colleague, and/or beloved is not at first glance an obvious response to Holtby's needs, her positioning as such enabled Holtby to feel needed. Moreover, in *Honourable Estate* the connection with the older woman functions to distance the friendship, and remove it from the possibility of sexual desire, while in *South Riding* it is a way of making connections across the differences which divide women – age, marital status, class, politics.

The restructuring of the friendship around the time of Brittain's marriage entailed a negotiation of the distinction between homosocial and homosexual behaviour and language which can be traced through their letters. Both Marion Shaw and Jean Kennard show how Brittain suppressed the more emotional language in their letters when she edited them for publication. She removed terms of endearment which included, as well as 'darling', 'sweetieheart' and 'beloved', the terms 'lover', 'spouse' and 'husband' (Shaw, n.d., 38; Kennard, 1989, 7). These suggest an appropriation of a heterosexual model for the friendship, which, once Brittain had a male lover, was no longer available without constructing Holtby as Catlin's rival. Holtby's subsequent deferral to Catlin's right as Brittain's husband to use such language works to neutralise any such rivalry.

Holtby's earlier use of such a heterosexual discourse was one of a range of positions she took up in response to Brittain's needs. Writing in December 1923 after an early letter from Catlin, Brittain comments: 'I do hope that, after this lovely period of peace, some devastating male is not going to push into my life and upset it again' and appeals to Holtby to act as 'a bulwark' (Brittain and Handley-Taylor, 1960, 28) to protect her. In return, Holtby takes a protective brotherly attitude towards Brittain, promising: ' I'll be your bulwark for as long as you want me. I regret that I have no Syren charms to entice away embarrassing suitors' (Brittain and Handley-Taylor, 1960, 30). Holtby here constructs herself as sexually unattractive in comparison to Brittain, and, significantly, as Pam Johnson points out, wishes for 'Syren charms' not to tempt men on her own account but to keep them away from Brittain (1989, 155).

In a later letter Holtby asks: 'do I seem cold to you?' and explains that she is torn between 'the exacting demands of love' and her 'invincible belief that no one person should lay too heavy claims upon another' (Brittain and Handley-Taylor, 1960, 36). What follows reads like a love letter:

> I believe you know I love you. Do you want me to say I know that you love me? Sweet child, do you think I dream for a moment that you could have endured my limitations all these years if you had not loved me?
>
> (Brittain and Handley-Taylor, 1960, 36)

This balancing act – reassuring Brittain without laying claim to her – is repeated in many of Holtby's letters. Her use of 'child' suggests a maternal attitude, but it also recalls the heterosexual love discourse used by Roland, again younger than Brittain: 'Dear child', he wrote to her, 'I have always liked this name for you, though I ought not to call you "child" ought I?' (Brittain, 1981, 228). In echoing this name Holtby combines the positions of mother and lover to Brittain.

Holtby's letters hint at her need to suppress the strength of her feeling for Brittain. She writes after Brittain's engagement:

> If you must spend yourself completely now upon a personal emotion and I must sublimate an emotion that I may not otherwise expend, do not think that my star rises or yours sets. We have both our ways to take and they will not be similar...
>
> (Brittain and Handley-Taylor, 1960, 40–1)

It is not clear exactly what emotion Holtby is being called upon to suppress – her feeling for Brittain, or her own capacity for heterosexual passion.

Holtby's letters to Jean McWilliam provide more insight into how acutely Holtby felt the loss of Brittain. 'My little Vera is going to be married after all' (1937a, 263) she writes, the 'my' still asserting possession. The impending marriage sparks off a crisis in her own life as she asks 'how shall I live' (1937a, 289). The answer is work: 'I am fierce for work. Without work I am nothing' (1937a, 301). Her letters to Jean become increasingly affectionate, frequently ending with 'I love you', and she seems, understandably, to be turning to McWilliam to replace Brittain. Her view of the damaging nature of the romance plot is clear in her description of Brittain and Catlin's relationship:

This is the most charming love-story that I have yet encountered. When I saw [Catlin] yesterday, slim, charming, brilliant, with his blue eyes ablaze with happiness, and his arm across the shoulders of his little love, I almost believed that the romance of fiction was less perniciously untruthful than I had thought. Even if marriage proves catastrophic, this parting and meeting has at least been lovely.

(1937a, 345)

Significantly, Holtby's 'little Vera' has become Catlin's 'little love'. And Holtby's distrust of romance is only 'almost' assuaged.

Brittain's letters hint at disillusion even during the honeymoon. Taking Catlin to visit Edward's grave, she writes to Holtby:

Thus I introduced my husband to all that remains of my dear, dear brother, and whether the future suffers by comparison with the past or vice versa, I am not prepared to say. But someday, perhaps, my husband will help me create another Edward...

(Brittain and Handley-Taylor, 1960, 45)

Brittain identified Catlin, as well as Holtby, with Edward, noting that their first meeting took place on the anniversary of Edward's death (TY 617). But her letter suggests that Catlin, unlike Holtby, proved an inadequate 'deputy' for Edward and her hopes now centre on the son she would christen 'John Edward'.

Following their honeymoon, Brittain and Catlin briefly stayed with Holtby in the London flat prior to leaving for America. This was clearly a difficult position for Holtby, and noting her lack of spirits afterwards, Brittain wrote, 'I do hate you being miserable [...] what was it really my dear?' (Brittain and Handley-Taylor, 1960, 48). She offers several possibilities, including (juxtaposed with a bad haircut) Holtby's anxiety over Harry Pearson's failure to keep an appointment. Holtby's reply offers an analysis of her feelings for Harry which recalls Muriel's failure to feel desire for Godfrey: 'Curious how, though I do not love nor respect as lovers love, I yet feel my personality so strangely linked to him. I do not particularly want to see him, and in his company I am a little bored' (Brittain and Handley-Taylor, 1960, 49). The following analysis of her feelings for Brittain, while acknowledging Catlin, contrasts vividly with this lukewarmness:

I like to be with you both – you give me exquisite joy. As for you, do you not realise that I don't care twopence whereabout in the scale of your loves I come, provided that you love me enough to let me love you, and that you are happy? I love you in a way that part of me has become part of you.

(Brittain and Handley-Taylor, 1960, 50)

Again Holtby balances the need to reassure Brittain of her love and the need to recognise that she is now the outsider in this triangle.

In this exchange Pearson is being used, by both women, as an alibi, a cover for feelings (whether sexual or not) neither of them wants to admit. If Holtby has a lover, however unsatisfactory, he provides a balance to Catlin, transforming an unbalanced triangle into two socially acceptable heterosexual couples and defusing the possibility of rivalry between Catlin and Holtby.

Brittain's letters from America detail her growing certainty that Holtby, rather than Catlin, enabled her writing. In *The Land of Green Ginger* (1927), the novel Holtby was writing at this point, Joanna (an idealised version of Holtby herself) reflects that men 'just won't *do*. Not as friends' (1983, 119, original emphasis) – a conclusion both Brittain and Holtby were reaching. In the novel, once again, it is the death of the man, in this case Joanna's husband, Teddy (who resembles both Catlin and Pearson), which leaves Joanna free for work and female friendship. For Brittain the solution was a return to England and the establishment of their *ménage à trois*.

One of the strategies Holtby used to cope with the strains of this unconventional living arrangement was to adopt a maternal role. Indeed, as Marion Shaw has noted, both Holtby and Catlin adopted a quasi-parental and oddly conspiratorial role towards Brittain, referring to her in letters as 'the child' (Shaw, 1999, 125). Holtby increasingly developed a role as mediator in the triangle, coaching Catlin on how to cope with Brittain, and even, as Shaw notes, describing Vera to him in erotic terms which cast Holtby as the 'purveyor and connoisseur of Vera's charms' (1999, 123). This clearly defines Holtby's role in a way which avoids constructing her as a rival to Catlin. But it also allowed her to continue enabling Brittain's work, not least by pointing out to Catlin that Brittain's sparse literary output during the marriage was related to her responsibilities as wife and mother: 'She has corrected your proofs and typed your articles [...] she has taken complete responsibility for your children. Surely this is a fair *quid pro quo* for your six months in (or out of) America?' (quoted in Berry and Bostridge, 1995, 258) The success of Brittain's marriage, as well as her writing, may well be attributed to such support from Holtby.

The short story, 'Episode in West Kensington', originally written for *Mandoa, Mandoa!*, offers a telling dialogue between women. Going to spend an evening with her spinster friend Evelyn, Jean, newly-married, pregnant and wrapped in expensive furs, observes:

> Girl typists, hurrying home to boil their supper eggs over gas-rings, gazed wistfully at the young mothers pushing prams back from the park; and the young mothers, tired and depressed, gazed wistfully at the smart unburdened typists.
>
> (1937b, 289)

The painful, edgy conversation between the two women reaches the understanding that both single and married states necessitate losses, but that their friendship is still a valuable support system. Evelyn refuses to accept an inferior status simply because she is unmarried, telling Jean:

> 'I'll warm myself at your fires. But I warn you, I shall resent that always. [...] there's one thing I promise I won't do [...] I won't be meek. I won't be a useful "aunty" to your children.'
>
> (1937b, 309–10)

Holtby was, of course, a 'useful "aunty"' to Brittain's children. This story expresses in miniature precisely the painful processes of their ongoing negotiations, as well as their competitive nature. The story's final, tentative reconciliation is based on the recognition that neither woman should be allowed to feel superior or inferior because of their marital status – a lesson which Brittain, in fact, never seemed to accept.

Brittain's diaries of 1932/3 record another potentially explosive triangle when she attempted to cultivate a closer friendship with the Yorkshire novelist Phyllis Bentley, originally a friend of Holtby's. While Brittain felt inferior to Bentley as a best-selling author, Bentley felt inferior to Brittain because

> Vera was beautiful; she had a husband, two children and an Oxford degree; she was admirably dressed, spoke and wrote fluent, pointed, expressive, Oxford English and knew hosts of people in literary London.
>
> (quoted in Brittain, 1986, 18)

As a recipe for female rivalry this cocktail has everything – differentials of beauty, marital status, literary achievement and class. There were inevitable misunderstandings and, finally, bitter quarrels between Brittain and Bentley during which it was Holtby who acted as mediator and peace-maker.

It is impossible not to sympathise with Holtby, when after one quarrel between Brittain and Bentley, she told Brittain 'You've been the most important person in too many people's lives, you little bitch!' (Brittain, 1986, 86). Brittain, one suspects, was a flirt who liked to be surrounded by admirers of both sexes. It would be easy to see Holtby as the victim here, but to be the calm, still centre to which Brittain returned after flirtations with people like Bentley or Storm Jameson and, indeed, Catlin, indicates Holtby's strength and power in the relationship. Moreover, Holtby had a large circle of friends of her own – Lady Rhondda, St John Ervine, Hilda Reid and others – who valued her highly and many of whom resented Brittain's treatment of her. And she was acutely aware, as 'Episode in West Kensington' shows, that the envy between married and single women flowed both ways. Clearly, Holtby needed to be needed as much as Brittain needed to be loved. While it seems to have been Holtby's ability to adapt herself to Brittain's needs, acting as mother, brother, lover, friend or colleague, which enabled the friendship, Holtby was the first to pay testament to all that she had gained from Brittain's friendship, not least her feminism. Within their 'shared working existence' their differences and, indeed, their rivalry could be transformed through dialogue into enabling forces.

The intertextual dialogue between *South Riding* and *Honourable Estate* centres around what was their greatest difference in both personal and political terms – Brittain's advocacy of marriage and Holtby's defence of spinsterhood.

South Riding (1936)

In *South Riding* Holtby offers a vision of life as connection: 'we are members one of another' (SR 509). In the central triangle with Sarah Burton at its apex, which is an explicit and ironic rewriting of *Jane Eyre*, Holtby again turns the rivalry of the triangle plot on its head and replaces it with female friendship, developing further her 'work-and-friendship ethic' (Shaw, 1986, 189). In the theorisation of female friendship Holtby's most important contribution is to move away from the familial models of female friendship as sisterhood, or a mother–daughter relationship, to offer a new ideal of professional partnership. In Alderman Mrs Beddows and Sarah Burton Holtby offers a picture of two able women, bonded by their work in the community. Work is not a consolation prize offered to the woman who fails to find a husband, nor friendship based on pity. Instead, shared work can bridge differences between women, connecting women of different ages, classes, marital status, even politics. *South Riding* situates friendship between women in a political and public context – that of local government, 'the first-line defence thrown up by the community against our common enemies – poverty, sickness, ignorance, isolation, mental derangement and social maladjustment' (SR 5–6). Holtby shows how women bear the brunt of these 'common enemies' but also how, through their growing political and social presence, they can fight them. Local government, education and the advancement of women, are all part of a web of connection.

Sarah is Holtby's most engaging heroine. Brittain claimed that 'Winifred thought of Sarah Burton as herself', although she gave her the appearance of the red-headed MP Ellen Wilkinson (TF 421). But Sarah actually merges the best of Holtby and Brittain, especially their political commitment and capacity for work. Like Brittain, Sarah has lost a lover in the war and she has Brittain's confidence in her attractiveness. Despite this, she has chosen to be single – 'I was born to be a spinster and by God, I'm going to spin' (SR 67).

The text centralises Holtby's belief in education for women through Sarah's work as headmistress of Kiplington High School for Girls. Sarah's theories are 'founded on experience':

> Sarah believed in action. She believed in fighting. She had unlimited confidence in the power of the human intelligence and will to achieve order, happiness, health and wisdom. It was her business to equip the young women entrusted to her by a still inadequately enlightened state for their part in that achievement.
>
> (SR 66)

Sarah's overriding characteristic is her ability to make connections with people across differences of gender, class and age: Mrs Beddows, the working-class Lydia Holly, the Socialist councillor, Astell, her colleague, Miss Sigglesthwaite. This reflects Holtby's humanist belief that 'it is what unites human beings that is firstly important and only secondly their differences, including their gender' (Shaw, 1986, 190).

Sarah's love for Robert Carne is one of those connections. It is part of Holtby's vision of connection and reconciliation that Sarah should love this 'natural and inevitable' (SR 193) enemy, who stands for everything she opposes – 'feudalism, patronage, chivalry, exploitation' (SR 193) –

and acknowledge even his political integrity. Heterosexual desire here becomes one of a range of connections, but not the ultimate connection. The parallels with *Jane Eyre* are made ironically explicit when Carne, mounted on a large black horse, accuses Sarah of trespassing on his land: 'Into Sarah's irreverent and well-educated mind flashed the memory of Jane Eyre and Mr Rochester' (SR 138). Carne's mad, aristocratic wife, Muriel, is the antithesis of Sarah, a blacksmith's daughter. Again, men and sex spell death or destruction to women – Muriel goes mad when Carne forces her to conceive a child.

This is, again, a double triangle. The third woman is 72–year-old Alderman Mrs Beddows, a school governor who supports Sarah's appointment as headmistress. Despite her age, Mrs Beddows is also in love with Carne. Radically reversing *Jane Eyre*, the novel ends with Carne dead of a heart attack and an image of connection between Sarah and Mrs Beddows:

> In Mrs Beddows' smile was encouragement, gentle reproof, and a half-teasing affectionate admiration. Sarah, smiling back, felt all her new-found understanding of and love for the South Riding gathered up in her feeling for that small sturdy figure. She knew at last that she had found what she had been seeking.
>
> (SR 510)

Kennard reads this as a reconciliation with the 'mother', as Sarah 'comes to appreciate the values of Mrs Beddows, a character based on Alice Holtby' (1989, 162). This is substantiated by Holtby's dedication of the book to her mother and her comment that 'when I described Sarah's vision of [Mrs Beddows] in the final paragraph, it was you upon whom, in that moment, my thoughts were resting' (SR 5).

However, to develop a psychoanalytic reading further through comparison with the more conservative *Rebecca,* it is the 'father' who is killed here to facilitate a return to the 'mother'. Sarah 'kills' Carne through over-excitement – first in the hotel when he has a heart attack in her bedroom, then in their quarrel before he rides to his death. Yet Carne is courageous, honest and kind and his love for his mad wife, which asks only 'the privilege of service' (SR 430), is an echo of Holtby's own conception of love. Carne is also, like Holtby's father, a Yorkshire farmer. It is possible to read *South Riding* as Holtby's reconciliation with *both* parents. Reconciliation with the mother is achieved through a recognition that both women can love the 'father', that they do not have to be rivals as in the Freudian paradigm. The crucial question here is: is such a reconciliation possible without the death of the father?

Carne's death is necessary because he negates Sarah's independent identity, as she recognises in the hotel:

> He has forgotten who I am or who he is; he thinks I am a little tart. Well? I am Sarah Burton; I have Kiplington High School; he is a governor. This may destroy me. [...]
> I will be his little tart; I will comfort him for one night.
>
> (SR 369–70)

To allow herself to be inscribed into this romance narrative Sarah must lose her identity as a headmistress and become a 'little tart'. However, marriage would also negate Sarah's identity. She has already broken one engagement because, prior to the 1935 lifting of the marriage bar, marriage would have meant the loss of her job. In contrast to Carne, Mrs Beddows affirms Sarah's identity and vocation, telling her: 'Now perhaps you are fit to teach a little' (SR 494). Situated in a female genealogy, Sarah's identity is constructed in relation to another woman through their work in the community. This gives them a professional identity which is not based on their relation to a man, and allows them to relate as equal subjects rather than as rivalrous objects.

To read the ending of the novel only as a reconciliation with the 'mother' actually obscures what Holtby is doing. The final image is one of affiliation between women which is precisely *not* based on a familial model, but on shared work in the public sphere. In this sense, the friendship between Sarah and Mrs Beddows resembles Holtby and Brittain's 'shared working existence'.

Sarah and Mrs Beddows sit at the centre of a web of connections between women in the novel which cross differences of class, education and marital status. Sarah's position as a teacher allows her to enable her female pupils but she refuses to be a 'mother' to them. Instead, she offers the role model of a working woman as a subject in her own right. Again, this is a relationship which is based on shared work, not on emotional attachment. What Holtby is advocating here is a form of networking as women taking up professional positions help other women.

Sarah's realisation that 'we are members one of another' (SR 509), reflects Holtby's recognition in *Virginia Woolf* (1932), the first critical study of Woolf in English, of Woolf's conception of identity as relatedness: 'we dwell in the mirror that lies in the eyes of our friends regarding us' (1932, 135). In Holtby's work it is most often women who find themselves reflected in the eyes of other women. And it is specifically through work that women can escape their positioning as rival commodities in the male economy and mirror each other as equal subjects. In narrative terms Carne functions as a conduit to bring Mrs Beddows and Sarah together in an exchange where each woman is able to give the other something of him. Mrs Beddows gives Sarah a last message from Carne and in return Sarah tells Mrs Beddows about Carne's angina, disabusing her of the fear that Carne committed suicide. As in the kiss between Margaret and Jenny in *The Return of the Soldier*, they make contact through the mediation of the man. But while in West's novel this exchange takes place in the private sphere, in Holtby's the women's affiliation is based on a respect for each other's public work. In this it has more in common with *Summer Will Show*, where Sophia's contact with Minna politically radicalises her. Holtby goes further than Warner in suggesting that homosocial relations between women are also strong enough to disrupt women's position as rivals. In contrast to the failed exchanges in *The Three Sisters, Harriett Frean* or *The Judge*, this exchange can take place because it does not involve self-sacrifice and both women have a subjectivity which is established in the public world. The novel's epigraph – ' "Take what you want", said God. "Take it – and pay for it" ' – is an encouragement to women to take their place in the mainstream economy and trade in their own right.

So, in narrative terms can a man function as a conduit within the triangle without dying? The texts of this period seem to indicate not. In texts where the male object of rivalry remains alive – *Summer Will Show, The Three Sisters, The Constant Nymph, Vera, Rebecca* and *The Weather in the Streets* – connection between women is frustrated, sometimes to the extent that one women is dead or dies. It is only when the man dies that connections between women are established. Moreover, in texts where the rivalry is between one woman and the man over another woman – *The Well of Loneliness, Regiment of Women,* or *The Love Child* – the women are parted, often as a result of one marrying.

It could be argued that in *South Riding* the two women's love for Carne, as well as Mrs Beddows's age and marriage, provide proof of their heterosexuality – an alibi. However, I think that Holtby's point is precisely the fact that it is the connections between women based on work rather than personal relations which offer a way forward. This emphasis on shared work is also to be found in *A Room of One's Own*, but Woolf's insistence that Chloe and Olivia shared a laboratory has been lost in subsequent commentary on the possibility of erotic attachment. Holtby offers us not only a model for relations between women as workers, but also the possibility of a new narrative by which women might start to rewrite their lives.

It is in this, and in her treatment of the spinster, that Holtby is most radical, and where she moves furthest away from Brittain. The single life chosen by Sarah is more fulfilling than married life as represented by Mrs Beddows or the fatally-pregnant Mrs Holly. Holtby offers a courageous validation of the importance of women teachers, particularly spinster teachers, at a time when they were under increasing attack as embittered, sexually frustrated and deviant. What Dale Spender perceives as the increasing radicalism of Holtby's politics in the 1930s (1983a, 626) can be seen as a response to the increasingly vicious attacks on spinsters. Holtby's *Virginia Woolf* and her historical survey, *Women*, as well as *South Riding*, consciously dispute the ideology which positioned spinsters as frustrated and dangerous. She pin-pointed the damage done by Freudian views of sexuality, especially to the woman writer:

> At the very moment when an artist might have climbed out of the traditional limitations of domestic obligations by claiming to be a human being, she was thrust back into them by the authority of the psychologist. A woman, she was told, must enjoy the full cycle of sex experience, or she would become riddled with complexes like a rotting fruit.
>
> (1932, 29)

This thinking diminishes the common humanity between men and women who become 'separated by the unbridgeable gulf of sex' (1932, 29). It also creates a gulf between married and single women. Elsewhere Holtby calls the 'legend of the Frustrated Spinster' 'one of the most formidable social influences of the modern world' (1934, 125), and links it to Fascist ideology.

Holtby's rejection of this stereotype, too easily accepted by Brittain, is a constant in her writing. *Poor Caroline* gives the comic figure of the spinster depth and dignity, and in *South Riding* Holtby works a similar magic with Agnes Sigglesthwaite, the ineffectual science mistress, who works to support a widowed mother. Thus refuting what Holtby scathingly referred to as the 'happy legend [...] that a woman has no dependants and therefore requires a lower salary than men who have families to keep' (1934, 85), a 'legend' which was used to justify paying women teachers four-fifths of what their male counterparts earned (Beddoe, 1989, 80). The second mistress, Dolores Jameson, secure that her engagement gives her 'a complete alibi in all charges of frustration and virginity' (SR 266), uses it to pull rank over the unmarried teachers. Sarah's remark that 'There's too much fuss about virginity and its opposite altogether' (SR 269) was a view Holtby strongly endorsed and Sarah superbly illustrates Holtby's argument that: 'The spinster may have work which delights her, personal intimacies which comfort her, power which satisfies her' (1934, 131). Moreover, the novel engages with the fears about 'Schwärmerei' which informed *Regiment of Women*. Asked how she deals with 'Schwärmerei', Sarah replies: 'I control them all by monopoly [...] We needs must love the highest when we see it. I take good care to be the highest in my school' (SR 129). Lydia Holly's love for Sarah is a positive emotion which can be utilised by Sarah for the girl's own benefit.

Ultimately, Holtby calls for greater tolerance, a more complex notion of sexuality, and a sense of common humanity which transcends difference. The conclusion of *Women* argues that:

> the real object behind our demand [for female emancipation] is not to reduce all men and all woman to the same dull pattern. It is rather to release their richness of variety. We are still greatly ignorant of our own natures. We do not know how much of what we usually describe as 'feminine characteristics' are really 'masculine', and how much 'masculinity' is common to both sexes [...] We do not even know [...] whether the 'normal' sexual relationship is homo- or bi- or heterosexual.
>
> (1934, 192)

In *South Riding* Holtby consciously uses a realist novel to create a sense of that 'richness of variety' – radical politics conveyed through a traditional form. It's a vision which does not erase difference but encompasses it.

Honourable Estate (1936)

If Holtby's most mature statement is in *South Riding*, Brittain's response to the novel in *Honourable Estate* makes her difference from Holtby's views most clear. Unlike Sarah, Ruth Allyndene is not a merging of what was best in both Brittain and Holtby, but another idealised self-portrait of Brittain. Ruth's brother, Richard, and her lover, the American Captain Eugene Meury (based partly on Roland, but more on Brittain's American publisher, the married George Brett, with whom she was in love at this time), are killed in the war. Ruth marries Denis Rutherston, an idealised version of Catlin, but it is she who becomes an MP, whereas

Catlin's similar ambitions were thwarted. The first section of the novel and the character of Janet Rutherston, a suffragette, were inspired by Catlin's mother, Edith, and based on her diary. The only important element of Brittain's life missing is a friend like Holtby. (Ruth's friend, Madelaine, is another version of 'Nina' in *Testament of Youth*.) The key female friendship in the book is displaced back a generation and involves Janet and the playwright, Gertrude Ellison Campbell. The acknowledgement of relationships like Janet's with Gertrude, and Richard's with a fellow soldier, is an important theme and Kennard suggests that this is Brittain's response to Holtby's insistence on recognising 'other relationships than those called "normal"' and 'as such it witnesses to their own friendship' (1989, 177).

An attempt to come to terms with loss is the dominant note of the book. In the last entry in her 1935 diary, Brittain wrote:

Winifred in dying took with her that second life that she initiated for me just after the War; can I make a third? Can I, once more, begin again? Are children and books enough incentive for living?...Does one make new friends when the thirties are over? Does love, orthodox and unorthodox still abide?

(1986, 235)

Obviously, Holtby's death meant a substantial readjustment of Brittain's life. The silence concerning her husband is noticeable here, while other diary entries suggest friction. Given the fact that Holtby often mediated between husband and wife, it is possible that her death made their relationship more difficult.

Despite this, I want to suggest that *Honourable Estate*, dedicated to Catlin and his mother, is Catlin's book.[1] The text is primarily a justification of Brittain's ideal of 'semi-detached marriage'. In *Testament of Youth* Brittain's marriage is presented as a political decision, an attempt to discover whether marriage and career could be combined, and she saw it as an example for others. In her article 'Semi-detached marriage' (1928) Brittain advocated a marriage where both partners worked. This solved the problem of choosing between work and the 'sacrifice of marriage, motherhood and all her emotional needs', or marriage and 'intellectual starvation and monotony' (Berry and Bishop, 1985, 130). This ideal is, Martin Pugh thinks, Brittain's 'greatest contribution to feminism' (1992, 262). It is, however, an ideal which makes little allowance for the fact that working-class women might see their economic need to work as part of their oppression.

Honourable Estate, as the subtitle 'A Novel of Transition' suggests, is an attempt to map women's untold history, and especially what Brittain saw as the shift from 'the master-servant relationship' of nineteenth-century marriages to the twentieth-century ideal of 'companionship between equals' (Brittain, 1953, 170). The structure of the book hammers home this point. The first two parts, which tell the stories of Ruth and Denis's parents – Janet and Thomas Rutherston, and Stephen and Jessie Alleyndene – each include three subsections titled 'Husband', 'Wife' and then 'Son'/'Daughter'. The thrust of the text, like a Hegelian dialectic, is to bring together Ruth and Denis in the final section of Part III, called 'Husband and Wife'. Politically and structurally, their marriage is the climax of the book.

In Janet and Thomas Rutherston's 'master–servant' style marriage, Janet, young, uneducated and inexperienced, is forced into motherhood by Thomas, who believes that 'What was hers was his' (HE 42). This is a socially sanctioned merger of husband and wife which entails the loss of the wife's separate identity. In contrast to Chodorow and Abel's idealisation of merging, this shows that women have traditionally been *expected* to merge with others. Witnessing his mother's struggle makes Denis a fit mate for Ruth, offering her a new type of marriage where he supports her political career. Education is validated here in a way it is not in *The Dark Tide* because it makes Ruth a better mother and wife, as she tells Denis: 'Don't you see that it is just because I *am* better qualified than your mother and still able to go on with my work, that I care for the twins so much?' (HE 550, original emphasis). However, the sense of its value for the wider community of women, so important in *South Riding*, is lost.

In a passage which anticipates a similarly-worded passage in *Testament of Experience* (1957) where Brittain writes of owing her children to 'G' and that his 'loving-kindness' had laid Roland's ghost (1979, 91–2), Ruth reflects that:

> [Denis] had restored her to life after seven years of war and desolation; through him she had found the work which had brought her within sight of a coveted position of service to the State. He was the father of her beloved children [...] he had recognised the claims of a dead man on her restive spirit.
>
> (HE 603)

Bearing in mind Catlin's distress over Brittain's account of her love for Roland in *Testament of Youth* which he saw, Brittain wrote, 'as evidence that "you cannot love me"' (Brittain, 1979, 92), these passages are Brittain's testament to her gratitude for Catlin. However, in Denis, Brittain has re-written Catlin into the kind of husband she wanted, one prepared to forego his own career to support her – something Catlin did not do. Ruth has no need of a supportive female friend because Denis fulfils that role. Here Brittain has incorporated the support offered by Holtby into the portrait of Catlin – merging the female friend into the more socially acceptable figure of the husband.

Like *South Riding, Honourable Estate* ends with a public service, here a memorial for Gertrude Ellison Campbell. Echoing Sarah's exchange of looks with Mrs Beddows, Denis's eyes meet Ruth's and he reflects, 'At least we still have one another; let us work together while there is light' (HE 636). Like *South Riding*, it's an image of shared work and service, but Brittain rewrites Holtby's vision of female community to validate heterosexual marriage.

The book is structured by the connection between Janet and Ruth, which echoes that between Sarah and Mrs Beddows. Ruth's life mirrors but rewrites Janet's, rather as Ellen's does Marion's in *The Judge*. However, the problem with reading their connection as a positive validation of relationships between women is that they never meet. The relationship between mother and daughter-in-law is mediated by a man and contained within the institution of marriage, but Brittain does not, as West does, explore what this means. In contrast to *South Riding*, it is the other woman, Janet, not the man in this triangle, who is dead, leaving the heterosexual couple pre-eminent. In psychoanalytical terms Ruth takes the place of the dead mother and gains an emasculated father, much as the protagonist of *Rebecca* does. At the end of the novel Ruth is isolated from other women, including her mother, rather than connected, as Sarah Burton is, to the wider community.

Brittain's novel resembles two of the novels of female 'friendship' discussed by Elizabeth Abel (Ruth Prawer Jhabvala's *Heat and Dust* and Christa Wolf's *The Search for Christa T*) where the relationship is between a living woman and a dead women. Abel argues that because the process of identification through merging 'can engulf as well as shape identity, its course is smoothest when the object of identification is remembered or imagined rather than physically present' (1981, 426). This is exactly what happens in *Honourable Estate*, where Ruth identifies with the dead Janet, but remains distant from her living mother and other women.

Although *Honourable Estate* does attempt to come to terms with unorthodox loves, Brittain's commitment to heterosexual marriage actually undermines any acceptance of same sex relationships. The relationship between Janet and Ellison Campbell is a living interaction, but is distanced from Ruth by being placed in the past. This is perhaps necessary because Brittain explicitly portrays this as a 'passionate friendship' (HE 630) – a risky strategy in the inter-war period. Janet records: 'Gertrude told me today that I made her realise what Ruth meant when she said to Naomi, "The Lord do so to me and more also, if aught but death part thee and me"' (HE 627). The Biblical parallel, because it implies connection through a man, is not totally appropriate here. Reading Janet's diary and letters, Ruth uses the popularised discourse of psychoanalysis to tell Denis: 'I believe Ellison Campbell had some kind of complex about your mother' (HE 629). In the light of the trial of *The Well of Loneliness* just two years before this point (the novel ends in 1930), Brittain's emphasis on the greater tolerance of such feelings in the twentieth century is perhaps more founded on hope than reality. Moreover, Brittain's biographers have uncovered evidence that Richard's courting of death in battle to avoid court martial for homosexuality was based on what had happened to Brittain's brother, Edward, something she only discovered in 1934 (Berry and Bostridge, 1995, 130–1). *Honourable Estate* is clearly Brittain's attempt to come to terms with these facts. Since the penalty for sodomy or an act of gross indecency was ten years penal servitude (Berry and Bostridge, 1995, 131), Brittain's anxieties are again understandable.

However, *Honourable Estate* shows how little of Holtby's problematising of the 'normal' Brittain had assimilated. Ruth sees Janet as 'a *normal* woman whose talents had been thwarted, whose natural affections had been starved' (HE 628, my emphasis). Brittain here is drawing on the sexologists' argument that some lesbians were 'true inverts' while others were 'normal' but, because of a lack in their lives, could be drawn into lesbianism. Brittain's implication is that the tall, masculine Gertrude is the true lesbian but Janet, under more favourable circumstances, would have been 'normal'. Similarly, Richard's relationship with Valentine is attributed to abnormal conditions in wartime. Brittain's repeated use of the word 'normal' indicates either active disagreement with or a failure to understand Holtby's destabilising of the term.

   The text could be seen as Brittain's acknowledgement of, and distancing of herself from, the lesbianism with which she and Holtby had been associated by gossip. Or it could be read as evidence of a contradictory split in Brittain's own desires – between her need for heterosexual marriage, articulated through Ruth, and her desire for a passionate friendship, articulated through Janet; or, indeed, through Gertrude, whose possessive jealousy of Janet resembles Brittain's need for Holtby's exclusive friendship. But the novel also explores the effect of political differences between women. Gertrude and Janet are separated not because of Janet's marriage but because of their politics. Gertrude, who later becomes president of the National League for Opposing Women's Suffrage, breaks off the friendship when Janet fails to attend the opening of Gertrude's new play because she has collapsed after walking in Emily Wilding Davison's funeral procession. *Honourable Estate* is not only a tribute to the women who fought for the vote – Edith Catlin no less than Emily Wilding Davison – but also an attempt to understand women, like Brittain's mother, who opposed the suffragists.

The triangle of Ruth's affair with Eugene has key differences from that in Holtby's book. Ruth's agreement that Eugene cannot break his engagement to Dallas Lowell, has all the hallmarks of the Victorian ethos of self-sacrifice exemplified in *Life and Death of Harriett Frean*. Ruth's exultation that *'I'm* the person he loves – I, you understand, not Dallas!' (HE 399), resembles Harriett's sense of superiority over Priscilla. The meeting between Ruth and Dallas after Eugene's death does attempt to go beyond this. The scene rewrites and rejects the rivalry between Virginia and Daphne, and echoes the exchange between Mrs Beddows and Sarah. Ruth is able to give Dallas the reassurance that Eugene had a sexual experience based on love before he died. It's less clear what Dallas gives Ruth. Brittain suggests that Ruth has somehow acted as Dallas's deputy in sleeping with Eugene. Sex here is not a matter of female desire but another self-sacrifice – something 'given' by the woman and 'taken' by the man. Ruth's reflection that 'So that's the woman for whom I lost my virginity' (HE 585) even transforms her gesture into a self-sacrifice on behalf of Dallas.

It is not so much that Eugene acts as a mediator between the two women, but that each woman acts as a conduit to Eugene for the other. Dallas is only important to Ruth because of her relation to Eugene and this never becomes a partnership like that of Sarah and Mrs Beddows. Brittain still sees a man, not work, as central to a woman's life. Dallas's sublimation of her desires is presented as a second-best, recalling *The Dark Tide*. A scene at Eugene's grave indicates that a man remains central to Ruth too as she tells him: 'I have made someone else the axis round which everything I am and do will revolve' (HE 533). This endorses the centrality of the man in a way which starkly contrasts with Holtby's killing of her male characters.

The connections between women which Brittain does set up are based on the specificity of shared physical female experience, which links Ruth to Dallas, Janet, and even her grandmother's cook, Agnes, who, sacked when her pregnancy was discovered, gave birth in a cab and lost her baby. The nightmare of thinking herself pregnant teaches Ruth her 'kinship' (HE 433) with Agnes and other women. This cross-class shared female experience is unusual in Brittain's fiction, where working-class women are usually given short shrift. The portrayal of the nurse whose suicide inspires Ruth to consummate her love for Eugene, for instance, is shot through with class snobbery, emphasising her slovenliness and 'the shrill whine of her thin Cockney voice' (HE 354).

The problem with Brittain's vision of a shared female experience as the basis of a feminist politics is that it is an experience shared only by heterosexual, sexually active women, and excludes single women – such as Holtby. Brittain's spinsters are invariably frustrated, such as Ruth's embittered aunt Emily. Ultimately, *Honourable Estate* illustrates Brittain's belief that: 'Today... one happily married wife and mother is worth more to feminism ... than a dozen gifted and eloquent spinsters' (quoted in Berry and Bostridge, 1995, 235). This negates everything that Holtby stood for and especially the vision of *South Riding*.

Testament of Friendship (1940)

Brittain's prefatory allusions in *Testament of Friendship* to Gaskell's *Life of Charlotte Brontë* offer a precedent for her project which situates her and Holtby in a female genealogy both as writers and friends. However, it is in *Testament of Friendship* that Brittain takes direct control of the narrative of Holtby's life, even going so far as to attribute her own desires to Holtby, specifically in the way that she shapes Holtby's life, as she shaped her own writing, according to the romance narrative.

Testament of Youth ends with Brittain's engagement and a railway reunion with 'G', while *Testament of Experience* ends with their reunion at an airport and the promise of their Silver Wedding anniversary. Similarly, *Testament of Friendship* culminates with Harry Pearson (called 'Bill') proposing to Holtby on her deathbed. Brittain concludes: 'There was still time for their strange erratic story, constantly broken and as often resumed, to end in as much of contentment as most of us are destined to know' (TF 436). However, Berry and Bostridge's recent biography of Brittain confirms what is hinted at in the strangely polished account of Holtby's death in Brittain's diary – that Pearson's proposal was, in fact, suggested and stage managed by Brittain (Berry and Bostridge, 1995, 325–6). Holtby's reasons for acquiescing can only be guessed at.

Reading back over the text it is clear that Brittain has shaped it, as she shaped *Testament of Youth*, through hindsight. Frequent references to Pearson, often tenuous and rarely in Holtby's words, create a sense of inevitability. Pearson is introduced thus:

> The elder shall be known for the purposes of this volume as Bill, since years afterwards, when the long tale of her loyalty and devotion to his charming incorrigible personality was almost ended, Winifred recorded it in the story of Jean Stanbury and Bill Durrant in *Mandoa, Mandoa!*.
>
> (TF 22)

Brittain claims that *Mandoa, Mandoa!* 'explains the secret history of [Holtby's] emotional life' because

> In it she reveals the hidden love, the suppressed exasperation, the mingled pity and respect for the man contemptuous of feathering his own nest, aroused in her by the only individual whom, for two tantalising decades, she ever contemplated or desired as a husband.
>
> (TF 347)

This is a version of the 'right man' myth. Pearson, seen like Roland as representative of the generation lost or maimed by the war, is presented as destined for Holtby – the only man she wanted as a husband. As Brittain lost her 'right man' through death, Holtby lost hers because the war made him incapable of sustaining a relationship.

The discrepancy between this and Holtby's own writings has been noted by both Susan Leonardi (1989) and Pam Johnson (1989).[2] There are two probable reasons for Brittain's writing into Holtby's life a man who was never really there. Firstly, he provides an alibi against accusations of lesbianism. This function is explicit in Brittain's contention that 'Bill created throughout Winifred's life a situation utterly different from the one imagined by scandalmongers who invented for her a lurid series of homosexual relationships usually associated with Lady Rhondda or myself' (TF 328). Brittain had a political and personal stake in her own image as a 'markedly heterosexual woman' (Berry and Bishop, 1985, 13) and, as both Holtby and Catlin recognised, had a tendency to reconstruct the characters in her autobiographies to fit her own needs. In *Testament of Friendship* Pearson fulfils a similar function to that which Sedgwick describes women fulfilling in their role as mediators between

men within the erotic triangle. His presence serves to remove the relationship between Brittain and Holtby from the realm of homosexual
desire. This is very different from Holtby's use of the man in her novels as
a conduit to bring the women together.

There is a second explanation for Brittain's use of the romance plot in
her telling of Holtby's story. There is a tension in *Testament of Friendship*
between Brittain's need to praise and to downgrade, between an idealisation of Holtby as a 'saint' (TF 440) and a presentation of Holtby as
inferior to herself, which suggests Brittain's still strong competitive
streak. Her praise for Holtby's writing is often undercut, as when she
refers to Holtby's 'usual facile lyrics' (TF 100). Her estimate of *Mandoa,
Mandoa!* as the only novel which approaches *South Riding*'s quality seems
to be based on the fact that it holds the 'secret' of Holtby's emotional life,
while she badly underrates *The Crowded Street*.

In an extraordinary paragraph in *Testament of Experience* she sums up
Holtby's life:

> None of her books published in her lifetime had sold remarkably, so
> she helped mine to sell magnificently. The only man whom she really
> loved had failed her, so she identified herself with my married happi-
> ness [. . .] When she learned that she must never have children, she
> shared in the care of ours.
>
> (1979, 133–4)

This is a version of Holtby as Brittain's 'second self' – a lesser, inferior
copy of the original, a bit player in Brittain's life rather than principal
player in her own. To return to the mirror analogy used by Irigaray and
Woolf to figure how women function as men's 'other', Brittain uses
Holtby as a mirror in the same way. She records Holtby's comment on
being asked to write her autobiography:

> 'I don't see how I can write an autobiography,' [Holtby] said. 'I never
> feel I've really had a life of my own. My existence seems to me like
> a clear stream which has simply reflected other people's stories and
> problems.'
>
> (TF 1)

The contrast with Brittain, who made her name through her autobiography, is unavoidable. It was Brittain who finally wrote Holtby's story
and it was she who saw Holtby as a 'clear stream' or a mirror which
reflected Brittain herself.

Irigaray's theorisation of the Western male 'economy of the Same' where there are not two sexes but one is helpful here. Irigaray argues that because woman has always been theorised within male parameters the feminine has been obliterated. True difference is erased and the male subject regards the woman not as an equal but different Other, but as lack of the Same – as a lesser or inadequate copy. Similarly, in her writing Brittain theorises Holtby within her own parameters, obliterating their true difference, and presenting Holtby as a lesser copy of herself. While Holtby was alive and their intertextual dialogue was ongoing, Holtby was able to correct these versions of herself by rewriting them in her own novels. Only after Holtby's death could this image of her as the Same but lesser be fixed in *Testament of Friendship*. Brittain's presentation of Holtby as lesser depends crucially on Holtby's status as a spinster, and therefore incomplete compared to Brittain. In *Testament of Friendship*, as in *The Dark Tide*, it is precisely by positioning the Holtby character (for the Holtby of the biography is no less a creation of Brittain's than Daphne) within the romance plot which was so important to Brittain and which Holtby considered 'perniciously untruthful' that Brittain contrives to establish her own superiority.

Writing *Testament of Friendship* gave Brittain the power to recreate the woman who was both her dearest friend and her nearest rival – as Rebecca West recreated her sister in her writing. Since Holtby is dead Brittain has absolute power over her and can ensure that her pre-eminent claim to Holtby is recognised but she can also shape her version of 'Winifred Holtby' according to her own needs. Brittain and Holtby 'merge' after Holtby's death, but in the sense that Holtby is engulfed by Brittain. While Holtby is alive and the process of friendship is still ongoing, Brittain has to recognise Holtby's otherness, her differences – political and personal. After her death Brittain smoothes over those differences to produce a portrait of Holtby as a reflection of Brittain herself – her 'second self'. The very title of the book, *Testament of Friendship*, echoing Brittain's own autobiography, followed by the subtitle 'The Story of Winifred Holtby', indicates that Holtby is taking second place in her own story. As Brittain's last word in their dialogue, it is also Brittain's victory in the struggle over how the friendship should be understood.

7
The 'Recurring Dream' of Romance: Rosamond Lehmann

The youngest of these five writers, Rosamond Lehmann at first sight seems the most conservative, her work a flight back into the world of the private, the intimate and the subjective which has traditionally been the territory of the 'woman's novelist'. Her focus on the romantic desires of women initially seems out of step with the political commitment and social realism which marks the writing we have come to think of as characterising the 1930s.[1] However, the erotic triangle recurs repeatedly in Lehmann's fiction and is used, precisely as Sedgwick suggests, to explore 'the play of desire and identification by which individuals negotiate with their societies for empowerment' (1985, 27). Specifically, Lehmann uses the triangle romance to explore the male economic and social power which frustrates women's attempts to negotiate the fulfilment of their desire within historically shifting relationships of gender, class and sexuality.

The post-war sense of gender roles in flux is especially pronounced in her work. Dinah's comment in *The Echoing Grove* indicates that this is a profound change in consciousness: 'the difference between our grandmothers and us is far deeper than we realise – much more fundamental than the obvious social economic one' (EG 311–12). The alienation and sexual ambiguity of Lehmann's characters reflects their inability to reconcile their desirous inner selves with the social roles offered to them. In the case of the female characters the new post-war opportunities which promise so much, particularly university education and greater sexual freedom, lead nowhere because of the lack of new alternatives to the wife/mistress/spinster roles.

Lehmann's texts engage with precisely the problem which Brittain never confronts – the question of *why* the inter-war woman, despite her increased educational and career opportunities, remained in thrall to romance in both fiction and life. What Lehmann explores is the gap between what women desire and what men give them. Her unhappy endings articulate a nostalgia for a pre-lapsarian romance – a dream of love as it could have existed before the war, had a generation of young men not been slaughtered. This idealised romance is recognised as an illusion, something which had never, in fact, existed, but the internalised desire for it is no less determining.

Lehmann acknowledged the autobiographical element in her writing (Lehmann, 1982c, 65) but where this differs from Brittain or Holtby is that with Lehmann the fiction frequently *anticipates* her life. *The Weather in the Streets*, with its account of an affair with a married man, was published in 1936, before her affair with the married poet, Cecil Day Lewis, which began in 1941. This suggests the powerful nature of pre-determined scripts, especially the romance plot. Despite her university education, Lehmann records in her autobiography, *The Swan in the Evening* (1967), that she was brought up to believe her life would follow the romance script:

> Girls should be pretty, modest, cultivated, home-loving, spirited but also docile; they should chastely await the coming of the right man, and then return his love and marry him and live as faithful, happy wives and mothers, ever after. All this I knew and was by temperament and upbringing fervently disposed towards.
>
> (1982c, 68)

Lehmann's own life – two marriages, and a nine-year affair with Day Lewis – suggests a continually frustrated quest for the 'right man'. She shared with Brittain a sense that the best of a generation of young men had been destroyed:

> I had it lodged in my subconscious mind [as a young woman] that the wonderful unknown young man whom I should have married had been killed in France, along with all the other wonderful young men; so that any suitor – and quite a few uprose – would be a secondary substitute, a kind of simulacrum.
>
> (quoted in Tindall, 1985, 32)

Her work is haunted by the 'wonderful young men' – Charlie in *Dusty Answer*, Rollo's brother, Guy, in *The Weather in the Streets* (1936) – who were lost in the war. Their absent presence is marked in the shortage of male partners in *Invitation to the Waltz* (1932). In this buyers' market men, the buyers themselves, have become a particularly scarce commodity. The men left are not only 'simulacrums', but tend to be unattainable because they are married like Rollo, or Rickie in *The Echoing Grove*, or possibly homosexual like Roddy in *Dusty Answer* and Hugh in *A Note in Music* (1930), or war-damaged like Johnny in *A Sea-Grape Tree* (1976). The romance plot in Lehmann's work is both an economic and emotional necessity and yet inherently flawed because of the lack of the proper object of desire – the 'right' man.

Relations between women, including rivalry, are a key concern in Lehmann's work.[2] They are closely linked to the ties of what West called 'sibship' which were central to Lehmann's own life. Rivalry is traced back to the primary bonds of the family, bonds which are ultimately more determining than even the internalised romance plot. As well as her younger brother, John, the writer and editor, Lehmann had two sisters. Helen, the eldest, married a cavalry officer and 'moved into a different kind of social life – hunting, racing, country house parties' (Watts, 1988, 150). The younger, Beatrix, became a well-known actress. Her picture in Lehmann's *Album* is captioned: 'Beatrix, my youngest sister – our yet unpublished letters to one another show our life-long closeness' (1985, 48). This pattern of closeness to one sister, distance from the other is one I noted in my discussion of West. Like West, Lehmann uses versions of these sisters in her fiction. She saw the 'image' of one in creating a character in *Invitation to the Waltz* and *Weather in the Streets* (WS Introduction), while she had Beatrix physically in mind when envisaging Dinah, and Helen when envisaging Madelaine in *The Echoing Grove* (Tindall, 1985, 170).

Lehmann's fiction explores how childhood rivalries intersect with the gendered roles which cast women as rivals. *The Swan in the Evening* points to the formative nature of birth order and its intersection with gender in inculcating identity. In Lehmann's case it was the insecurity of being a middle child – she confided in her teacher: 'I don't like being in the middle [...] I'm not the oldest...and I'm not the youngest....' (1982c, 10) – and the knowledge that her mother had hoped for a son. In contrast to John Lehmann's memories of a 'fortunate childhood' (Lehmann, J, 1955, 87) which gave him 'the conception of a complete order of things; a full world' (88), Rosamond Lehmann's autobiography conveys a sense of isolation and alienation.

Competition between the talented Lehmann children appears to have been a given. John Lehmann refers to 'the inevitable, endless competition between us' (1955, 73), and he concentrated on poetry because 'Rosamond had established novels as her territory in a way I could never possibly rival' (134). This recalls the division between art and literature worked out by Woolf and Bell. Clearly, such divisions are not necessarily gender specific, although especially necessary to children who share a gender. Beatrix Lehmann did publish two novels. Her *Rumour of Heaven* (1934) deals with sibling bonds and the plight of an eldest sister, Clare, caught between her responsibility for her siblings and her desire for the man she loves. It is yet another inter-war novel which betrays an obsession with the Brontës. Viola, the younger sister, reads and rereads *Wuthering Heights*. Rosamond Lehmann's reaction to Beatrix's encroachment on her own area is perhaps hinted at in a remark about Dinah in *The Echoing Grove* who writes 'a subdued, not very interesting or well-written novel, semi-fantastic, about a deaf girl and a blind man' (EG 15).

In 1931 Lehmann published *A Letter to A Sister* in the Hogarth Letters series. Its very title (in a series which included Viscount Cecil writing to an MP on disarmament, Leonard Strong to W.B. Yeats, and Virginia Woolf to 'a young poet'), is an assertion that relationships between women, between *sisters*, are important. Lehmann's subject is the question (heard, interestingly, in Woolf's voice) 'What is Life?' (1931, 21), and she asserts the value of the subjective, domestic and private as a subject for literature. The writer thinks 'Obviously, life is *things that happen*' (1931, 22, original emphasis), such as reaching the North Pole, or flying alone to Australia. But she refuses to accept this, asserting, 'I cannot countenance a system of distribution which would give the bootlegger, the big-game hunter so large a share, and me so little' (1931, 24). It is, of course, the value system which asserts that only some things are Life-with-a-capital-L which is at fault.

Lehmann explores this distribution not through gender difference (as one might expect) but within sisterly difference and rivalry. She draws a contrast between her sister, 'an enterprising, courageous character' who has leapt into a flooded river to save a cat, been in a motor smash and set herself on fire, and her own 'pitiful' record – 'One fall out of the apple-tree, one fall into the fishpond; a few bee-stings (no wasps)' (1931, 22–3). Her refusal to accept that the adventurous life is more important than her own domestic interior life is a refusal to feel inferior to her sister, but it is also an assertion of different types of femininity. Lehmann emphasises the 'we' of the sisters, their shared memories which mean that only her sister can fully understand what she is trying to convey.

One key image in the pamphlet emphasises the life-long bonding between the sisters, from girlhood to death:

Living alone: as in girlhood, before one was broken in upon.... Do you remember that waiting? – that being caged up away from the rest of humankind, the dome of many-coloured glass pressing close all round one? [...] One stared out at the passing procession, hating, fearing, adoring it – crying: 'Nobody knows what I'm like. Nobody's going to stop and listen. In all the crowd no one will wait for me and walk in step....'[...]

Well – Time that let us out, will draw down the shutter once again. Behind the brittle panel we shall sit, quietly now, and look out upon the world. We shall see all, our children and all, through a glass – not too darkly, I hope – just through uncoloured glass. It won't be so bad really as long as we can take our places at about the same time and sit side by side.

(1931, 16–17)

All Lehmann's young women are longing for someone to 'wait for me and walk in step'. It is only when this happens, when they are inserted into the romance plot, that they feel they are part of the procession, part of 'life'.

In Elizabeth Bowen's *The House in Paris* (1935) Mrs Michaelis expresses a similar view: 'a woman's *real life* only began with marriage, that girlhood amounts to no more than a privileged looking on' (Bowen, 1946, 60, my emphasis). Jane Rule suggests that in Bowen's books 'lesbian experience bracket[s] the heterosexual experience of marriage and children' (1976, 119). Although Rule's identification of Bowen's fiction as lesbian is highly contentious, she makes the important point that relationships between women become central in precisely those stages in a woman's life which are not considered 'real life' (i.e. not taken up with marriage and children) – girlhood and old age.

Bowen and Lehmann, who were friends,[3] have much in common as writers within the tradition of the 'woman's novel' and a broadly similar pattern can be traced in their work. Both their first novels – Lehmann's *Dusty Answer* and Bowen's *The Hotel* (both 1927) – deal with a young girl's intense relationship with and betrayal by another woman. Similarly, their penultimate novels, Lehmann's *The Echoing Grove* and Bowen's *The Little Girls* (1964), deal with older women re-visiting relationships with friends/sisters to understand old rivalries and loves, which they come to understand as central to their lives.

Lehmann also explicitly situated herself in a *female* literary genealogy which reaches back through May Sinclair to the Victorians:

In those days I knew no other female writers, young or old; with the exception of May Sinclair whose novels excited me, I was singularly ill-read in fiction published in the twentieth century. With the Victorians I was well acquainted. I thought of the nineteenth century literary giants as my great ancestresses, revered, loved, and somehow intimately known.

(1982c, 68–9)

Comparing her critical reception with theirs, she found it comforting to feel 'if in no other sense their match, at least sisterly in suffering with such noble souls' (1982c, 69) – a recognition that women novelists have consistently not been given their due. She shared Sinclair's admiration for Elizabeth Gaskell. Her article on *Wives and Daughters* (1884–6), entitled 'A Neglected Victorian Classic' (1947), attempts to rescue Gaskell from the pejorative category 'a woman's author' again by asserting the validity of the domestic and the personal as a subject for literature. *Wives and Daughters* is, of course, another rival sisters romance where Molly Gibson unconsciously cedes the man she loves to her half-sister, Cynthia.

The awareness that Lehmann was 'in no sense their match', together with their safe chronological distance, obviates the possibility of rivalry with her 'great ancestresses'. With more contemporary writers (as between Brittain and Holtby) the question of comparison becomes more problematic. Lehmann's assessment of Woolf is interesting in its implied contrast with herself:

It is true that there was much which [Woolf] lacked, much which was outside the scope of her powers. She was not equipped for a broad grasp of humanity, she had not the kind of richness and sanity, the rooted quality which comes from living a completely fulfilled life as a woman and a mother.

(Noble, 1989, 81)

Similarly, Woolf assessed Lehmann against herself:

I am reading R. Lehmann with some interest and admiration.[. . .] I am as usual appalled by the machinery of fiction: it's much work for little result. Yet I see no other outlet for her gifts. And these books dont matter – they flash a clear light here and there; but I suppose no more. But she has all the gifts (I suppose) that I lack: can give story & development & character & so on.

(Woolf, 1977–1984, vol. III, 314–15)

Neither judgement is totally fair. Lehmann's comment echoes Woolf's own belief that 'telling the truth about my own experiences as a body, I do not think I solved' (Woolf, 1979, 62) but Lehmann's acceptance of the myth that one must experience heterosexual love and motherhood to write well prevents her recognising Woolf's exploration of other sexualities. Woolf, on the other hand, misses Lehmann's ability to evoke the physical experience of inhabiting a female body – of sexuality, pregnancy, childbirth and abortion – and to expose this as the suppressed underside of the romance 'story'.

Lehmann is also a far more technically complex writer than at first appears. The modernist techniques developed by Richardson, Sinclair and Woolf – internal monologue, stream of consciousness, shifts in chronology – are used by Lehmann to draw the reader into the text, into the subjective consciousness she is exploring, and to establish an emotional identification between reader and character which appears effortless. Frequent ellipses mark gaps, the endless 'not-saids' in conversations,[4] which are filled by the reader. In *Dusty Answer* the use of the second person 'you' (frequently used by Sinclair) establishes a dialogue which implicates the reader directly in Judith's thoughts. More than any other writer I have discussed here, Lehmann creates an effect of speaking directly to the reader as a woman, of a dialogue between women, intimate, confessional and private. It is this carefully crafted effect which explains the intense appeal that these books have for some women. Her books are, in a sense, all 'letters to a sister', and her readers frequently responded with letters to Lehmann – 'Oh Miss Lehmann, this is my story! – how did you know' (WS Introduction) – which carry on this dialogue.

Dusty Answer (1927)

Dusty Answer is not only a critique of the romance plot, as several critics have noted, but specifically of the triangle romance. The text is a chain of interlocked triangles where 'everybody love[s] someone who loves another person' (DA 294) and desire is endlessly deferred. Judith Earle, an isolated only child, differs from her nineteenth-century predecessors in having a university education but she is still in thrall to romance. The novel's overriding mood is a nostalgia for something which has never happened, never existed – a dream of romance, whether it is with a man, a woman or Cambridge itself. It exposes as an illusion that possibility of unity with another human being, of possession of them, which is the *raison d'être* of the romance plot. At the heart of the novel is a paradox:

the deconstruction of romance is accompanied by an intense desire for romance. The novel was published the year before *The Well of Loneliness*, but while it was a *succès de scandale*, partially because of the intense relationship between Judith and her fellow student, Jennifer, there was no suggestion of prosecution. This probably had much to do with the fact that whereas Hall makes Stephen's homosexuality explicit in order to frame a plea for tolerance, Judith's attraction to Jennifer is not only ambiguous, but is paralleled by her relations with the three Fyfe brothers, especially Roddy. Thus her longings could be interpreted as an adolescent crush, a rehearsal for heterosexual romance.

Dusty Answer has frequently been read autobiographically – Lehmann recalled that early reviewers said 'This is obviously this young girl's autobiography and she's not likely to write any more' (Watts, 1988, 154). Such readings miss its close relationship with contemporaneous schoolgirl and college fiction, recognised by Muriel Bradbrook who noted that its three-women triangle (Judith, her fellow student Jennifer and the older, sophisticated Geraldine Manners) 'is precisely the story of *A Sweet Girl Graduate* [written by L. T. Meade (1901)]' (1984, 113). *Dusty Answer*, then, draws on established tropes and patterns from the school or college story. These offered a female world, controlled by women, where 'women's friendships are seen as positive, not destructive or competitive, and sufficient unto themselves' (Auchmuty, 1992, 7). Dane's earlier *Regiment of Women* also used the three-women triangle, but to articulate anxieties about this female world and specifically about the pupil–teacher relationship as destructive and competitive compared to the healthy heterosexuality of co-educational schools.

In contrast, *Dusty Answer* depicts a friendship between peers set in a nostalgic, glamorised version of university life. This intense nostalgia, expressed through an evocation of the beauties of Girton and the Cambridge landscape, is, like that of Sayers's *Gaudy Night*, partly to do with a sense of exclusiveness, the entry of a privileged few women to a new world. But it is also to do with exclusion – a nostalgia for a university which women, even as students, never actually possessed because it belonged to men. When Sayers went up to Somerville in 1912 and Lehmann to Girton in 1919, women were not granted degrees by the universities, nor allowed membership of the university. Lehmann wrote to her mother when women were granted a 'titular degree' that the women at Newnham College had had to lock themselves in against a protesting mob who 'smashed the lovely memorial gate and did 700 pounds worth of damage – and *that* is the superior sex!!!' (quoted in

Ginden, 1992, 95). Far from proffering a 'healthy' alternative to single-sex female education, men were more concerned to keep women out of their territory. This sense of exclusion is summed up in Judith's final visit to Cambridge:

> Farewell to Cambridge, to whom she was less than nothing. She had been deluded into imagining that it bore her some affection. Under its politeness, it had disliked and distrusted her and all other females; and now it ignored her. It took its mists about it, folding within them Roddy and Tony and all the other young men; and let her go.
>
> (DA 302)

Whereas both Holtby and Sayers validate education, Cambridge, although it offers an initial sense of freedom and privilege, ultimately fails Judith, providing neither career, friendship, nor lover.

Geographically set apart by its position outside Cambridge itself, Girton is presented as an almost pre-oedipal world of women which echoes that of the girls' school. Removed from parental control, the girls inhabit a brief Eden-like space, a 'quiet safe pool' where 'time seems to have stood still'(DA 188), before they take up the drudgery of teaching or enter the marriage market. The 'room of one's own', insisted on by Girton's founder, Emily Davies, provided a 'psychological sense of freedom' (Vicinus, 1985, 142), as well as an important space for female bonding. Jennifer and Judith's rooms are as stamped with their identity as those of Rebecca or Vera: 'How like Jennifer was her room!' Judith reflects (DA 140). They are also class signifiers – Judith's blue, purple and rose room is nicer than many others simply because she has more money.

Within this female world the friendship between Judith and Jennifer is presented as idyllic and natural. Jennifer, associated with beauty, colour and sensuality, is contrasted with the other students who are 'all alike, commonplace creatures in the mass' (DA 110).The only other student identified by name is the awful Mabel Fuller with her lank hair, spots, envy of her pretty sister, Freda, and her eventual nervous breakdown. This portrait is riven with class-snobbery, yet there is a clear parallel between Mabel's desire for Judith's friendship and Judith's for Jennifer's. Judith responds particularly to Jennifer's physical beauty: ' "Glorious, glorious pagan that I adore!" whispered the voice in Judith that could never speak out' (DA 137) – an echo of Lord Alfred Douglas's famous phrase 'the love that dare not speak its name'. Jennifer embodies, or calls to, the repressed part of Judith:

She was the part of you which you had never been able to untie and set free, the part that wanted to dance and run and sing, taking strong draughts of wind and sunlight; and was, instead, done up in intricate notes and overcast with shadows.

(DA 137)

Indeed, the novel's emphasis on the physical and feminine beauty of both Judith and Jennifer, in contrast to Hall's masculine Stephen, is another possible reason for its relatively benign reception.

Gillian Tindall suggests that Lehmann wrote the book 'wrapped in the kind of innocence [...] that today has become impossible' (1985, 40). But, in fact, the text clearly indicates awareness of contemporary debates around sexuality. Jennifer remarks that Mabel has 'sex-repression' (DA 117), while Judith writes to Martin that 'curious things are apt to happen to strictly maiden aunts as all we *enlightened moderns* know' (DA 141, my emphasis). Knowledge of Freudian ideas is part of being 'modern'. Placed in its historical context the text can be read as expressing a nostalgia for a (non-existent?) time before Freudian ideas became common currency, when passionate friendship between women was unremarkable, as in the girls school story. Geraldine Manners then represents the 'intrusion of the lesbian stereotype' (Jeffreys, 1985, 121) which makes such 'innocent' friendships impossible. She has the physical appearance of one of the vampire lesbians which Faderman sees as specific to this post-war period, although Frith notes that they occur earlier (Frith, 1988, 16). She is named, of course, for Coleridge's serpentine Geraldine in 'Christabel', the mysterious and possibly vampiric lady who shares Christabel's bed and bewitches her.

Masculine and exotic, beautiful and ugly, fascinating and repulsive, Geraldine blurs the boundaries of gender and sexuality:

The hair was black, short, brushed straight back from the forehead, leaving small, beautiful ears exposed. The heavy eyebrows came low and level on the low broad brow; the eyes were long slits, dark-circled, the cheeks were pale, the jaw heavy and masculine. All the meaning of the face was concentrated in the mouth, the strange wide lips laid rather flat on the face, sulky, passionate, weary, eager. She was not a young girl. It was the face of a woman of thirty or more; but in years she might have been younger.

(DA 161)

This sexually ambiguous appearance echoes that of Roddy's rather effeminate friend, Tony Baring, who has 'a wide mouth with beautiful sensuous lips, thick black hair and a broad wide forehead' (DA 95). Both are intensely jealous, reflecting the fact that they too are unsure of their possession of Jennifer and Roddy. However, Geraldine at first fails to recognise Judith as a rival for Jennifer at all, misreading the situation as a schoolgirl quarrel: ' " So you've all sent Jennifer to Coventry" ' (DA 165).

Gill Frith argues that *Dusty Answer* creates space for the sensuous yet 'healthy' friendship of Judith and Jennifer by playing it against the 'real' lesbian relationship of Geraldine and Jennifer (1988, 301). This is supported by Jennifer's final letter, which admits her feelings for the 'innocent' Judith: 'I loved you frightfully from the very first. [...] I couldn't explain to you how I felt [...] You'd have hated it really, wouldn't you? You are pure and ethereal and I am not. Nor was Geraldine' (DA 288–9). Lehmann's novel, however, is both more complex and more ambivalent, and it sets up this contrast only to destabilise it further.

The conversation between the two rivals, Judith and Geraldine, is another of those key dialogues between women which is shadowed by another person, the absent Jennifer, who is the object of their exchange. But Judith's 'surrender' of Jennifer to Geraldine is informed by an understanding that:

> Perhaps after all you [Judith] had been unlucky to Jennifer, committed that crime of trying to possess her separateness, – craved more than even she could give without destroying herself. So in the end she had gone to someone more wholesome for her nature. [...] Perhaps she should be surrendered to Geraldine now, ungrudgingly.
> (DA 170)

Judith has attempted to break down the ego boundaries between herself and Jennifer. This merger is not an idyllic state which facilitates self-identification but a destructive possession of the other's 'separateness'. In this sense, the 'innocent' Judith is actually *more* dangerous to Jennifer, more of a vampire, than Geraldine. Judith, then, cedes Jennifer to Geraldine, much as Hall's Stephen cedes Mary to Martin – but, in this case, the exchange takes place between women, and it is the lesbian relationship which is, ironically, seen as more 'healthy'.

One of the difficulties in offering a consistent reading of the novel is that the text itself is unstable and ambiguous. This is partly because of the juxtaposition of two opposing discourses – the school or college story, which values female friendship and the newly emergent discourse of 'inversion' or deviancy. The distinction between homosocial and homosexual bonds is blurred in a way which was impossible after the *Well* trial. The temptation is to read *Dusty Answer either* as a gynaeceum novel, which foregrounds the primary bonds of women, *or* as a heterosexual romance plot, however fractured. The difficulty is to reconcile the two, and yet the two central triangles – Judith, Jennifer and Geraldine, and Judith, Roddy and Tony – are directly paralleled. The two central objects of desire, Jennifer and Roddy, are similarly glamorous, work-shy, sexually ambiguous and elusive, and in each case the rival is a same-sex lover.

As Judy Simons points out, Lehmann undermines the romance plot by providing *three* potential lovers for Judith (1992, 51): Roddy; Martin, who offers her marriage; and Julian, who asks her to become his mistress. None of these can answer Judith's desires. Lehmann exposes, as Holtby does, the perceived *inevitability* of the romance plot as a script for women: '[Judith] had always known that the play of Roddy must be written and that she must act in it to the end – the happy end' (DA 51). But what follows the sexual consummation of this desire is not the 'happy end' of marriage, but a painful scene which exposes the incompatibility of female and male needs. What for Judith has been all-encompassingly important, is to Roddy a matter of giving her 'what you wanted: what you were asking for' (DA 227). Ultimately, Judith realises that: 'He had never been for her. He had not once, for a single hour, become a part of real life. He had been a recurring dream, a figure seen always with abnormal clarity and complete distortion.' (DA 301) The 'dream' of the romance plot is just that – a 'recurring dream'.

The romance plot is fractured further by the fact that the text offers Judith a fourth potential lover – Jennifer – only to expose bonding between women as equally impossible. While other texts of the period which critique the romance plot (like Holtby's) use friendship or love for a woman as an alternative to marriage, the parallel between Roddy and Jennifer makes it clear that a relationship with a woman is not an alternative to a relationship with a man. This is not because of the social sanctions against it, but because both are equally elusive. In this chain of triangles Judith herself eludes those who love her: Martin, Julian and even Jennifer. Julian's cry 'oh Judith! You were a pleasure; never quite real' (DA 284) directly echoes Judith's feelings about Roddy.

Furthermore, Lehmann deconstructs the traditional notion of the romance rival as it is explored by Girard or Sedgwick. First in terms of gender – Judith's rival for Roddy is another man, just as her rival for Jennifer is another woman. But more importantly, the ostensible rival is also exposed as a chimera. There can be no competition for the love object because he or she is never possessable, and thus cannot be 'surrendered' or exchanged. Jennifer leaves Geraldine just as she left Judith. Roddy never indicates that Tony's love for him is reciprocated. Desire is always frustrated, not because the beloved is taken by another, but because the beloved him/herself is always 'other', always unattainable.

If the popular romance novel, as Janice Radway (1987) suggests, expresses the female desire to return to the state of oneness with the mother, through a socially approved union with the man, then *Dusty Answer* can be read as an expression of the impossibility of recreating that primary bond – with either a man, or another woman. In psychoanalytic terms the problem here is not that (as in *The Unlit Lamp*) the mother is suffocating, but that she is unattainable. Both Judith and Jennifer have unsatisfactory, distant mothers and Judith's lonely isolation is strongly foregrounded. Jennifer's comment to Judith that 'You used to look after me and kiss me as if you were my mother' (DA 289) puts their friendship on a level of maternal caring. But the recreation of the primary bond with the mother is impossible, not because it would mean rivalry with the father who forbids it, as in the Freudian paradigm, but because the *mother* is ultimately and always 'other', and that primary bond has itself never existed. This is not a lost Eden, but one we have never in fact possessed. The repetitive nature of romance reading is echoed in *Dusty Answer*'s chain of triangles, each offering, then frustrating, fulfilment.

While the ending of *Dusty Answer* resembles that of *Mary Olivier* in its emphasis on the separation of the female self from others – Judith is rid of 'the futile obsession of dependence on other people' (DA 303) – it offers no compensation through work or creativity. The reader is left to decide whether Judith's 'emptiness' (DA 303) is a positive shedding of illusions preparatory to adulthood, as Tindall suggests (1985, 38), or a death of the heart. But the suggestion of the text is that although the dream of romance is only a dream it is all we have, and that makes any other option – 'find work, write a book, something . . .' (DA 280) – a 'dusty answer'.

The Weather in the Streets (1936)

The Weather in the Streets is another revision of the *Jane Eyre* romance: a déclassé woman in love with an older, richer man with an invalid wife. By making her protagonist the 'Other Woman' – Olivia Curtis, 27, separated from her husband and living on the fringes of Bohemian London –

Lehmann is (to borrow Rachel Blau DuPlessis's phrase) 'writing beyond the ending' of the marriage plot with a vengeance. Judy Simons comments that Lehmann's reassessment of the familiar romance formula exposes romance as 'a protracted form of anguish rather than as a source of fulfilment' and adds that 'the text comprises a savage attack on the patriarchal establishment, complacent and hierarchical, that conspires against vulnerable women' (1992, 78).

Lehmann's analysis of the economies of class and gender makes it clear that Olivia, despite her status as a modern, sexually liberated woman, is worse off than Jane Eyre. As Patsy Stoneman suggests, Jane Eyre's love sharpens her sense of identity, while Olivia's erodes hers (1996, 98) – as an affair with Carne would have destroyed Sarah's. Rollo's final car accident does not bring him down to Olivia's level nor free her, it merely reinstates his hold over her. Olivia's reading of *Pride and Prejudice* while waiting for the abortion to take effect is the cruellest cut of all. The novel is in dialogue not only with the discourse of the romance novel but with that of the new women's magazines of the 1930s. As Olivia says:

> 'Well, it's all worked out like they tell you in *Woman's World*. A husband may stray, but home ties are strongest, and if you hang on he'll come back. It's the Other Woman who gets had for a mug.'
>
> (WS 336)

What Lehmann's text makes clear through its exploration of Olivia's imaginary construction of Rollo's wife as 'Other' is the continuing commodification of women as rival sexual objects to be used by men.

This, however, is set against a network of female bonds which make it clear how primary such bonds are to women. Olivia's story begins in *Invitation to the Waltz* (1932) where her first dance is a rite of passage signalling her movement into the marriage market. Lehmann's conception of identity as contingent on relations with others is close to the Bakhtinian concept, as well as Holtby's notion. It is, again, imaged through mirrors and the reflective gaze of others. Olivia remarks:

> '*We* don't know what we look like. We're not just ourselves – we're a tiny nut of self, and the rest a mass of unknown quantities – according to who's looking at us.'
>
> (WS 17, original emphasis)

The subject is part of a web of interconnections within which identity is constructed and endlessly reconstructed in relation to others, and to earlier selves. Olivia's sense of identity is particularly fluid. The question she asks in *The Weather in the Streets* – 'Do I exist? Where is my place?' (WS 78) – is at the heart of *Invitation to the Waltz* where she was 'so in a flux....Seeing myself in dozens of distorting mirrors....' (WS 134). These 'mirrors' offer her different possible versions of herself as seen by others.

The most important of the mirroring others in *Invitation to the Waltz* is her elder sister, Kate, in relation to whom Olivia is struggling to construct an appropriately feminine identity. According to McConville, the key question sisters ask is 'Will I be like her – or different?' (1985, 33). For Olivia, the answer at this point seems to be 'different'. While Olivia is awkwardly half-way between child and woman, Kate makes the transition easily. It is Kate who tries to help Olivia make the leap into adulthood, choosing flame-coloured silk for Olivia's dress. Femininity here is not natural but a learned masquerade, constructed through clothes.

Dressed for the dance, the two sisters are clearly commodities packaged for the market. They stand together in front of the mirror:

> After a bit Kate said:
>   'Thank heaven, anyway, we don't look alike.'
> Olivia ventured:
>   'We set each other off really rather well, don't you think?' She thought: The younger girl, with her gypsy colouring, afforded a rich foil to her sister's fair beauty.
>
> (IW 134)

This is a version of the mirror ritual Frith has identified, which opens up 'the possibility of a feminine identity which is *not* unitary' but a split 'between two kinds of femininity' (1988, 13, original emphasis). While in nineteenth-century novels the two women look together in a moment of 'simultaneous identification and separation, defining a difference between "true" and "false" femininity' (1988, 11), in twentieth-century versions the heroine is more usually alone, but sees herself through the eyes of another woman.

Lehmann's version is rather different. Kate's relief that they do not look alike is part of the sisterly anxiety about sameness and an assertion of her difference. Olivia, on the other hand, uses the discourse of romantic fiction which constructs the two girls as rival commodities competing for male attention. She sees herself not through Kate's eyes, but through an imaginary *male* gaze. This imagined 'third term' transforms the sisters into a triangle within which female identity is constructed in terms of the difference of romance rivalry. Here Lehmann subverts the traditional distinctions between the virginal romance heroine and her rival by taking Olivia, a 'scarlet woman' in her red dress, as her heroine. Clearly, others see them in terms of this romance rivalry. The dressmaker tells Olivia 'You'll be cutting your sister out' (IW 59) and even Mrs Curtis measures the two sisters against each other to gauge their success at the dance. Yet, again, there is another side to this economy. Men are also commodified by the marriage market – as the unpleasant Podge tells Olivia: 'You're all alike, you girls. Just a lot of scalp-hunters' (IW 220–1).

In *The Weather in the Streets* Olivia's sense of fluid identity is the result of her ambiguous marital status – separated but not divorced. No longer definable in terms of her relation to a man, she is, like her cousin Etty, a 'superfluous woman' (WS 232), in contrast to the happily-married Kate. Other people, Olivia believes, think Kate is 'the sensible sister... [...]: so different from the younger one....' (WS 93–4). As in Holtby's 'An Episode in West Kensington', the dialogue between the two sisters is a negotiation of power differentials of marriage and spinster-hood. Olivia's remark, 'We sex-starved women have cravings you com-fortable wives and mothers don't dream of' (WS 36), suggests a superiority to Kate in Olivia's independent openness to experience, but Kate's 'And vice versa' immediately undercuts it.

Despite these tensions, Olivia, Kate and their mother have a strong sense of the bonds of their family unit:

> Across the table they began to ply a peaceful shuttle between the three of them, renewing, re-enforcing, patching over rents and frayed places with old serviceable thread. They were tough still; they were a family. That which had chanced to tie them all up together from the start persisted irrevocably, far below consciousness, far beyond the divergences of the present, uniting them in a mysterious reality, independent of reason.
>
> (WS 59–60)

This dialogically constructed identity remains a constant presence throughout life. Looking back on her childhood, Olivia feels that: 'All that was important: had made an experience of emotion more complex, penetrating and profound, yes, than getting married' (WS 129). The lifelong nature of the sister bond means that Olivia feels she knows Kate better than anyone, even her husband: 'I alone know her' (WS 258).

Their relationship echoes those in the earlier generation: Mrs Curtis still misses her sister, May, and even the dignified Lady Spencer and her sister Blanche are bonded by shared memories of childhood games. Olivia's friendship with Anna is an idealised version of supportive sister-hood, lacking the tension of sibling rivalry, while Etty is genuinely kind to Olivia, despite her frivolity. By placing these female bonds within the context of the romance plot, Lehmann shows how that plot keeps women apart. Olivia cannot share her love for Rollo with anyone, even Kate, and she finds that she loses her friends because they think of her as 'under a glass case' (WS 316).

In contrast, men fail to either understand or fulfil female needs. When Olivia tells Rollo 'You don't like women really, do you?' he replies, kissing her ear, 'There's one or two things I quite like about them' (WS 161). In other words, he sees them as objects to satisfy his sexual needs. He rarely uses Olivia's name, always calling her 'darling or something' (WS 192) and, similarly, usually refers to Nicola as 'my wife'. Both women become anonymous, their identities negated by their position as 'wife' or 'mistress' in relation to the man.

Olivia's attraction to Rollo is tangled with the class glamour with which his whole family is suffused, especially his sister Marigold. Olivia is 'in love with the whole lot of them' (WS 281). Like Jennifer, Marigold is sexually ambiguous, telling Olivia: 'I bet if I were like that [i.e. lesbian] I'd make a pass at you' (WS 106). Though Olivia feels foolish and uneasy with Marigold's approach, there is again a blurring of homosocial/homo-sexual desire. This oblique pass mirrors Rollo's later move and Marigold's suggestion that Rollo and Olivia should have an affair suggests that Rollo acts out his sister's desire. The funnelling of possibly lesbian desire into a heterosexual relationship is one more thread in the pattern which draws Olivia to Rollo.

The relationship with Rollo is the classic erotic triangle – man, wife, mistress – where the identity of both women depends on their relation to the man and to each other. As Rollo's mistress Olivia risks moving into the role of 'prostitute' identified by Irigaray. Her refusal to take money or expensive presents from Rollo indicates her determination to maintain her integrity. Ironically, when Olivia first goes to dinner at the Spencers' she wears a white dress (borrowed from Kate) which, as Rollo indicates when he tells her 'You're like a young girl' (WS 132), reinserts her into the position of 'virgin'. Again, femininity is manufactured by clothes. Like Judith, Olivia has internalised the romance plot, telling Rollo: 'I always knew I should meet you again' (WS 134). The white dress signals both her belief in the romance plot and her ironic unsuitability for the role of the heroine. But it also links her with Rollo's wife, Nicola. When Rollo tells Olivia 'I love white. Dark ladies in white dresses'

(WS 124) she remembers that Nicola wore white satin to the dance. White satin, expensive and exotic among the pastel-coloured debutantes, connotes not just Nicola's frigidity but her class status.

Nicola appears directly only once in the two novels. In *Invitation to the Waltz* Olivia sees her posing on the stairs in a classic film scenario and summoning Rollo merely by lifting her hand. Nicola is the 'archetypal Other Person' (Tindall, 1985, 93). She is, like du Maurier's Rebecca, an absent presence, existing as a sign – 'wife' 'rival' – rather than as a person. She is present in *The Weather in the Streets* only through the repetition of the image of her on the stairs and through the speech and thoughts of the other characters. The nearest we get to her is when Olivia looks into her bedroom. In both *Rebecca* and *Vera* the first wife's room serves a mediating function, allowing identification between the women. Here it serves to indicate Nicola's otherness, and the fact that no connection, no dialogue, can be established with her.

Yet Nicola's existence as the third corner of the triangle which structures the novel determines Olivia's identity. Within the text they functions as mirror opposites – 'wife'/'mistress' – both in relation to the 'third term' Rollo. Olivia's construction of Nicola as the 'other woman' – her rival – depends on that opposition, within which she can construct herself as different and therefore preferred by Rollo. She thinks of Nicola as a 'beautiful protected doll [...] not a wife' (WS 164), an 'Upper-class parasite! Hysterical little vampire!' (WS 204). Hence Olivia prides herself on never making a fuss or being jealous. Yet she recognises that her image of Nicola is a construction: 'I put her like that, a wax figure immune in a show case, to account for her, to make her harmless...' (WS 158). Specifically, Olivia constructs herself as the sexual woman in opposition to Nicola's supposed frigidity. As in *The Return of the Soldier*, there is an opposition of sexual/non-sexual, lower-class/upper-class woman. As Olivia constructs her, Nicola resembles Kitty – exquisite, well-bred, cold and non-sexual – while Olivia is both lower in class status and sexual. This sexual opposition, as Nicola's pregnancy reveals, is a delusion.

The Weather in the Streets exposes the class and economic power differentials on which the classic romance is based. These are evident from Rollo and Olivia's initial meeting on the train when he has a full breakfast while she, having only one and sixpence in her purse, has just a cup of coffee. Despite her Oxford education, Olivia exists in a genteel and specifically feminine poverty. The glamour of Rollo's wealthy country-gentry background is part of his masculinity and his attraction. His appearance and manner ensure good service from waiters and porters who know they can expect liberal tips, and, tellingly, he would 'never eat anywhere inferior or female' (WS 162). The title of the novel is taken from an image used to convey Olivia's sense of the time when they were in love:

> Beyond the glass casing I was in, was the weather, were the winter streets in rain, wind, fog, in the fine frosty days and nights, the mild, damp grey ones. Pictures of London winter the other side of the glass – not reaching the body; no wet ankles, muddy stockings, blown hair, cold-aching cheeks, fog-smarting eyes, throat, nose...not my usual bus-taking London winter. It was always indoors or in taxis or in his warm car; it was mostly in the safe dark, or in half-light in the deepest corner of the restaurant, as out of sight as possible.
>
> (WS 145)

The dream of romance forms a glass case around Olivia but her access to this comfort and class status is conditional on her relationship with Rollo. The half-lit restaurants are chosen, of course, to conceal them from people of his own class.

The text explores the eroticisation of this power differential. During their first meeting Olivia becomes aware that he is 'Fighting, subduing me....What'll happen? He might hit me, kiss me....' (WS 26). And then just before they do kiss, when he grabs her hand in the car, 'Overtaken, caught, punished....' (WS 131). This slippage between the male desire to hit and to kiss is a standard convention in romance fiction. Tania Modleski (1984) suggests that it offers women a way of explaining male brutality by revealing it as the result of love, not contempt. The eroticisation of male domination and female submission in this period is at its most blatant in E. M. Hull's best-seller, *The Sheik* (1919). In Hull's novel the boyish and independent heroine suffers abduction and repeated rape at the hands of an inscrutable Arab sheik, who tames her, as he breaks his horses, into submissive womanliness. Her reward is not only his love for her, and the power over him that gives her, but the revelation that he was born a British aristocrat. As Margaret Jackson (1994) has shown, the eroticisation of male domination and female submission as 'natural' in the work of the sexologists, especially Ellis, and the marriage guidance literature of the inter-war period was an important strategy in the control of female sexuality. *The Weather in the Streets* examines this eroticisation of women's oppression, economic and sexual, and exposes as illusory the final power reversal of the romance novel, whereby the man's desire for the woman renders him vulnerable. Unlike the Sheik's passion, Rollo's love for Olivia is merely 'fun' (WS 383).

Olivia's abortion is the culmination of Lehmann's deconstruction of the power differential of the romance plot – an exposure of its suppressed underside. Although *The Weather in the Streets* was not the first novel to depict an abortion (both F. Tennyson Jesse's *A Pin To See the Peepshow* (1934) and Jean Rhys's *Voyage in the Dark* (1934) preceded it), this was still radical enough for Lehmann's publishers to demand that half a page be cut from the English version (Tindall, 1985, 76). The economics of the situation are made painfully clear by the abortionist's fingering of the bronze semi-nude female figures he collects. His trade, like that of Sinclair's Rowcliffe, is in female bodies, and it will pay for his son's education at Harrow and the perpetuation of the system.

The abortion initiates Olivia into an under-class of women, including her cousin Etty, at the mercy of their bodies and the abortionist's illegal trafficking. Olivia and Nicola's parallel pregnancies mark both their common membership of this female conspiracy, and their different social and legal status. Both women are commodities used by the male, but Nicola, as the 'precious vessel for the heir' (WS 333), is cosseted and protected. However, it is the discovery of Nicola's unrequited love for Archie which forces Olivia fully to realise that they share an oppressed status: 'Now one must accept her as real, as human and suffering' (WS 341). This is a conception of Nicola, not as the Other Woman as a mad-woman in an attic, but as a woman who, like Olivia herself, suffers from loving men who will not or cannot fully return that love.

Even so, the identification with Olivia's point of view is such that Nicola always remains 'other' in the text. The narrative form of *The Weather in the Streets*, with its sophisticated use of interior monologue, draws the reader into an identification with Olivia. Maroula Joannou suggests that *The Weather in the Streets* 'interpellates the woman reader whose perspective the familiar narrative of seduction has traditionally failed to recognise' (1995, 144). Another way of putting this might be to say that the text itself *seduces* the reader into identification with the protagonist, as does the popular romance, only to break that contract with the abrupt and shocking shift from 'I' to 'She' between parts two and three. The shift signals the end of the dream of romance and the surfacing of its silenced underside – a shift from the supposedly transhistorical romance to the historically specific.

Despite this, it is striking that the one important conversation Olivia never has is with Nicola. Not only is there is no dialogue between them, but we never hear Nicola's speech reported by others. We only see her making that mute gesture of command to Rollo. The key conversation Olivia does have is with Lady Spencer who, acting on behalf of Nicola (though without her knowledge), suggests that Olivia 'sacrifice' (WS 278) her love for Rollo by giving him up – another version of the nineteenth-century self-sacrifice motif. Only in one instance does Olivia imagine talking to Nicola and that is when she attempts to imagine the affair going on into old age when, after Rollo's death, 'Nicola would turn to me for comfort, we'd set up together. I'd look after her....God knows what muck went through my head....' (WS 196). Female bonding comes before or after the romance plot but, as in *South Riding*, it seems to be only the death of the man, the object of rivalry, which can bring the two women together. It is in this brief passage that we find the seeds of *The Echoing Grove* where Lehmann combines the figures of the sister and the rival, establishing a reconciliatory dialogue.

Conclusion

Rosamond Lehmann's *The Echoing Grove* (1953) brings together the themes I have been discussing and offers a retrospective on the inter-war period. The novel's framework is a reconciliatory dialogue between two sisters, Madelaine and Dinah Burkett, set over twenty-four hours in November 1946, but the main action and the reason for their fifteen-year estrangement – Dinah's affair with Madelaine's husband Rickie – takes place in the 1930s. This central triangle revises that in *The Weather in the Streets* and fuses the female rival with the sister to explore the intersection of sibling rivalry and romance rivalry.

Plot and character similarities, as well as a direct reference, suggest that *The Echoing Grove* also revises Sinclair's *The Three Sisters*. Sinclair's novel is evoked by Georgie in a conversation with Rickie, just three days before he dies:

> '[...] then you said, was the human condition always frustration then? And I said yes, but could be like *The Three Sisters* or that story *The Dead* – the kind that starts echoes afterwards, backwards and forwards for ever wherever you strike it – one echo picking up another till the whole thing *sounds out* like a fulfilment ...'
>
> (EG 231, original emphasis)

As I noted, Lehmann was influenced by her early reading of Sinclair. This, as well as the rival sisters theme and echoes in the names of parallel characters (Mary/Madelaine, Gwenda/Dinah, Cartaret/Burkett, Rowcliffe/Rickie, Amy/Georgie), confirm that it is Sinclair's novel rather than Chekhov's *Three Sisters* that Georgie is invoking.

Sinclair's novel could be regarded as the 'strike' which re-echoes, decades later, in Lehmann's novel as she continues Sinclair's project of exploring female desire. The frustrated affair between Dinah and Rickie is the catalyst which starts 'echoes' moving backwards and forwards. The novel's remarkable circular narrative is made up of the echoes of memory, moving from one character's consciousness to another until 'the whole thing sounds out like a fulfilment'. The past is revisited through Madelaine and Dinah's memories but also, as key scenes are told through a memory of one character retelling them to another, through the consciousnesses of others. The meaning of the novel is thus constructed dialogically through a process of remembering previous utterances, and (because the reader knows the end from the beginning) anticipating future ones.

Where *The Echoing Grove* moves on from *The Three Sisters* is in establishing a dialogue between the two sisters, both through juxtaposing their consciousnesses in the text (as in *The Judge*) and through their reconciliation. Like West, Lehmann refuses to allow the reader to sympathise with only one woman. Both Madelaine and Dinah occupy the position of 'heroine' and 'the other woman' simultaneously, a subversion of the binary opposites of the romance plot. The book is, to borrow the phrase coined by 'Anna O', a 'talking cure' (Freud and Breuer, 1991, 83), but one which takes place between women rather than male doctor and female patient. It breaks the silence which Lynne Pearce sees as 'the great enemy' (1994, 171) but this can only be broken once the sisters have moved out of the romance stage of their lives, and, as in *South Riding*, after the death of the man. By entering into a reciprocal dialogue the two sisters are reconstructing their identities in relation to each other through an acknowledgement of both self and other as equal subjects.

The initial meeting between the sisters illustrates how the shifting power dynamics of competition can co-exist with the easy banter of a shared family background: 'Unspoken, the challenging testing exchange went on beneath the ripple of superficial commentary and question, the small bursts of laughter that exploded between them like bubbles released under pressure' (EG 11–12). The ghost or shadow fracturing the sisters' conversation is Rickie, whose name is initially a 'not said' in their discourse: 'Now the name was said. Perfectly simple. Now the tension would drop' (EG 11). However, a host of other ghosts, including their mother, hover over their discourse.

Dinah's affair with her sister's husband is the ultimate betrayal, transgressing not just sisterly loyalty but also religious and legal taboos, as Madelaine indicates:

'One's own sister... It does seem a bit – out of the ordinary. This letter
seems to imply her intention is – or your joint intention is – to break
up our marriage. It's rather frowned on, isn't it? – in that list of
relations, I mean, in the Prayer Book.'
   'Oh yes,' [Rickie] agreed politely. 'That's putting it mildly.'
   'Not even *deceased* wife's sister.'

(EG 98–9)

According to the table of kindred and affinity in the Book of Common
Prayer, the wife's sister became by marriage a 'sister' to the husband and
sexual relations with her therefore became incest. The Deceased Wife's
Sister Bill in 1907 made it legal for a man to marry his deceased wife's
sister but not the sister of a living wife. The central question in this text,
which Madelaine obliquely asks Dinah in the final pages, is *why*? *Why*
did Dinah have an affair with her sister's husband, when such an affair is
so strongly tabooed?

While Sinclair's text is informed by psychoanalysis, Lehmann's characters themselves are *au fait* with psychoanalytical jargon: 'Death wish.
Birth trauma. Narcissism, sadism, masochism: the terms of
reference were all available' (EG 181). Even Rickie corrects his 'old-
fashioned' comment that Madelaine is 'singularly unsuspicious' to
'I mean, she's an escapist' (EG 104). As his flippancy indicates, such
labels are inadequate in the face of the complexities of human
behaviour.

Psychoanalytic ideas were a releasing force for May Sinclair, but by the
1930s, as Holtby indicated, they had become a straitjacket. Whereas
Sinclair's Gwenda sacrifices her desire for her sister's sake, Dinah could
be said to sacrifice her sister for her desire in line with the popularised
Freudian ideology that modern women should act on their sexual needs,
regardless of other loyalties. Madelaine blazes at Rickie: '*She*'ll tell you
nothing matters – trust, marriage, children, nothing. Not even *decency*.
Experience is the great thing!' (EG 99, original emphasis). As Mrs Burkett
sees it, her daughters' generation are bent on 'fulfilling themselves with
the aid of textbooks' (EG 155). Freudian values have superseded not only
the morality of the Prayer Book, but also the sisterly loyalty valued by the
Victorian novelists. Dinah does indeed at one point suggest that she has
attempted to cede Rickie to Madelaine – 'I did, so to speak, deliberately
relinquish him and hand him back' (EG 38) – but the novel makes clear
the impossibility of this exchange because of the impossibility of ever
possessing another person.

The unspoken question 'Why?' is answered in the sisters' final conversation in a way which evokes the labels of psychoanalysis but moves beyond them:

'What happened happened because...' [Dinah] paused. 'I suppose a number of things contributed to it.'

'For instance?'

'Propinquity. Hysteria. Escapism. Sense of failure. Impulse of self-destruction. Me. You. Rickie...' She sniffed again; then sighed. 'Can't think of any more.'

[...]

'I suppose,' continued Dinah, 'my jealousy of you had gone on growing. I couldn't compete in your world. And you made it so plain I wasn't really acceptable. I don't mean you particularly – all of you.'

'Oh, nonsense! Anyway, *you* were the one; you despised my friends. At least you behaved as if you did.'

'Yes I did.' Her voice was brisk. 'They didn't like me. I tried so hard too! They couldn't stomach me. Plain, highbrow and intense...'

'You weren't plain. You can't have been. You were always very attractive. Much more attractive than me really – anyway, to men.'

'That's nonsense. Simply more business-like. More determined not to fail. I was bound to feel more competitive, with a handicap like you know who.'

(EG 300)

It is the sibling rivalry between Madelaine and Dinah which has been the determining factor in this triangle. The sister bond is more powerful, long-lasting and determining than the sexual bond between men and women. To put it at its most basic, Dinah has the affair with Rickie *because* he is her elder sister's husband.

Within the patriarchal economy their sibling rivalry is doubled by romance rivalry, by competition over who is more attractive to men. This complicates the stereotype that women will betray even those closest to them in order to catch a husband because heterosexual love overrides all other loyalties. Here, echoing Girard's contention that it is the bond with the rival which is determining, not that with the beloved, it is the sister bond which actually determines the betrayal. Rickie is the conduit here, a pawn in their game. Madelaine's comment to him, 'Don't you see this is just another move in the same old game?' (EG 85), assumes that Dinah's actions are determined by this game-playing rather than by her desire for Rickie. Rickie's sense of his position is articulated when, having left Dinah in one taxi, he and Madelaine get into another and for a fleeting moment he thinks it is the same vehicle: 'He smelt a rat. Dinah was inside, in ambush, hugging herself with laughter, preparing with Madelaine's connivance to disclose herself. In another moment he would be stripped, raked by their deadly cross-fire.' (EG 49) The 'rat' Rickie smells here recalls/anticipates the rat killed by the sisters in the opening scenes. Rickie himself (a 'rat' in the slang sense) is killed by the two women, as surely as Carne is killed by Sarah. His first illness, a burst ulcer, is precipitated when he leaves Madelaine for Dinah. Thus his position as an object of exchange within their rivalry leads directly to his death.

So, what is the nature of the bond between the sisters and what exactly was their childhood rivalry for? The relationship between the two women as blood sisters precludes a Freudian interpretation, similar to that given of *Rebecca*, of their rivalry as the daughter's competition with her mother for the attention of the father. Instead, the novel explores the competition between two economies – the 'male hom(m)osexual economy' in which women are constructed as rival commodities, and a female economy of primary bonds between women. Romance rivalry maps onto and re-enforces sibling rivalry.

Toni McNaron's suggestion that 'sisters [...] may well be jealous over their mother' (1985, 6) suggests one interpretation. The relationship between the sisters and their mother is certainly problematic, while their father, who never appears directly, favoured Madelaine. Mrs Burkett is, like most of Lehmann's Edwardian generation mother figures, rather distant. Her conversation with Dinah after Rickie's death, for instance, is conducted in 'the dry tone that was part of the game – the particular type of backhand volley they practised enjoyably together' (EG 158). Game-playing seems endemic to this family. Mrs Burkett relaxes into warmth towards only two objects, both male. The first is Rickie, her 'spirit's son' (EG 155) with whom she is more than a little in love, positioning her as in some senses a rival to her daughters. The second is her male cat, Griswold. Given that Dinah and Madelaine have two brothers, the barely-mentioned Henry and Charles, it would not be surprising if they had had to compete for their mother's attention.

This is never spelt out in the novel. It is one of its strengths that the text resists exactly the kind of analysis which I am trying to generate and (in contrast to Sinclair) refuses to pigeonhole its characters as psychoanalytic types: 'I'm not an *hystérique*,' Dinah asserts (EG 114). In Lehmann's final novel *A Sea Grape Tree* (1976) one character tells another, 'Steer clear of Freud [...] There are more constructive ways of getting to know yourself' (1982d, 63). Another passage in this novel provides a background for the childhood rivalry of Madelaine and Dinah:

> Strange but true, families are the cruellest company in these predicaments: forcing you back to the roots, and oh! how the roots tug, threaten, ache; whispering the old competitive comparisons, guilts, atavisms, insecurities. Plain, pretty; clever, stupid; naughty, good; bad marks, top marks; spiteful; selfish; jealous; unfair; unkind; unjust; your fault; my fault; his fault; her fault; best loved, not loved, lonely, lonely, failure, FAILURE...
>
> (1982d, 85)

Family life is the crucible within which identity is formed, and the labels or roles then affixed, like those in the romance plot, work by binary oppositions: pretty/plain, clever/stupid. Like Woolf and Bell, though in different ways, Madelaine and Dinah are polarised into opposites: mother/barren, non-sexual/sexual, wife/mistress, fair/dark, conventional/Bohemian. The divisive and restrictive labels imposed by adults are the distorting mirrors from which we construct our identities. And in a world where women's value is always determined by their relation to men, it is the issue of sexual attractiveness which is the most divisive.

Yet it is Rickie, the 'third term' against whom their 'value' as wife/ mistress is constructed, who notes how similar the two sisters are and understands their common identity as part of a family unit. His reflection that 'There was never any knowing what went on between those sisters' (EG 268) clearly indicates that they are involved in a game in which he merely acts as a conduit. When they talk to him the shadow fracturing their discourse is that of the other sister, to whom their speech is in some ways addressed. The strength of their bond, based in the roots of a shared childhood, is indicated by their assertions of their primary knowledge of the other in terms that echo Olivia's feelings about Kate. Madelaine tells Rickie, 'I know her better than you do' (EG 85).

It is significant, then, that the sisters, who had faced each other across Rickie's deathbed as rivals (an ironic comment on Olivia's fantasy that she and Nicola could become friends after Rollo's death), begin their reconciliation over their mother's deathbed. The novel's central theme of reconciliation is emblematised by the jade cufflinks with their Maltese crosses (a symbol of forgiveness (Tindall 1985, 181)), which are used to 'link' sections together, and in the Blake quotation which Rickie had intended to have inscribed on a bracelet for Dinah: 'And throughout all

Eternity/I forgive you, you forgive me' (EG 256). It is also symbolised by the moon, echoing *The Three Sisters*, and, again, a circular image. During their final conversation Madelaine watches the moon: 'Before the intentness of her stare the globe in the sky divided: twin moons swam in and out of one another. [...] She focused carefully; the twin discs slid together like a pair of folding lenses' (EG 304). It is an image of the two women as *'neither one nor two'* (Irigaray, 1985, 26) which almost anticipates Irigaray's 'Living mirrors'.

This image suggests a further interpretation of the text – that the two sisters are not only versions of Lehmann's sisters, but also, as Tindall suggests, 'two aspects of their creator's own personality' (1985, 192). That Lehmann herself denies the latter suggestion and emphasises Dinah's similarity to Beatrix (Guppy, 1993, 162) does not preclude its being true on an unconscious level. McNaron suggests that between sisters there is often an 'unspoken, probably unconscious, pact that neither sister need develop all her potential [as] each can see some of herself being acted out by her sibling' (1985, 8). As a writer Lehmann can use fictional characters as 'sisters' to act out different parts of herself, creating a dialogue between them which is sometimes competitive, sometimes supportive. The woman writer may see as her 'sisters' not only her literary ancestresses, but also her characters. Like blood sisters, they are both 'self' and 'other', and thus offer the possibility of a dialogue within which the exchange which Irigaray desires can be enacted: two women 'play[ing] together at being the same and different. You/I exchanging selves endlessly and each staying herself. Living mirrors' (Irigaray, 1981, 61).

However, *The Echoing Grove* goes further than any of the other novels I have discussed in that it gives a voice to the man in the triangle. In the other novels the man remains silent, 'other', even if he is a sympathetic character. Although Rickie is 'killed' by the sisters he is not erased from the text because major sections of the novel are filtered through his consciousness. The text is fully dialogic in the sense that the viewpoints offered are not reconcilable into clear 'right' and 'wrong'. Caught between the two women, Rickie is aware that male identity too is transitional and fluctuating and hazards that 'Sometimes I think a new thing is happening: men aren't any good to women any more' (EG 245). Dinah suspects, rightly, that the key to Rickie's character lies in his class dislocation following the sale of his family estate: 'a whole way of life gone – not just his own personal one: all his racial memories' (EG 163). Masculinity, like femininity, is closely interwoven with class and subject to historical process.

Rickie's voice comes through most clearly in his blitz-time conversation with Georgie, where she plays the psychoanalyst, encouraging him to talk out his part in the affair in a process which parallels the reconciliation of Madelaine and Dinah. Georgie offers an explanation of the male need to 'keep women in their proper place':

'[...] you start at a disadvantage. It *is* kind of unmanly being carried around the way you are all those nine months. And then having no choice but to submit to all those female processes – being born, fed and all the rest. It must be a big humiliation – confusing too. No wonder you're scared you may be women in disguise.'

(EG 246)

This suggests that the fear of the feminine, of *being* feminine, is at the root of the irreconcilability of male and female needs, and thus of the oppression of women. The cufflinks, symbol of reconciliation, will be given in turn by Madelaine to her and Rickie's son, Colin, indicating a hope for the future in the new generation. Within this new generation, as gender roles resettle, the death of the man will, possibly, become unnecessary...?

To return, finally, to the question of canons. That the novels I have been discussing, even such a technically sophisticated novel as *The Echoing Grove*, have not become part of the canon but remain marginalised as 'women's novels', supports my contention that the subject of women's homosocial bonds actively marks a text as uncanonical. Unlike Terry Castle, I do not see the female-identified triangle as a specifically lesbian form, but rather as one which is especially attractive to women writers because it offers a narrative form within which women's own bonds and powers, including those of rivalry, are foregrounded and can be explored. In the female-identified triangle the issues of female identity, desire and power are negotiated in relation to both a man and another woman, who can be either a rival or an object of desire and sometimes both simultaneously. Within this narrative space the conflict between female bonding and the desire for fulfilment through heterosexual romance can be explored.

In Bakhtinian terms, the woman in the triangle can be in dialogue simultaneously with both a man and a women. Likewise, women writers themselves during the inter-war period were in dialogue with both the dominant masculine ideology within which women were constructed as rivals, and with other feminine discourses (such as the novels of their nineteenth-century predecessors), where the bonds between women might be highly valued. Thus, in Irigaray's terms, the triangle makes explicit the fact that women exist simultaneously in a dominant male hom(m)osexual economy and an almost submerged female economy which has the potential to disrupt the former. The bonds between sisters such as Dinah and Madelaine, colleagues like Sarah Burton and Mrs Beddows, friends such as Delia and Muriel, as well as lovers such as Sophia and Minna, are all shown as strong enough to disrupt the male economy which constructs woman as rivals.

The answer to Irigaray's question 'Why are men not objects of exchange among women' (1985, 171) is that they are – at least between the covers of women's novels. The texts I have examined track a problematising of the nineteenth-century motif of self-sacrifice and exchange of the man which includes an understanding that men are as much commodities on the marriage market as women. Acting as a conduit between women, however, almost inevitably leads to the man in the triangle being erased, possibly through death. It is as if during the interwar years women writers could see no way of bringing female rivals together without killing off the male element in the triangle. Over a decade later in *The Echoing Grove* Lehmann makes this explicit but also counters that erasure by giving Rickie a voice in the text. By doing this she suggests that the object in the exchange is never just an object but also a subject with his or her own autonomy, powers and affiliations.

As this examination of the female-identified triangle makes clear, rivalry plays an important part in both the bonds between women and their struggles for empowerment but it is not necessarily always imposed by patriarchal structures. It may, on the contrary, come out of the strength of primary female bonds. This can make it as important and determining a factor as sexual attraction, whether heterosexual or lesbian. To dismiss rivalry between women as automatically a bad thing buys into patriarchal notions of women as 'nice' – non-competitive and self-sacrificing. We need a more complex understanding of rivalry between women which takes into account the fact that there are different kinds of rivalry and that these may not necessarily be bad. As Sinclair shows, Harriett Frean's refusal of rivalry is inspired by a Victorian ethic of female self-sacrifice which leads ultimately to frustration and neurosis. In contrast, as the writing relationship of Vera Brittain and Winifred Holtby shows, rivalry encompassed within a supportive friendship can be a productive spur to achievement. Likewise, the factory girls West watched displayed a rivalry which was not only productive in terms of their work but actually a form of female bonding as it welded them into teams.

Furthermore, there is a clear disjunction between the plots or scripts available to women and their lived experience. The lived writing rivalry of Brittain and Holtby is transmuted in both the 'fiction' of *The Dark Tide* and the 'fact' of *Testament of Friendship* into romance rivalry. As the work of Keller and Moglen suggests, we still lack scripts for positive and friendly rivalry between women in the workplace today. Winifred Holtby's depiction of the working partnership between Mrs Beddows and Sarah Burton, who are bonded by shared aims and beliefs not by a pseudo mother–daughter or sister relationship, offers us one possible way ahead. While an understanding of the reality of blood sister relationships problematises the often sterilised feminist notion of sisterhood, we need other, non-familial based, models for relations between women.

Finally, I believe that this study indicates a pattern which can be traced in women's fiction, not just of the inter-war period but also of other eras and areas. Within the fiction of the inter-war period the theme of female rivalry is defined particularly sharply because of the cluster of historical factors I have outlined and because it is a key moment in the shift from the Victorian motif of self-sacrifice to a more complex understanding of the determining nature of female desire. We need other studies to examine how the female-identified erotic triangle might be utilised by other women writers in other periods, and how this reflects women's powers, bonds and rivalries.

Appendix 1: Census Population of the United Kingdom

Date	Total	Male	Female
1841	18,534,332	9,019,448	9,514,884
1851	20,816,351	10,156,704	10,659,647
1861	23,128,518	11,226,107	11,902,411
1871	26,072,284	12,662,077	13,410,207
1881	29,710,012	14,439,377	15,270,635
1891	33,028,206	16,003,135	17,025,071
1901	36,999,946	17,902,368	19,097,578
1911	40,831,396	19,754,447	21,076,949
1921	42,769,196	20,422,881	22,346,315
1931	44,795,357	21,458,533	23,336,824
1939 (estimate)	46,466,689	22,332,244	24,134,445
1951	48,854,303	23,449,991	25,403,312

Appendix 2: Chronology of Main Legislation Relating to Women, 1914–39

1918   Representation of the People Act – enfranchised all men over 21, and women over 30 subject to a property qualification
Parliament (Qualification of Women) Act – allowed women to become MPs
Maternal and Child Welfare Act – enabled local authorities to provide grant-aided ante-natal and child welfare clinics
Midwives Act – made training more rigorous
Education ('Fisher') Act – raised school-leaving age to 14 and legislated for all children between 14 and 16 to attend compulsory part-time 'continuation schools'

1919   Sex Disqualification (Removal) Act – made it unlawful to bar women from public office, civil or judicial posts

1920   Employment of Women, Young Persons and Children Act – prohibited night work and limited shift work

1922   Married Women (Maintenance) Act – extended Affiliation Orders Act to children of separated wives

1923   Matrimonial Causes Act – allowed women as well as men to sue for divorce on grounds of adultery

1925   Guardianship of Infants Act – established legal equality between parents in the event of marital breakdown
Widows, Orphans and Old Age Contributory Act – introduced weekly pension for widows

1926   Midwives and Maternity Homes Act – tightened up regulations against unqualified midwives and required nursing homes to be registered

1928   Representation of the People (Equal Franchise) Act – enfranchised all women over 21

1929   Infant Life (Preservation) Act – stated that abortion over 28 weeks was infanticide, with perpetrators liable to life imprisonment

1933   British Nationality and Status of Aliens Bill – made it possible for a women who did not acquire her husband's nationality to retain her own

1936   Midwives Act – set up service of salaried midwives and barred unqualified midwives
Employment of Women and Young Persons Act – relaxed some prohibitions on shift work but retained ban on night work

1937   Matrimonial Causes ('Herbert') Act and Divorce (Scotland) Act – made divorce easier to obtain

Notes

Introduction

1 Studies of female friendship and community in women's literature include: Nina Auerbach, *Communities of Women: An Idea in Fiction* (1978), Janet Todd, *Women's Friendship in Literature* (1980), Elizabeth Abel, '(E)merging Identities: the Dynamics of Female Friendship in Contemporary Fiction by Women' (1981), Pauline Nestor, *Female Friendship and Communities: Charlotte Brontë, George Eliot, Elizabeth Gaskell* (1985), Tess Cosslett, *Woman to Woman: Female Friendship in Victorian Literature* (1988) and Gill Frith, 'The Intimacy Which is Knowledge: Female Friendship in Novels by British Women Writers' (1988); as well as chapters in Louise Bernikow, *Among Women* (1980) and Annis Pratt, *Archetypal Patterns in Women's Fiction* (1982). A useful summary of theoretical work can be found in Pat O'Connor's *Friendships Between Women: A Critical Review* (1992). Nancy Chodorow's *The Reproduction of Mothering* (1978) has been particularly influential. Janice Raymond's *A Passion for Friends: Towards a Philosophy of Female Affection* (1986), which utilises Chodorow's work, does identify the blindspot around conflict between women and theorises it as a result of patriarchal structures. Raymond's book also illustrates a common slippage between the terms 'friendship' and 'lesbian relationship', a slippage which itself leads to 'rivalry' between feminists who wish to claim as either 'lesbian' or 'just friendship' the relationship between, for instance, Vera Brittain and Winifred Holtby. Relevant work on lesbian relationships in literature includes Lillian Faderman, *Surpassing the Love of Men: Romantic Friendship and Love Between Women from the Renaissance to the Present Day* (1981) and Emma Donoghue, *Passions Between Women: British Lesbian Culture 1668–1801* (1993). Gabriele Griffin's *Heavenly Love? Lesbian Images in Twentieth-Century Women's Writing* (1993) offers a survey and critique of work on female friendship which suggests that the celebration of *non-sexual* female friendship by 1980s feminist literary critics was itself a retrenchment from more radical stances in the early 1970s.

2 One of the earliest texts of second-wave feminism, *Sisterhood is Powerful*, edited by Robin Morgan (1970), included an essay by Frances M. Beal, 'Double Jeopardy: To Be Black and Female', which made the point that feminism ignored the needs and perspectives of Black women. Later key critiques include Hazel Carby, 'White Women listen! Black feminism and the boundaries of sisterhood' (1982), bell hooks, *Ain't I a Woman: Black Women and Feminism* (1981) and *Feminist Theory: From Margin to Centre* (1984), Alice Walker, *In Search of Our Mothers' Gardens* (1984) and Audre Lorde, *Sister Outsider* (1984). Toni Morrison's *Sula* (1974) has been particularly central to discussions of both female friendship and black women's fiction.

3 Sociological and biographical studies of sister relationships include Elizabeth Fishel, *Sisters: Shared Histories, Lifelong Ties* (1979), Doris Faber, *Love and Rivalry:*

Three Exceptional Pairs of Sisters (1983), Toni McNaron, *The Sister Bond: A Feminist View of a Timeless Connection* (1985) and Brigid McConville, *Sisters: Love and Conflict Within the Lifelong Bond* (1985). Literary studies include Amy K. Levin, *The Suppressed Sister* (1992) and Masako Hirai, *Sisters in Literature: Female Sexuality in* Antigone, Middlemarch, Howard's End *and* Women in Love (1998). Helena Michie's *Sorophobia: Differences Among Women in Literature and Culture* (1992) is a wide-ranging study of differences among women which carefully interrogates the concept of sisterhood, but which explicitly avoids examining the rivalry between women over a man which is the subject of this book.

Chapter 1

1 The critical topography of this period is currently undergoing a radical reworking. Sandra Gilbert and Susan Gubar, Bonnie Kime Scott, Alison Light, Jane Eldridge Miller, Janet Montefiore and Maroula Joannou among others have written illuminatingly about women writers of the period, their relation to traditional mappings of 'Modernism' and 'the 1930s', and the need for a more complex understanding of the 'gendering' of both.

Chapter 2

1 Gilbert and Gubar are here reworking Harold Bloom's model in *The Anxiety of Influence* (1973).
2 My interpretation of Irigaray's work is indebted to Margaret Whitford's *Luce Irigaray: Philosophy in the Feminine* (1991) and her introductions in *The Irigaray Reader* (1991), and to Elizabeth Grosz's *Sexual Subversions: Three French Feminists* (1989). Following them, I would argue that Irigaray is not an essentialist but that her work is above all concerned with the issue of representation, which makes it of particular interest to the literary critic.
3 For simplicity's sake, the name 'Bakhtin' is used to encompass the cluster of work which was also contributed to by Medvedev and Voloshinov.

Chapter 3

1 Although there are currently only two full-length studies of her work – T. E. M. Boll, *Miss May Sinclair: Novelist* (1973) and Hrisey Dimitrakis Zegger, *May Sinclair* (1976) – the task of reassessing Sinclair's work has been started, especially by Jean Radford (in her useful introductions to Virago's reprints), Penny Brown (1992), Jane Eldridge Miller (1994) and Diane Gillespie (1985). Several of Sinclair's critical essays are included in Bonnie Kime Scott, ed., *The Gender of Modernism* (1990). Suzanne Raitt's forthcoming study, *May Sinclair: A Modern Victorian,* will be published by Oxford University Press in 2000.
2 An honourable exception to this neglect is Virginia Blain's 'Thinking Back Through Our Aunts: Harriet Martineau and Tradition in Women's Writing' (1990). Blain not only explores Martineau's importance as a literary 'Aunt'

but also discusses *Deerbrook* as a subversion of the conventional 'rival sisters romance' in a way which has been particularly helpful for my own project.

Chapter 4

1 Gordon Ray, *H. G. Wells and Rebecca West* (1974) and J. R. Hammond, *H. G. Wells and Rebecca West* (1991) focus on her relationship with Wells. Much of the early criticism – Peter Wolfe, *Rebecca West: Artist and Thinker* (1971), Motley F. Deakin, *Rebecca West* (1980), Harold Orel, *The Literary Achievement of Rebecca West* (1986) and Samuel Hynes, *Rebecca West: A Celebration* (1978, introduction) – tended to disparage, regret or ignore West's feminism. The collecting of West's witty and iconoclastic early journalism in *The Young Rebecca* (1982) by Jane Marcus made available to scholars a valuable body of material which has enabled a revaluation of her work. Two particularly important studies are Bonnie Kime Scott's *Refiguring Modernism* (1995), which places West, along with Woolf and Djuna Barnes, at the centre of a 'second flourishing of modernism' in 1928, and Janet Montefiore's *Men and Women Writers of the 1930s* (1996), which examines *Black Lamb and Grey Falcon* in the light of the 1930s.
2 Ray (1974), Hammond (1991), Deakin (1980) and Rollyson (1995) all rely on this reading.
3 Pamela Cotterill, *Friendly Relations?: Mothers and Their Daughters-in-Law* (1994) offers a rare sociological study.
4 Wolfe sees *The Judge* as 'poor in drama' (1971, 41); Orel calls it 'the glummest type of thesis novel' (1986, 130) and condemns Book II as 'profoundly dissatisfying and incomplete' (131); Hammond remarks that 'The rather overelaborated prose has a florid texture, as if one is reading Lawrence heavily laced with James' (1991, 126). Scott, however, offers a valuable reading of it as a modernist text concerned with 'maternal politics' (1995b, 130–9).

Chapter 5

1 The jacket blurb for the Virago reprint of *Testament of Friendship* iconises it as 'a perfect friendship', while Muriel Mellown calls the book a 'glowing tribute to Holtby' (1983, 327). Carolyn Heilbrun cites *Testament of Friendship* as an 'ideal, rare counterexample' (1989, 99) of female friendship based on shared work in the public sphere, which offers an alternative to the romance plot in the project of 'writing a woman's life'.
2 Rosalind Delmar in her Afterword to *Testament of Friendship* comes down squarely behind Brittain, remarking on the 'tenacity' with which such friendships are 'attributed to hidden lesbianism' (TF 446). Likewise Paul Berry refers to the lesbian 'myth' and writes that 'to understand fully the friendship between Vera and Winifred it is nonetheless necessary to understand that it was not a lesbian one' (Berry and Bishop, 1985, 13). Hilary Bailey thinks it 'highly unlikely' that the relationship was lesbian (1987, 71). Deborah Gorham catagorises it as 'non-lesbian', arguing that there is evidence that Brittain 'found lesbian sexuality repellent', and that Holtby believed that 'passion' for another women should not be gratified (1996, 162–5). On the other hand,

Lillian Faderman asks what contemporary reader, faced with the evidence, could 'not conclude that the two women had a lesbian relationship?' (1985, 310). More cautiously, Pam Johnson suggests that it is tempting to see *Testament of Friendship* as 'a clever cover-up of a long-term lesbian relationship' (1989, 156). Most useful for my project is Marion Shaw's careful distinction: 'Vera and Winifred were not lovers but Winifred had a lover-like relation to Vera' (1999, 120).

Chapter 6

1 Kennard argues that *Honourable Estate* is 'the novel Brittain and Holtby wrote together' (1989, 177). For Hilary Bailey it is 'George Brett's book' (1987, 95).
2 Leonardi argues that the account of Pearson's proposal turns Holtby into 'a character in a Brittain romance plot' and denies the centrality of the women's relationship (1989, 221). Johnson exposes the 'heterosexism' which makes it 'more acceptable for [Holtby's] primary emotional attachment to be to a man with whom she had no viable relationship for fifteen years, than to the woman with whom she shared 'sixteen incomparable years' of life and work' (1989, 157).

Chapter 7

1 Early studies of the 1930s – Samuel Hynes, *The Auden Generation: Literature and Politics in England in the 1930s* (1976), Valentine Cunningham, *British Writers of the Thirties* (1988) – barely mention women writers. Lehmann's work has also been badly misread. John Atkins, for instance, condemns her 'snobbism' (1977, 128) and her 'contempt' for the lower classes (127). More recent work by Alison Light, Janet Montefiore, James Ginden, Maroula Joannou and others has enabled a remapping of the period. Judy Simons especially has allowed us to see Lehmann as 'a bitter analyst of the British class system and of its impact on gender and identity' (1992, 137), while Wendy Pollard (1999) makes a convincing case for Lehmann's 'political philosophy'.
2 The importance of mother–daughter bonds in Lehmann's work has been shown by Sydney Janet Kaplan (1981) who examines the Demeter and Persephone myth in *The Ballad and the Source* (1944).
3 And also, for a while, romantic rivals. Victoria Glendinning records a house party of Bowen's where Goronwy Rees, invited because Bowen was attracted to him, began an affair with Lehmann (1988, 113–6). After a period of awkwardness the two writers became close friends again.
4 The term 'not-said' comes from the work of Pierre Macherey (1978).

Bibliography

Abel, Elizabeth, 1981, '(E)Merging Identities: The Dynamics of Female Friendship in Contemporary Fiction by Women', *Signs*, 6, 3, 413–35

Adler, Alfred, 1962 [1932], *What Life Should Mean to You*, ed. Alan Porter, London: Unwin

Alcott, Louisa May, 1953 [1869], *Little Women*, Harmondsworth: Penguin

Aldington, Richard, 1984 [1929], *Death of a Hero*, London: Hogarth

Atkins, John, 1977, *Six Novelists Look at Society*, London: John Calder

Auchmuty, Rosemary, 1989, 'You're a Dyke, Angela! Elsie J. Oxenham and the rise and fall of the schoolgirl story', in Lesbian History Group, *Not a Passing Phase: Reclaiming Lesbians in History 1840–1985*, London: The Women's Press, 119–40

——, 1992, *A World Of Girls*, London: The Women's Press

Auerbach, Nina, 1978, *Communities of Women: An Idea in Fiction*, Cambridge, MA and London: Harvard University Press

Austen, Jane, 1975 [1954], 'The Three Sisters: A Novel', in *The Works of Jane Austen, Vol. VI, Minor Works*, ed. R. W. Chapman, London, New York, Toronto: Oxford University Press

——, 1985 [1813], *Pride and Prejudice*, Harmondsworth: Penguin

Bagnold, Enid, 1978 [1918], *A Diary Without Dates*, London: Virago

Bailey, Hilary, 1987, *Vera Brittain*, Harmondsworth: Penguin

Bakhtin, Mikhail, 1994, *The Bakhtin Reader: Selected Writings of Bakhtin, Medvedev, Voloshinov*, ed. Pam Morris, London: Edward Arnold

Bank, Stephen and Michael D. Kahn, 1982, *The Sibling Bond*, New York: Basic Books

Beauman, Nicola, 1983, *A Very Great Profession: The Woman's Novel 1914–39*, London: Virago

Beddoe, Deirdre, 1989, *Back to Home and Duty: Women Between the Wars, 1918–1939*, London: Pandora

Benjamin, Jessica, 1990 [1988], *The Bonds of Love: Psychoanalysis, Feminism and the Problem of Domination*, London: Virago

Benstock, Shari, 1987 [1986], *Women of the Left Bank: Paris, 1900–1940*, London: Virago

Berry, Paul and Alan Bishop, eds, 1985, *Testament of a Generation: The Journalism of Vera Brittain and Winifred Holtby*, London: Virago

Berry, Paul and Mark Bostridge, 1995, *Vera Brittain: A Life*, London: Chatto and Windus

Bernikow, Louise, 1981 [1980], *Among Women*, New York: Harper Colophon

Blain, Virginia, 1990, 'Thinking Back Through Our Aunts: Harriet Martineau and Tradition in Women's Writing', *Women: A Cultural Review*, 1, 3 (Winter), 223–39

Bloom, Harold, 1973, *The Anxiety of Influence: A Theory of Poetry*, New York: Oxford University Press

Boll, Theophilus E. M., 1970, 'The Mystery of Charlotte Mew and May Sinclair: An Inquiry', *Bulletin of the New York Public Library*, 74 (September), 445–53

——, 1973, *Miss May Sinclair: Novelist: A Biographical and Critical Introduction*, New Jersey: Fairleigh Dickinson University Press

Bowen, Elizabeth, 1931, *Friends and Relations*, London: Constable

——, 1943 [1927], *The Hotel*, Harmondsworth: Penguin

——, 1946 [1935], *The House in Paris*, Harmondsworth: Penguin

——, 1982 [1964], *The Little Girls*, Harmondsworth: Penguin

Bradbrook, M. C., 1984 [1969], *'That Infidel Place': A Short History of Girton College, 1869–1969*, Cambridge: Girton College

Braybon, Gail and Penny Summerfield, 1987, *Out of the Cage: Women's Experiences in Two World Wars*, London and New York: Pandora

Bristow, Joseph, ed., 1992, *Sexual Sameness: Textual Differences in Lesbian and Gay Writing*, London and New York: Routledge

Brittain, Vera, 1923, *The Dark Tide*, London: Grant Richards

——, 1933, *Testament of Youth*, London: Victor Gollancz

——, 1936, *Honourable Estate: A Novel of Transition*, London: Victor Gollancz

——, 1953, *Lady into Woman: A History of Women from Victoria to Elizabeth II*, London: Andrew Dakers

——, and Geoffrey Handley-Taylor, eds, 1960, *Selected Letters of Winifred Holtby and Vera Brittain (1920–1935)*, London and Hull: A. Brown

——, 1968, *Radclyffe Hall: A Case of Obscenity?*, London: Femina

——, 1979 [1957], *Testament of Experience*, London: Virago

——, 1980 [1940], *Testament of Friendship*, London: Virago

——, 1981, *Chronicle of Youth: War Diary 1913–1917*, ed. Alan Bishop with Terry Smart, London: Victor Gollancz

——, 1986, *Chronicle of Friendship: Diary of the Thirties 1932–39*, ed. Alan Bishop, London: Victor Gollancz

Brontë, Charlotte, 1967 [1847], *Jane Eyre*, London: Pan

——, 1985 [1849], *Shirley*, Harmondsworth: Penguin

——, 1909 [1853], *Villette*, intro. May Sinclair, Everyman Library, London: Dent

Brontë, Emily, 1981 [1847], *Wuthering Heights*, Oxford and New York: Oxford University Press

Brown, Penny, 1992, *The Poison at the Source: The Female Novel of Self-development in the Early Twentieth Century*, London and Basingstoke: Macmillan

Carby, Hazel, 1982, 'White Women Listen! Black feminism and the boundaries of sisterhood', in Centre for Contemporary Studies, *The Empire Strikes Back: Race and Racism in 70s Britain*, London: Hutchinson

Castle, Terry, 1992, 'Sylvia Townsend Warner and the counterplot of lesbian fiction', in Joseph Bristow, ed., *Sexual Sameness: Textual Differences in Lesbian and Gay Writing*, London and New York: Routledge, 128–47

Chamberlain, Mary, ed., 1988, *Writing Lives: Conversations Between Women Writers*, London: Virago

Chekov, Anton, 1959, 'Three Sisters' in *Plays*, trans. Elisaveta Fen, Harmondsworth: Penguin

Chodorow, Nancy, 1978, *The Reproduction of Mothering: Psychoanalysis and the Sociology of Gender*, Berkeley: University of California Press

Cockburn, Claud, 1972, *Bestseller: The Books That Everyone Read 1900–1939*, London: Sidgwick and Jackson

Cosslett, Tess, 1988, *Woman to Woman: Female Friendship in Victorian Fiction*, Brighton: Harvester

Cotterill, Pamela, 1994, *Friendly Relations?: Mothers and Their Daughters-in-law*, London and Bristol, PA: Taylor and Francis

Cunningham, Valentine, 1988, *British Writers of the Thirties*, Oxford and New York: Oxford University Press

Curran, James and Jean Seaton, 1985, *Power Without Responsibility: The Press and Broadcasting in Britain*, London and New York: Methuen

Dane, Clemence, 1995 [1917], *Regiment of Women*, intro. Alison Hennegan, London: Virago

Deakin, Motley F., 1980, *Rebecca West*, Boston: Twayne

de Beauvoir, Simone, 1983 [1949], *The Second Sex*, trans. and ed. H. M. Parshley, Harmondsworth: Penguin

Delafield, E. M., 1984 [1930], *The Diary of a Provincial Lady*, London: Virago

——, 1988 [1927], *The Way Things Are*, London: Virago

Donoghue, Emma, 1993, *Passions Between Women: British Lesbian Culture, 1668–1801*, London: Scarlet Press

du Maurier, Daphne, 1975 [1938], *Rebecca*, London: Pan

Dunn, Jane, 1991[1990], *A Very Close Conspiracy: Vanessa Bell and Virginia Woolf*, London: Pimlico

DuPlessis, Rachel Blau, 1985, *Writing Beyond the Ending: Narrative Strategies of Twentieth Century Writers*, Bloomington: Indiana University Press

Dyhouse, Carol, 1989, *Feminism and the Family in England 1880–1939*, Oxford: Basil Blackwell

Eliot, George, 1979 [1860], *The Mill on the Floss*, Harmondsworth: Penguin

Ellis, Havelock, 1901a, *Studies in the Psychology of Sex: Vol. I: Sexual Inversion*, Philadelphia: F. A. Davis

——, 1901b, *Studies in the Psychology of Sex: Vol. II: The Evolution of Modesty, The Phenomenon of Sexual Periodicity, Autoeroticism*, Philadelphia: F. A. Davis

Faber, Doris, 1983, *Love and Rivalry: Three Exceptional Pairs of Sisters*, New York: Viking Press

Faderman, Lillian, 1985 [1981], *Surpassing the Love of Men: Romantic Friendship and Love between Women from the Renaissance to the Present Day*, London: The Women's Press

Farrell, M. J. [Molly Keane], 1984 [1934], *Devoted Ladies*, London: Virago

Faulkner, Peter, 1977, *Modernism*, London: Methuen

Fishel, Elizabeth, 1994 [1979], *Sisters: Shared Histories, Lifelong Ties*, Berkeley, CA: Conari

Fitzgerald, Penelope, 1984, *Charlotte Mew and Her Friends*, London: Collins

Ford, Ford Madox, 1972 [1915], *The Good Soldier: The Saddest Story Ever Told*, Harmondsworth: Penguin

Fortunati, Vita and Gabriella Morisco, eds, n.d., *The Representation of the Self in Women's Autobiography*, University of Bologna (Erasmus Occasional Paper)

Freud, Sigmund, 1961, *Letters of Sigmund Freud, 1873–1939*, ed., Ernst L. Freud, trans. Tania and James Stern, London: Hogarth

——, 1973 [1964], *New Introductory Lectures on Psychoanalysis*, Pelican Freud Library, Vol. 2, Harmondsworth: Penguin

——, 1977, *On Sexuality: Three Essays on the Theory of Sexuality and Other Works*, Pelican Freud Library, Vol. 7, Harmondsworth: Penguin

——, 1990 [1977], *Case Histories I: 'Dora' and 'Little Hans'*, Penguin Freud Library, Vol. 8, Harmondsworth: Penguin

——, 1991 [1979], *Case Histories II: The 'Rat Man', Schreber, The 'Wolf Man', A Case of Female Homosexuality*, Penguin Freud Library, Vol. 9, Harmondsworth: Penguin

——, and Josef Breuer, 1991 [1974], *Studies on Hysteria*, Penguin Freud Library, Vol. 3, Harmondsworth: Penguin

Frith, Gill, 1988, 'The Intimacy Which is Knowledge: Female Friendship in the Novels of Women Writers', unpublished Ph.D thesis, Warwick University

Fuss, Diana, 1989, *Essentially Speaking: Feminism, Nature and Difference*, London and New York: Routledge

Gallop, Jane, 1982, *Feminism and Psychoanalysis: The Daughter's Seduction*, London and Basingstoke: Macmillan

Gardiner, Judith Kegan, 1981, 'The (US)es of (I)dentity: A Response to Abel on "(E)Merging Identities" ', *Signs*, 6, 3, 436–42

——, 1990 [1985], 'Mind mother: psychoanalysis and feminism', in Gayle Greene and Coppélia Kahn, eds, *Making a Difference: Feminist Literary Criticism*, London and New York: Routledge, 113–45

Gaskell, Elizabeth, 1908 [1857], *The Life of Charlotte Brontë*, intro. May Sinclair, Everyman Library, London: Dent

——, 1969 [1884–86], *Wives and Daughters*, Harmondsworth: Penguin

Gilbert, Sandra M. and Susan Gubar, 1988, *No Man's Land: The Place of the Woman Writer in the Twentieth Century: Vol. I: The War of the Words*, New Haven and London: Yale University Press

Gillespie, Diane F., 1985, ' "The Muddle of the Middle": May Sinclair on Women', *Tulsa Studies in Women's Literature*, 4, 2, 235–51

Ginden, James, 1992, *British Fiction in the 1930s: The Dispiriting Decade*, London and Basingstoke: Macmillan

Girard, René, 1976 [1961], *Deceit, Desire and the Novel: Self and Other in Literary Structure*, trans. Yvonne Freccero, Baltimore and London: Johns Hopkins University Press

Glendinning, Victoria, 1988 [1987], *Rebecca West*, London and Basingstoke: Macmillan

——, 1993 [1977], *Elizabeth Bowen: Portrait of a Writer*, London: Phoenix

Gorham, Deborah, 1996, *Vera Brittain: A Feminist Life*, Oxford and Cambridge, MA: Blackwell

Graves, Robert, 1960 [1929], *Goodbye to All That*, Harmondsworth: Penguin

Graves, Robert and Alan Hodge, 1941, *The Long Week-End: A Social History of Great Britain 1918–1939*, London: Readers Union by arrangement with Faber and Faber

Greene, Gayle and Coppélia Kahn, eds, 1990 [1985], *Making a Difference: Feminist Literary Criticism*, London and New York: Routledge

Griffin, Gabriele, 1993, *Heavenly Love? Lesbian Images in Twentieth-Century Women's Writing*, Manchester and New York: Manchester University Press

Grosz, Elizabeth, 1989, *Sexual Subversions: Three French Feminists*, Sydney and London: Allen and Unwin

Guppy, Shusha, 1993 [1991], *Looking Back: A Panoramic View of a Literary Age by the Grandes Dames of English Letters*, London: Touchstone

Hall, Radclyffe, 1981[1924], *The Unlit Lamp*, London: Virago

——, 1982 [1928], *The Well of Loneliness*, London: Virago

Hammond, J. R., 1991, *H. G. Wells and Rebecca West*, London: Harvester Wheatsheaf

Hanscombe, Gillian, 1991, 'Katherine Mansfield's Pear Tree', in Elaine Hobby and Chris White, eds, *What Lesbians do in Books*, London: The Women's Press, 111–33

Harding, M. Esther, 1933, *The Way of All Women: A Psychological Interpretation*, intro. C. G. Jung, London, New York and Toronto: Longmans, Green and Co.

H.D. [Hilda Doolittle], 1984 [1960], *Bid Me to Live*, London: Virago

Heilbrun, Carolyn G., 1989 [1988], *Writing a Woman's Life*, London: The Women's Press

Herrmann, Ann, 1989, *The Dialogic and Difference: "An/Other Woman" in Virginia Woolf and Christa Wolf*, New York: Columbia University Press

Hirai, Masako, 1998, *Sisters in Literature: Female Sexuality in* Antigone, Middlemarch, Howards End *and* Women in Love, Basingstoke: Macmillan

Hoagland, Sara Lucia, 1988, *Lesbian Ethics: Toward New Value*, Palo Alto: Institute of Lesbian Studies

Hobby, Elaine and Chris White, eds, 1991, *What Lesbians do in Books*, London: The Women's Press

Holtby, Winifred, 1932, *Virginia Woolf*, London: Wishart

——, 1933, *Mandoa, Mandoa! A Comedy of Irrelevance*, London: Collins

——, 1934, *Women*, London: John Lane

——, 1935, 'The Native Women', *The Listener*, vol.XIII, no. 334, 5 June, 946–7

——, 1937a, *Letters to a Friend*, ed. Alice Holtby and Jean McWilliam, London: Collins

——, 1937b, *Pavements at Anderby: Tales of 'South Riding' and Other Regions*, eds H.S. Reid and Vera Brittain, Bath: Lythway Press

——, 1974 [1936], *South Riding: An English Landscape*, Glasgow: Fontana

——, 1981a [1923], *Anderby Wold*, London: Virago

——, 1981b [1924], *The Crowded Street*, intro. Clare Hardisty, London: Virago

——, 1983 [1927], *The Land of Green Ginger*, London: Virago

——, 1985 [1931], *Poor Caroline*, London: Virago

hooks, bell, 1981, *Ain't I a Woman: Black Women and Feminism*, London: Pluto Press

——, 1984, *Feminist Theory: From Margin to Center*, Boston: South End Press

Hull, E. M., 1919, *The Sheik*, London: Eveleigh Nash and Grayson

Hynes, Samuel, 1976, *The Auden Generation: Literature and Politics in the 1930s*, London: Faber

Ibsen, Henrik, 1988, *An Enemy of the People, The Wild Duck, Rosmersholm*, trans. and ed. James McFarlane, Oxford and New York: Oxford University Press

Ingman, Heather, 1998, *Women's Fiction Between the Wars: Mothers, Daughters and Writing*, Edinburgh: Edinburgh University Press

Irigaray, Luce, 1981, 'And the One Doesn't Stir Without the Other', trans. Hélène Vivienne Wenzel, *Signs*, 7, 1, 60–7

——, 1985 [1977] *This Sex Which is Not One*, trans. Catherine Porter with Carolyn Burke, Ithaca, New York: Cornell University Press

——, 1991, *The Irigaray Reader*, ed. Margaret Whitford, Oxford: Basil Blackwell

——, 1993a [1984], *An Ethics of Sexual Difference*, trans. Carolyn Burke and Gillian C. Gill, London: Athlone

——, 1993b [1987], *Sexes and Genealogies*, trans. Gillian C. Gill, New York: Columbia University Press

——, 1993c [1990], *Je, Tu, Nous: Toward a Culture of Difference*, trans. Alison Martin, New York and London: Routledge

——, 1994 [1989], *Thinking the Difference: For a Peaceful Revolution*, trans. Karin Montin, London: Athlone

Jackson, Margaret, 1994, *The Real Facts of Life: Feminism and the Politics of Sexuality c.1850–1940*, London and Bristol, PA: Taylor and Francis

Jameson, Storm, 1982 [1934], *Company Parade*, London: Virago

——, 1984 [1935], *Love in Winter*, London: Virago

Jeffreys, Sheila, 1985, *The Spinster and Her Enemies: Feminism and Sexuality 1800–1930*, London: Pandora

Jesse, F. Tennyson, 1979 [1934], *A Pin to See the Peepshow*, London: Virago

Joannou, Maroula, 1995, *'Ladies Please Don't Smash These Windows': Women's Writing, Feminist Consciousness and Social Change 1918–38*, Oxford: Berg

——, ed., 1999, *Women Writers of the 1930s: Gender, Politics and History*, Edinburgh: Edinburgh University Press

Johnson, Pam, 1989, ' "The Best Friend Whom Life Has Given Me": Does Winifred Holtby have a place in lesbian history?', in Lesbian History Group, *Not a Passing Phase: Reclaiming Lesbians in History 1840–1985*, London: The Women's Press, 141–57

Kaplan, Sydney Janet, 1975, *Feminine Consciousness in the Modern British Novel*, Urbana, Chicago, London: University of Illinois Press

——, 1981, 'Rosamond Lehmann's *The Ballad and the Source*: A Confrontation With "The Great Mother" ', *Twentieth Century Literature*, 27, 2, 127–45

Keller, Evelyn Fox and Helen Moglen, 1987, 'Competition and Feminism: Conflicts for Academic Women', *Signs*, 12, 3, 493–511

Kennard, Jean, 1978, *Victims of Convention*, Hamden, Conn.: Archon

——, 1989, *Vera Brittain and Winifred Holtby: A Working Partnership*, Hanover and London: University Press of New England

Kennedy, Margaret, 1924, *The Constant Nymph*, London: Heinemann

——, 1981a [1923], *The Ladies of Lyndon*, London: Virago

——, 1981b [1936], *Together and Apart*, London: Virago

Lasser, Carol, 1988, ' "Let Us Be Sisters Forever": The Sororal Model of Nineteenth Century Female Friendship', *Signs*, 14, 11, 158–81

Lawrence, D. H., 1934, *The Tales of D. H. Lawrence*, London: Martin Secker

——, 1948 [1913], *Sons and Lovers*, Harmondsworth: Penguin

——, 1949 [1915], *The Rainbow*, Harmondsworth: Penguin

——, 1981, *The Letters of D. H. Lawrence*, vol. 2, ed. George J. Zytaruk and James T. Boulton, Cambridge: Cambridge University Press

——, 1982 [1920], *Women in Love*, Harmondsworth: Penguin

Lee, Hermione, 1996, *Virginia Woolf*, London: Chatto and Windus

Lehmann, Beatrix, 1987 [1934], *Rumour of Heaven*, London: Virago

Lehmann, John, 1955, *The Whispering Gallery: Autobiography I*, London, New York, Toronto: Longman

Lehmann, Rosamond, 1931, *A Letter to a Sister*, London: Hogarth Press

——, 1936 [1927], *Dusty Answer*, Harmondsworth: Penguin

——, 1947, 'A Neglected Victorian Classic', *The Penguin New Writing, 32*, London: Penguin, 89–101

——, 1953, *The Echoing Grove*, London: Collins
——, 1981a [1932], *Invitation to the Waltz*, London: Virago
——, 1981b [1936], *The Weather in the Streets*, London: Virago
——, 1982a [1930], *A Note in Music*, London: Virago
——, 1982b [1944], *The Ballad and the Source*, London: Virago
——, 1982c [1967], *The Swan in the Evening: Fragments of an Inner Life*, London: Virago
——, 1982d [1976], *A Sea-Grape Tree*, London: Virago
——, 1985, *Rosamond Lehmann's Album*, London: Chatto and Windus
Leonardi, Susan J., 1989, *Dangerous by Degrees: Women at Oxford and the Somerville College Novelists*, New Brunswick and London: Rutgers University Press
Lesbian History Group, 1989, *Not a Passing Phase: Reclaiming Lesbians in History 1840–1985*, London: The Women's Press
Levin, Amy K., 1992, *The Suppressed Sister: A Relationship in Novels by Nineteenth and Twentieth Century British Women*, London and Toronto: Associated University Presses
Lévi-Strauss, Claude, 1969 [1949], *The Elementary Structures of Kinship*, trans. James Harle Bell and John Richard von Sturmer, ed. Rodney Needham, London: Eyre and Spottiswoode
Lewis, Jane, 1984, *Women in England 1870–1950: Sexual Divisions and Social Change*, Sussex: Wheatsheaf; Bloomington: Indiana University Press
——, ed., 1987, *Before the Vote Was Won*, New York and London: Routledge
Liddington, Jill and Jill Norris, 1978, *One Hand Tied Behind Us: The Rise of the Women's Suffrage Movement*, London: Virago
Light, Alison, 1991, *Forever England: Femininity, Literature and Conservatism Between the Wars*, London and New York: Routledge
Lorde, Audre, 1984, *Sister Outsider*, New York: The Crossing Press
Ludovici, Anthony M., 1923, *Woman: A Vindication*, London: Constable
Macaulay, Rose, 1965 [1923], *Told by an Idiot*, London: Collins
——, 1986 [1916], *Non-Combatants and Others*, London: Methuen
Macherey, Pierre, 1978, *A Theory of Literary Production*, London: Routledge and Kegan Paul
Malinowski, Bronislaw and Robert Briffault, 1931, 'The Present Crisis in Marriage', *The Listener*, V, 104, 7 January, 7–8
Mansfield, Katherine, 1945, *Collected Stories*, London: Constable
——, 1990, 'The New Infancy (Review of May Sinclair's *Mary Olivier*)', in Bonnie Kime Scott, ed., *The Gender of Modernism: A Critical Anthology*, Bloomington and Indianapolis: Indiana University Press, 311–12
Martineau, Harriet, 1983 [1839], *Deerbrook*, intro. Gaby Weiner, London:Virago
Mayor, F. M., 1980 [1913], *The Third Miss Symons*, London: Virago
——, 1987 [1924], *The Rector's Daughter*, London: Virago
McConville, Brigid, 1985, *Sisters: Love and Conflict Within the Lifelong Bond*, London: Pan
McNaron, Toni A. H., 1985, *The Sister Bond: A Feminist View of a Timeless Connection*, Oxford: Pergamon Press
Mellown, Muriel, 1983, 'Vera Brittain: Feminist in a New Age (1896–1970)', in Dale Spender, ed., *Feminist Theorists: Three Centuries of Women's Intellectual Traditions*, London: The Women's Press, 314–33

Melman, Billie, 1988, *Women and the Popular Imagination in the Twenties: Flappers and Nymphs*, Basingstoke and London: Macmillan

Michie, Helena, 1992, *Sorophobia: Differences Among Women in Literature and Culture*, New York and Oxford: Oxford University Press

Miller, Jane Eldridge, 1994, *Rebel Women: Feminism, Modernism and the Edwardian Novel*, London: Virago

Mitchison, Naomi, 1934, 'The Reluctant Feminists', *The Left Review*, 1.3 (December), 93–4

——, 1935, *We Have Been Warned*, London: Constable

——, 1986 [1979], *You May Well Ask: A Memoir 1920–1940*, London: Fontana

Modleski, Tania, 1984, *Loving With a Vengeance*, London: Methuen

——, 1988, *The Women Who Knew Too Much: Hitchcock and Feminist Theory*, New York and London: Routledge

Montefiore, Janet, 1996, *Men and Women Writers of the 1930s: The Dangerous Flood of History*, London and New York: Routledge

Monteith, Moira, ed., 1986, *Women's Writing: A Challenge to Theory*, Brighton: Harvester

Morgan, Robin, ed., 1970, *Sisterhood is Powerful: An Anthology of Writings from the Women's Liberation Movement*, New York: Vintage

Morrison, Toni, 1982 [1974], *Sula*, London: Triad/Panther

Nestor, Pauline, 1985, *Female Friendships and Communities: Charlotte Brontë, George Eliot and Elizabeth Gaskell*, Oxford: Clarendon Press

Nicolson, Nigel, 1990 [1973], *Portrait of a Marriage*, London: Weidenfeld and Nicolson

Noble, Joan Russell, ed., 1989 [1972], *Recollections of Virginia Woolf by Her Contemporaries*, London: Cardinal

O'Brien, E. J. ed., 1932 [1930], *Modern English Short Stories,* London: Jonathan Cape

O'Brien, Kate, 1988 [1934], *The Ante-Room*, London: Virago

O'Connor, Pat, 1992, *Friendships Between Women: A Critical Review*, Hemel Hempstead: Harvester Wheatsheaf

'Olivia' [Dorothy Strachey], 1987 [1949], *Olivia*, London: Virago

Olivier, Christiane, 1989, *Jocasta's Children: The Imprint of the Mother*, trans. George Craig, London and New York: Routledge

Olivier, Edith, 1981 [1927], *The Love Child*, London: Virago

Oram, Alison, 1989, ' "Embittered, Sexless or Homosexual": Attacks on spinster teachers 1918–39', in Lesbian History Group, *Not a Passing Phase: Reclaiming Lesbians in History 1840–1985*, London: The Women's Press, 99–118

Orbach, Susie and Luise Eichenbaum, 1994 [1987], *Between Women: Love, Envy and Competition in Women's Friendships*, London: Arrow. First published as *Bittersweet*

Orel, Harold, 1986, *The Literary Achievement of Rebecca West*, London and Basingstoke: Macmillan

Ouditt, Sharon, 1994, *Fighting Forces, Writing Women: Identity and Ideology in the First World War*, London and New York: Routledge

Overton, Bill, 1996, *The Novel of Female Adultery: Love and Gender in Continental European Fiction, 1830–1900*, London and Basingstoke: Macmillan

Pankhurst, Sylvia, 1977 [1931], *The Suffragette Movement: An Intimate Account of Persons and Ideals,* London: Virago

Pearce, Lynne, 1994, *Reading Dialogics*, London: Edward Arnold

Poems of To-Day: An Anthology, 1931 [1915], London: Sidgwick and Jackson

Pollard, Wendy, 1999, 'Rosamond Lehmann's Political Philosophy: From *A Note in Music* (1930) to *No More Music* (1939)', in Maroula Joannou, ed., *Women Writers of the 1930s: Gender, Politics and History,* Edinburgh: Edinburgh University Press, 87–99

Pratt, Annis, 1982, *Archetypal Patterns in Women's Fiction,* Brighton: Harvester

Pugh, Martin, 1992, *Women and the Women's Movement in Britain: 1914–1959,* Basingstoke and London: Macmillan

Radford, Jean, ed., 1986, *The Progress of Romance: The Politics of Popular Fiction,* London: Routledge and Kegan Paul

——, 1986, 'An Inverted Romance: *The Well of Loneliness* and Sexual Ideology', in Jean Radford, ed., *The Progress of Romance: The Politics of Popular Fiction,* London: Routledge and Kegan Paul, 97–111

Radway, Janice, 1987 [1984], *Reading the Romance: Women, Patriarchy and Popular Literature,* London and New York: Verso

Raitt, Suzanne, 1993, *Vita and Virginia: The Work and Friendship of Vita Sackville-West and Virginia Woolf,* Oxford: Clarendon Press

Rathbone, Eleanor F., 1924, *The Disinherited Family: A Plea for the Endowment of the Family,* London: Edward Arnold

Ray, Gordon N., 1974, *H. G. Wells and Rebecca West,* London: Macmillan

Raymond, Janice, 1991[1986], *A Passion for Friends: Towards a Philosophy of Female Affection,* London: The Women's Press

Reiter, Rayna R., ed., 1975, *Toward an Anthropology of Women,* New York and London: Monthly Review Press

Rhys, Jean, 1969 [1934], *Voyage in the Dark,* Harmondsworth: Penguin

——, 1969 [1928], *Quartet,* London: Andre Deutsch. First published as *Postures*

Rich, Adrienne, 1980, 'Compulsory Heterosexuality and Lesbian Existence', *Signs,* 5, 4, 631–60

Richardson, Dorothy, 1979 [1915–35], *Pilgrimage,* 4 vols, London: Virago

Robertson, E. Arnot, 1962 [1933], *Ordinary Families,* London and Glasgow: Fontana

——, 1982 [1931], *Four Frightened People,* London: Virago

Robins, Elizabeth, 1980 [1907], *The Convert,* London: The Women's Press

Roe, Sue, ed., 1987, *Women Reading Women's Writing,* Brighton: Harvester

Rollyson, Carl, 1995, *Rebecca West: A Saga of the Century,* London: Hodder and Stoughton

Romero, Patricia W., 1990 [1987], *E. Sylvia Pankhurst: Portrait of a Radical,* New Haven and London: Yale University Press

Rubin, Gayle, 1975, 'The Traffic in Women: Notes on the "Political Economy" of Sex', in Rayna R. Reiter, ed., 1975, *Toward an Anthropology of Women,* New York and London: Monthly Review Press, 157–210

Rule, Jane, 1976 [1975], *Lesbian Images,* New York: Pocket Book

Russell, Bertrand, 1930, *The Conquest of Happiness,* London: George Allen and Unwin

Sackville-West, Vita, 1974 [1924], *Challenge,* London: Collins

Sayers, Dorothy L., 1981 [1935], *Gaudy Night,* London: New English Library

——, 1989 [1927], *Unnatural Death,* London: Hodder and Stoughton

——, 1988 [1937], *Busman's Honeymoon,* London: Hodder and Stoughton

Schreiner, Olive, 1978 [1911], *Woman and Labour,* London: Virago

Scott, Bonnie Kime, 1987, 'The Strange Necessity of Rebecca West', in Sue Roe, ed., *Women Reading Women's Writing*, Brighton: Harvester, 265–86

——, ed., 1990, *The Gender of Modernism: A Critical Anthology*, Bloomington and Indianapolis: Indiana University Press

——, 1995a, *Refiguring Modernism: Vol. 1, The Women of 1928*, Bloomington and Indianapolis: Indiana University Press

——, 1995b, *Refiguring Modernism, Vol. 2, Postmodern Feminist Readings of Woolf, West and Barnes*, Bloomington and Indianapolis: Indiana University Press

Sedgwick, Eve Kosofsky, 1985, *Between Men: English Literature and Male Homosocial Desire*, New York: Columbia University Press

Shaw, Marion, (n.d.) ' "A Noble Relationship": Friendship, Biography and Autobiography in the Writings of Vera Brittain and Winifred Holtby', in Vita Fortunati and Gabriella Morisco, eds, *The Representation of the Self in Women's Autobiography*, University of Bologna (Erasmus Occasional Paper), 29–42

——, 1986, 'Feminism and Fiction Between the Wars: Winifred Holtby and Virginia Woolf', in Moira Monteith, ed., *Women's Writing: A Challenge to Theory*, Brighton: Harvester, 175–91

——, 1999, *The Clear Stream: A Life of Winifred Holtby*, London: Virago

Showalter, Elaine, 1987 [1985], *The Female Malady: Women, Madness and English Culture 1830–1980*, London: Virago

Simons, Judy, 1992, *Rosamond Lehmann*, London and Basingstoke: Macmillan

Sinclair, May, 1911 [1904], *The Divine Fire*, London: Everleigh Nash

——, 1910, *The Creators*, London: Constable

——, 1912a, *Feminism*, London: Women Writers Suffrage League

——, 1912b, *The Three Brontës*, London: Hutchinson

——, 1915, *A Journal of Impressions in Belgium*, London: Hutchinson

——, 1916a, 'Symbolism and Sublimation I', *Medical Press and Circular*, 9 August, 118–22

——, 1916b, 'Symbolism and Sublimation II', *Medical Press and Circular*, 16 August, 142–45

——, 1917, *A Defence of Idealism: Some Questions and Conclusions*, London: Macmillan

——, 1918, 'The Novels of Dorothy Richardson', *The Egoist*, V, 4 (April), 57–9

——, 1920, *The Romantic*, London: The Literary Press

——, 1921, *Mr Waddington of Wyck*, USA: Grosset and Dunlap

——, 1924a, *Arnold Waterlow*, London: Hutchinson

——, 1924b, *The Dark Night*, London: Jonathan Cape

——, 1926, *Far End*, New York: Macmillan

——, 1927, *History of Anthony Waring*, London: Hutchinson

——, 1932 [1930], 'Lena Wrace', in E. J. O'Brien, ed., *Modern English Short Stories*, London: Jonathan Cape, 217–29

——, 1980a [1919], *Mary Olivier: A Life*, intro. Jean Radford, London: Virago

——, 1980b [1922], *Life and Death of Harriett Frean*, intro. Jean Radford, London: Virago

——, 1982 [1914], *The Three Sisters*, intro. Jean Radford, London: Virago

——, 1996 [1985], 'Where Their Fire is Not Quenched', in Sandra M. Gilbert and Susan Gubar, eds, *The Norton Anthology of Literature by Women: The Traditions in English*, 2nd ed., New York and London: Norton

Smith, Helen Zenna [Evadne Price], 1988 [1930], *Not So Quiet: Stepdaughters of War*, London: Virago

Spender, Dale, 1983a [1982], *Women of Ideas and What Men Have Done to Them: From Aphra Behn to Adrienne Rich*, London: Arc

——, ed.,1983b, *Feminist Theorists; Three Centuries of Women's Intellectual Traditions*, London: The Women's Press

——, 1984, *Time and Tide Wait for No Man*, London: Pandora

Stevenson, John, 1977, *Social Conditions in Britain Between the Wars*, Harmondsworth: Penguin

——, 1990 [1984], *British Society 1914–45*, Harmondsworth: Penguin

Stoneman, Patsy, 1996, *Brontë Transformations: The Cultural Dissemination of* Jane Eyre *and* Wuthering Heights, Hemel Hempstead: Prentice Hall, Harvester Wheatsheaf

Stopes, Marie, 1918, *Married Love: A New Contribution to the Solution of Sex Difficulties*, London: A. C. Fifield

——, 1934 [1928], *Enduring Passion: Further New Contributions to the Solution of Sex Difficulties*, 5th edn., London: Putnam

Strachey, Ray, 1978 [1928], *The Cause: A Short History of the Women's Movement in Great Britain*, London: Virago

Struther, Jan, 1939, *Mrs Miniver*, London: Chatto and Windus

Tindall, Gillian, 1985, *Rosamond Lehmann: An Appreciation*, London: Chatto and Windus

Todd, Janet, 1980, *Women's Friendship in Literature*, New York: Columbia University Press

Trefusis, Violet, 1992 [1986], *Broderie Anglaise,* trans. Barbara Bray, London: Minerva

Tylee, Claire, M., 1990, *The Great War and Women's Consciousness: Images of Militarism and Womanhood in Women's Writings 1914–64*, London: Macmillan

Vicinus, Martha, 1985, *Independent Women: Work and Community for Single Women 1850–1920*, London: Virago

von Arnim, Elizabeth, 1983 [1921], *Vera*, London: Virago

Walker, Alice, 1984, *In Search of Our Mothers' Gardens*, London: The Women's Press

Wallace, Diana, 1999, 'Revising the Marriage Plot in Women's Fiction of the 1930s', in Maroula Joannou, ed., *Women Writers of the 1930s: Gender, Politics and History*, Edinburgh: Edinburgh University Press, 63–75

Warner, Marina, 1988, 'Rebecca West', in Mary Chamberlain, ed., *Writing Lives: Conversations Between Women Writers*, London: Virago, 262–75

Warner, Sylvia Townsend, 1993 [1926], *Lolly Willowes: or The Loving Huntsman*, London: Virago

——, 1987 [1936], *Summer Will Show*, London: Virago

Watts, Janet, 1988, 'Rosamond Lehmann', in Mary Chamberlain, ed., *Writing Lives: Conversations Between Women Writers*, London: Virago, 150–9

Wells, H. G., 1980 [1909], *Ann Veronica*, London: Virago

——, 1912, *Marriage*, London: Macmillan

——, 1984, *H. G. Wells in Love: Postscript to an Experiment in Autobiography*, ed. G. P. Wells, London and Boston: Faber and Faber

West, Rebecca, 1928, *The Strange Necessity: Essays and Reviews*, London: Jonathan Cape

——, 1942 [1941], *Black Lamb and Grey Falcon*, 2 vols, London: Macmillan

——, 1954, 'The Role of Fantasy in the Work of the Brontës', *Brontë Society Transactions*, 12, 64, 255–67

——, 1978 [1977], *Rebecca West: A Celebration,* ed. Samuel Hynes, Harmondsworth: Penguin

——, 1980a [1918], *The Return of the Soldier,* intro. Victoria Glendinning, London: Virago

——, 1980b [1922], *The Judge,* intro. Jane Marcus, London: Virago

——, 1982, *The Young Rebecca: Writings of Rebecca West 1911–1917,* ed. Jane Marcus, London: Macmillan

——, 1984 [1957], *The Fountain Overflows,* London: Virago

——, 1987 [1984], *This Real Night,* London: Virago

——, 1988 [1985], *Cousin Rosamund,* London: Virago

——, 1992 [1987], *Family Memories,* ed. Faith Evans, London: Lime Tree

White, Evelyne, 1938, *Winifred Holtby as I Knew Her: A Study of the Author and Her Works,* London: Collins

Whitford, Margaret, 1991, *Luce Irigaray: Philosophy in the Feminine,* London and New York: Routledge

Wilkinson, Ellen, 1989 [1929], *Clash,* London: Virago

Wiltsher, Anne, 1985, *Most Dangerous Women: Feminist Peace Campaigners of the Great War,* London: Pandora

Wolfe, Peter, 1971, *Rebecca West: Artist and Thinker,* Carbondale and Edwardsville: Southern Illinois Press

Woolf, Virginia, 1966–67, *Collected Essays,* 4 vols, ed. Leonard Woolf, London: The Hogarth Press

——, 1968 [1937], *The Years,* Harmondsworth: Penguin

——, 1975–80, *The Letters of Virginia Woolf,* 6 vols, ed. Nigel Nicolson, London: The Hogarth Press

——, 1976a [1925], *Mrs Dalloway,* London: Granada

——, 1976b, *Moments of Being: Unpublished Autobiographical Writings,* ed. Jeanne Schulkind, Sussex: The University Press

——, 1977a [1927], *To the Lighthouse,* London: Granada

——, 1977b [1928], *Orlando: A Biography,* London: Granada

——, 1977c [1929], *A Room of One's Own,* London: Granada

——, 1977d [1933], *Flush,* Harmondsworth: Penguin

——, 1977–84, *The Diary of Virginia Woolf,* 5 vols, ed. Anne Olivier Bell, London: The Hogarth Press

——, 1978, *The Pargiters: The Novel–Essay Portion of* The Years, ed. Mitchell A. Leaska, London: The Hogarth Press

——, 1979, *On Women and Writing: Her Essays, Assessments and Arguments,* ed. Michèle Barrett, London: The Women's Press

——, 1986 [1938], *Three Guineas,* London: The Hogarth Press

——, 1992 [1915], *The Voyage Out,* Harmondsworth: Penguin

Wright, Sir Almroth, 1912, 'Suffrage Fallacies: Sir Almroth Wright on militant hysteria', *The Times,* 28 March, 7–8

Young, E. H., 1984a [1922], *The Misses Mallett,* London: Virago

——, 1984b [1930], *Miss Mole,* London: Virago

——, 1990 [1937], *Celia,* London: Virago

Zegger, Hrisey Dimitrakis, 1976, *May Sinclair,* Boston, USA: Twayne

Index